ROUTLEDGE LIBRARY EDITIONS:
ARTIFICIAL INTELLIGENCE

Volume 9

THE ARTIFICIAL LIFE ROUTE TO ARTIFICIAL INTELLIGENCE

THE ARTIFICIAL LIFE ROUTE TO ARTIFICIAL INTELLIGENCE

Building Embodied, Situated Agents

Edited by
LUC STEELS AND RODNEY BROOKS

Routledge
Taylor & Francis Group
LONDON AND NEW YORK

First published in 1995 by Lawrence Erlbaum Associates, Inc.

This edition first published in 2018
by Routledge
2 Park Square, Milton Park, Abingdon, Oxon OX14 4RN

and by Routledge
711 Third Avenue, New York, NY 10017

Routledge is an imprint of the Taylor & Francis Group, an informa business

British Library Cataloguing in Publication Data
A catalogue record for this book is available from the British Library

ISBN: 978-0-8153-8566-0 (Set)
ISBN: 978-0-429-49236-5 (Set) (ebk)
ISBN: 978-1-138-54578-6 (Volume 9) (hbk)
ISBN: 978-1-351-00188-5 (Volume 9) (ebk)

Publisher's Note
The publisher has gone to great lengths to ensure the quality of this reprint but points out that some imperfections in the original copies may be apparent.

The Artificial Life Route to Artificial Intelligence: Building Embodied, Situated Agents

Edited by
Luc Steels
University of Brussels
Rodney Brooks
Massachusetts Insitute of Technology

LEA
LAWRENCE ERLBAUM ASSOCIATES, PUBLISHERS
1995 Hillsdale, New Jersey Hove, UK

Lawrence Erlbaum Associates, Inc., Publishers
365 Broadway
Hillsdale, New Jersey 07642

cover design by Cheryl Minden

Library of Congress Cataloging in Publication Data

The Artificial life route to artificial intelligence : building embodied, situated agents / edited by Luc Steels and Rodney Brooks.
p. cm.
ISBN 0-8058-1519-8 (pbk. : alk. paper). — ISBN 0-8058-1518-X (alk. paper)
1. Artificial intelligence. I. Steels, Luc. II. Brooks, Rodney Allen.
Q335.A789 1994
006.3—dc20 94-11644
CIP

Books published by Lawrence Erlbaum Associates are printed on acid-free paper, and their bindings are chosen for strength and durability.

Printed in the United States of America
10 9 8 7 6 5 4 3 2 1

Contents

Preface

In April 1991, a number of researchers from Artificial Intelligence (AI) and biology came together in the old Priory of Corsendonck, north of Brussels. The meeting was originally scheduled to be held in Dubrovnik but the early beginnings of the Yugoslavian war made a last minute change of location necessary. The researchers gathered to examine whether there was any ground to assume that a new AI paradigm was forming itself and what the essential ingredients of this new paradigm were. A great deal of scepsis is justified when researchers, particularly in the cognitive sciences, talk about a new paradigm. Shifts in paradigm mean not only new ideas but also shifts in what constitutes good problems, what counts as a result, the experimental practice to validate results, and the technological tools needed to do research. Due to the complexity of the subject matter, paradigms abound in the cognitive sciences, connectionism being the most prominent newcomer in the mid-1980s.

In the years before the meeting, there had been a number of indications that a relatively small group of people who had an earlier record of work in "classical AI" were indeed shifting their attention and scientific research methodology in a profound way. These researchers have built up some strong alliances with recent work in artificial life because of the strong biological bias in their work. The link with biology is not in terms of modeling biological phenomena but rather in exploiting principles underlying living organisms.[1] The workshop brought together some of the key players of this vanguard group in order to clarify the common ground, see what had been achieved so far, and examine in which way the research could move further. The participants were Rodney Brooks, William Clancey, John Hallam, Stevan Harnad, Leslie Kaelbling, Chris Langton, Maja Mataric, Rolf Pfeifer, Tim Smithers, Luc Steels, Charles Taylor, Francis Van Aeken

[1]Two prominent artificial life researchers were present at the workshop: Chris Langton and Charles Taylor (see Langton & Taylor, 1992). They unfortunately did not find the time to contribute to the present workshop proceedings. Instead a contribution by McFarland has been added to the workshop proceedings.

and Francisco Varela.

The workshop was organised by Luc Steels and Rodney Brooks and sponsored by NATO as part of a joint project between the VUB (Vrije Universiteit Brussel) and the MIT (Massachusetts Institute of Technology) AI laboratories on intelligent autonomous agents (1990-1992). The workshop was partly intended to be a follow up of an earlier workshop organised by the VUB AI laboratory in Lagos (Portugal) in 1988 and sponsored by the European Communities as part of the COST 13 programme (action on the fundamentals of knowledge representations).[2] This collection of papers is a reflection of the Corsendonck workshop. It contains contributions that were distributed before the workshop but then substantially broadened and revised to reflect the workshop discussions and more recent technical work.

The book starts with an introductory philosophical statement by F. Varela. Then there are three parts. The first part contains statements of research programmes. The second part contains technical work. The third part contains position papers. They are written in a polemic form, sometimes even criticising the work done so far within the new paradigm.

Prologue

Francisco Varela

The collection starts with a contribution by Francisco Varela, who in a philosophical, sometimes even poetical, way outlines some of the major shifts suggested by the new paradigm:

Embodiedness.

"Cognition depends on the kinds of experience that come from having a body with various sensorimotor capacities." (Varela, p. 17) The new AI paradigm takes this statement seriously and has consequently shifted the attention from the "higher level" cognitive activities typically studied in AI (chess playing, logical reasoning, expert problem solving, etc.) to the "lower level" capabilities associated with sensorimotor intelligence. In order to seriously investigate these using the synthetic method practised in AI, researchers have turned to the construction of physical autonomous agents. These robotic agents are not built with the prime goal of automating parts of sensory processing or action control, but as a first step toward the study of full cognitive agents.

---

[2]Reports of this workshop have appeared in the *Journal of Robotics and Autonomous Systems*, Vol. 6 (1&2) (pp.1-196) and Vol. 8 (1&2) (pp.1-165). They have been reprinted in books published by the MIT Press (Bradford Books), respectively edited by P. Maes and W. Van de Velde.

Situatedness

"The individual sensorimotor capacities are themselves embedded in a more encompassing biological and cultural context" (Varela, p. 17). Researchers in the new paradigm wholeheartedly agree. Being situated within a specific context and drawing as much as possible on this context to relate appropriate actions to environmental circumstances are two key ideas exploited in the construction of complete agents. Behavior-oriented decompositions and new integrated architectures that directly couple perception and action have been proposed to make such situated agents possible.

The role of symbolic representations

The Cartesian tradition, in which early AI work has grown up, stresses abstractions and symbolic inferences based on representations that capture these abstractions. The relation with the world is viewed as a problem to be dealt with later. The new AI paradigm, because of its orientation toward sensorimotor competence and situatedness, has come to adopt very specialised representations, immediately relevant to achieve a specific competence and completely grounded within concrete experiences. Varela has called a specialised dedicated view of the world a microworld.[3] There is no longer a centralised representation built out of a priori Cartesian categories; instead the representations are built up interactively by behaving in the world, and they focus on supporting appropriate action.

Symbol grounding

A different stance viz à viz representations also induces a different view on the relation between symbols and sensorimotor activities: "The overall concern ... is not to determine how some perceiver-independent world is to be recovered; it is, rather, to determine the common principles or lawful linkages between sensory and motor systems that explain how action can be perceptually guided in a perceiver-dependent world"(Varela, p. 17). This does not mean that earlier work on pattern recognition or computational vision has become irrelevant. But it means that the overall context (i.e., what is expected from visual processing components) is seen in a new light and may therefore become much more doable.

Emergence

"The manner in which the cognitive agent will next be constituted is nei-

[3] This term is somewhat unfortunate because it was previously used in AI for experimental environments such as the blockworld.

ther externally decided nor simply planned ahead. It is a matter of it commonsensical emergence." (Varela, p. 17). Most of classical AI has been embedded in a strong engineering tradition where the designer analyses beforehand the possible situations, categorises these situations, designs solutions for each of them, and tries to handle all possible disturbances. The new AI paradigm searches for other mechanisms of organisation and other design principles that would allow the agent itself to handle the continuous novelty of the real world. This is why the topic of emergent functionality and self-organisation within the complex dynamical world constituted by the processes establishing sensor-action couplings has become so dominant.

1. Research Programmes

Varela has sketched in broad terms what he believes to be new post-Cartesian directions for cognitive science. But the distance from these philosophical statements to explicit mechanisms that can be built with current technology and thus validated in the context of concrete experiments is very wide. Filling this gap is the role AI has played for earlier theories of cognitive science, and it may play the same role now. The next group of contributions reports on AI research programmes and activities that try to bridge the gap. These research programmes have been the basis of experimental work in the various AI laboratories represented at the workshop. There are three contributions, from Brooks, Steels, and Smithers, respectively. These contributions point, on the one hand, to an emerging consensus on such points as a behavior-oriented versus a function-oriented decomposition and an emphasis on autonomy as the major research question. But there are also differences. For example, Brooks bases a lot of his work on the subsumption architecture whereas Steels advocates a parallel activation of behavior systems with control taking place in a nonhierarchical way. Brooks programs individual behaviors through finite state machines whereas Smithers and Steels advocate the use of dynamical systems to couple sensors with actuators. These are some of the major issues currently being debated and explored experimentally. The following is a summary of the three contributions in this section.

Rodney Brooks: Intelligence Without Reason

The MIT mobile robots group lead by Brooks has done more than any other group to develop the technological basis for carrying out concrete experiments in the spirit of the new AI paradigm. The contribution by Brooks gives a complete review of the agents built by the group so far, the hypotheses and assumptions that were explored, the problems encountered, as well as the achievements and open problems. Brooks also makes an effort to sketch out the different backgrounds leading up to the work of himself and his collaborators.

Luc Steels: Building Agents out of Autonomous Behavior Systems

At the Free University of Brussels (VUB) Artificial Intelligence lab, an autonomous agents group has been exploring the new paradigm since 1986. The group has been strongly influenced by work on self-organisation in complex dynamical systems going on at the Free University (ULB) and therefore emphasises more the problems of how an agent builds up its own structure and functioning by interaction with an environment. Steels reviews the major assumptions and principles of the group, particularly the idea that a complete agent is built out of behavior systems that have a direct coupling between sensors and effectors and that are themselves autonomous. Behavior systems can no longer be put together in a hierarchical fashion but interact in a nonhierarchical way, similar to the way of ants in an ant society. The chapter is illustrated with an example concerning navigation using taxis. A zig-zag behavior emerges by putting together simpler behavioral systems in a nonhierarchical way.

Tim Smithers: Are Autonomous Agents Information Processing Systems?

The contribution by Smithers is based on work at the department of AI in Edinburgh. Smithers makes a direct link to Varela by challenging the classical view that intelligent agents must be seen as information processing systems. The chapter contains a number of sketches that illustrate the concrete thinking that one goes through when designing and building a seemingly trivial but actually very hard to achieve basic competence in an autonomous physical agent. These sketches illustrate how new insights, such as letting action determine perception much in the same way advocated by Varela, can be implemented in a concrete robot.

2. Technical Contributions

The technical contributions intend to demonstrate how the work in the new paradigm is carried out in practice. There are two contributions, one by Mataric and one by McFarland.

Maja Mataric: Integration of Representation Into Goal-Driven Behavior-Based Robots

Mataric has been working for several years with Brooks to turn the major hypotheses into practice. The chapter gives a concrete illustration of the subsumption architecture. It also shows how an agent—in continuous operation with the environment—is capable of building distributed and specialised representations. The representations in this case are maps for navigation.

David McFarland: Autonomy and Self-Sufficiency in Robots

McFarland is a biologist who has enthusiastically started to contribute to the new paradigm out of his background as an ethologist. McFarland sharpens the notion of autonomy and relates it to self-sufficiency. He then goes on to introduce some major new technical ideas that come from viewing robots as cost-optimizing agents. The definition of cost-functions promises to be an important tool in the design and study of autonomous agents.

3. Position Papers

These chapters are short statements, mostly in a polemic form, written from the viewpoint of the various disciplines that are strongly relevant to the construction of intelligent autonomous agents. These chapters bring out the doubts surrounding the new paradigm: Is it really a new paradigm? Is the work done so far really that different? Will it ever get us to real intelligence? Some authors argue for more radical departures. Others point out that good engineering practice needs to be maintained.

John Hallam: Autonomous Robots: A Question of Design?

Hallam's background is in robotics. He goes beyond traditional robotics by considering autonomy as the primary question to be addressed in current research. Hallam focuses on attempts to combine symbolic reasoning and low-level motor skills. In contrast to traditional planners, which try to anticipate all possible problems, he relates the results of experiments that have tried to push the uncertainty and complexity into the lower layers, thus simplifing the planning process.

William Clancey: A Boy Scout, Toto, and a Bird: How Situated Cognition Is Different from Situated Robotics

Clancey's background is in AI, more specifically in knowledge engineering. Over the past years he has shifted his position more radically to become aligned with anthropologists and psychologists subscribing to the situated cognition hypothesis. Clancey first introduces this hypothesis, which appears to be closely related to the stance taken by the new AI paradigm discussed in the book. He critically examines the experiments that have been conducted so far in the new paradigm, particularly the experiments on mapbuilding discussed by Mataric. His conclusion is that the current technical work is still too much linked to the classical AI tradition and that more radical deviations are needed.

Rolf Pfeifer and Paul Verschuren: The Challenge of Autonomous Agents: Pitfalls and How to Avoid Them

Pfeifer and Verschuren have their roots in psychology. They attack in a polemic way the assumptions underlying traditional symbol processing models in artificial intelligence by identifying a number of pitfalls. Pfeifer and Verschuren then briefly discuss the directions they are currently exploring themselves to avoid the pitfalls. At the end of the chapter the authors ask whether the new approach is indeed so different from the traditional one and whether the study of low-level skills like wall following will ever lead us to intelligent behavior.

Leslie Kaelbling: The Importance of Being Adaptable

Kaelbling comes from a background of classical AI and robotics. She has also come to view the problem of autonomous agents as central to the understanding of intelligence. Kaelbling focuses on the problem of adaptability, which has been ignored in earlier AI work. Specifically she looks at the possibilities of exploiting reinforcement learning and outlines the issues and basic directions for future research.

Stevan Harnad: Grounding Symbolic Capacity in Robotic Capacity.

The last chapter rounds off the position chapters by returning to the philosophical issues with which the book started. Harnad defines the symbol grounding problem and its role in the debate of computationalism versus connectionism. He then points to his own work on categorical perception as a first step for resolving the symbol grounding problem.

Luc Steels
Rodney Brooks

Prologue

1. The Re-Enchantment of the Concrete

Some Biological Ingredients for a Nouvelle Cognitive Science

FRANCISCO J. VARELA
Ecole Polytechnique

1.1 Shifts in Cognitive Science

Rationalistic, *Cartesian*, or *objectivist*: These are some terms used to characterize the dominant tradition within which we have grown in recent times. Yet when it comes to a re-understanding of knowledge and cognition I find that the best expression to use for our tradition is *abstract:* Nothing characterizes better the units of knowledge that are deemed most natural. It is this tendency to find our way toward the rarified atmosphere of the general and the formal, the logical and the well defined, the represented and the planned-ahead, that makes our Western world so distinctly familiar.

The main thesis I pursue here is that there are strong indications that the loose federation of sciences dealing with knowledge and cognition—the cognitive sciences—are slowly growing in the conviction that this picture is upside down and that a radical paradigmatic or epistemic shift is rapidly developing. At the very center of this emerging view is that the proper units of knowledge are primarily *concrete*, embodied, lived. This uniqueness of knowledge, its historicity and context, is not a noise that occludes the brighter pattern to be captured in its true essence, an abstraction. The concrete is not a step toward anything: It is how we arrive and where we stay.

Let me unfold this emerging view, which revitalizes the role of the concrete by focusing on its proper scale: the cognitive activity as it happens in a very special space that we may call the hinges of the *immediate present*, for it is in the immediate present that the concrete actually lives. But before this unfolding we need to revise some entrenched assumptions inherited from the computationalist orthodoxy.

1.2 Minds and Disunited Subjects

If we turn to consider the living, there is considerable support for the view that brains are not logical machines, but highly cooperative, unhomogeneous, and distributed networks. The entire system resembles a *patchwork* of subnetworks assembled by a complicated history of tinkering, rather than an optimized system that results from some clean unified design. This kind of architecture also suggests that instead of looking for grand unified models for all network behaviors, one should study networks whose abilities are restricted to specific, concrete cognitive activities that interact with each other.

This view of cognitive architecture has begun to be taken seriously by cognitive scientists in various ways. For example, as is well known Minsky [15] presented a view in which minds consist of many *agents* whose abilities are quite circumscribed: Each agent taken individually operates only in small-scale or *toy* problems. The problems must be of a small scale because they become unmanageable for a single network when they are scaled up. This last point has not been obvious to cognitive scientists for long time. The task, then, is to organize the agents, who operate in these specific domains, into effective larger systems or agencies and then to turn these agencies into higher level systems. In doing so, mind emerges as a kind of *society*.

It is important to remember here that, although inspired by a fresh look at the brain, this is a model of the mind. In other words, it is not a model of neural networks or societies; it is a model of the cognitive architecture that abstracts (again!) from neurological detail and hence from the wet of the living and of lived experience. Agents and agencies are not, therefore, entities or material processes; they are abstract processes or functions. The point bears emphasizing, especially because Minsky sometimes wrote as if he was talking about cognition at the level of the brain. As I emphasize, what is missing is the detailed link between such agents and the incarnated coupling, by sensing and acting, that is essential to living cognition. But let us pause for the moment to follow some of the implications of the notions of fragmented and local cognitive subnetworks.

The model of the mind as a society of numerous agents is intended to encompass a multiplicity of approaches to the study of cognition, ranging from distributed, self-organizing networks up to the classical, cognitivist conception of symbolic processing. This encompassing view challenges a centralized or unified model of the mind, whether in the form of distributed networks, at one extreme, or symbolic processes, at the other extreme. This move is apparent for example when Minsky argued that there are virtues not only in distribution, but in insulation, (i.e., in mechanisms that keep various processes apart[1]). The agents within an agency may be connected in the form of a distributed network, but if the agencies were themselves connected in the same way they would, in effect, constitute one large network whose functions were uniformly distributed. Such uniformity, however, would restrict the ability to combine the operations of individual agencies in a productive way. The more distributed these operations are, the harder it is to have many of them active at the same time without interfering with each other. These problems do not arise, however, if there are mechanisms to keep various agencies insulated from each other. These agencies would still interact, but through more limited connections.

The details of such a programmatic view are, of course, debatable. But the overall picture it suggests is that of mind not as a unified, homogenous entity, or even as a collection of entities, but rather as a *disunified, heterogenous collection of processes*. Elsewhere I have discussed *in extenso* some important consequences of this idea [20]. Such a disunified assembly can obviously be considered at more than one level. What counts as an agency, (i.e., as a collection of agents) could, if we change our focus, be considered as merely one agent in a larger agency. And conversely, what counts as an agent could, if we resolve our focus in greater detail, be seen to be an agency made up of many agents. In the same way, what counts as a society will also depend on our chosen level of focus.

Having thus set the stage for this key issue in contemporary cognitive science, I want to develop its implications for the question at hand: the present-centeredness of the concrete.

1.3 Readiness-to-Action in the Present

My present concern is with one of the many consequences of this view of the disunity of the subject, understood as a cognitive agent. The question I have in mind can be formulated thus: Given that there is a myriad of contending subprocesses in every cognitive act, how are we to understand the moment of negotiation and emergence when one of them takes the lead and constitutes a definite behavior? In more evocative terms, how are we to understand the very moment of being there when something concrete and specific shows up?

[1]This idea has also been extensively explored, though in a somewhat different context, by Fodor [14].

Picture yourself walking down the street, perhaps going to meet somebody. It is the end of the day, and there is nothing very special in your mind. You are in a relaxed mood, in what we may call the readiness of the walker who is simply strolling. You put your hand into your pocket, and suddenly you don't find your wallet where it usually is. Breakdown: You stop, your mind setting is unclear, your emotional tonality shifts. Before you know it, a new world emerges: You see clearly that you left your wallet in the store where you just bought cigarettes. Your mood shifts now to one of concern for losing documents and money; your readiness-to-action is now to go back to the store quickly. There is little attention to the the surrounding trees and passersby; all attention is directed to avoiding further delays.

Situations like this are the very stuff of our lives. We always operate in some kind of immediacy of a given situation: Our lived world is so ready-at-hand that we don't have any deliberateness about what is and how we inhabit it. When we sit at the table to eat with a relative or friend, the entire complex knowhow of handling table utensils, the body postures, and pauses in the conversation, are all present without deliberation. Our having-lunch-self is transparent.[2] You finish lunch, return to the office, and enter into a new readiness with a different mode of speaking, postural tone, and assessments. We have a readiness-to-action that is proper to every specific lived situation. New modes of behaving and the transitions or punctuations between them correspond to mini- (or macro-) breakdowns we experience constantly.

I refer to any such readiness for action as *microidentities* and their corresponding *microworlds*. Thus, the way we show up *as* is the way things and others show up *to* us. We could go through some elementary phenomenology and identify some typical microworlds within which we move during a normal day. The point is not to catalogue them but rather to notice their *recurrence*: Being capable of appropriate action is, in some important sense, a way in which we embody a stream of recurrent microworld transitions. I am not saying that there aren't situations where recurrence does *not* apply. For example when we arrive for the first time in a foreign country there is an enormous lack of readiness-to-hand and recurrent microworlds. Many simple actions such as social talk or eating have to be done deliberately and learned. In other words, microworlds and identities are historically constituted. But the pervasive mode of living consists of the *already* constituted microworlds that compose our identities. Clearly there is a lot more that should be explored and said about the phenomenology of ordinary experience.[3]

My intention here is more modest, merely to point to a realm of phe-

[2] I borrow this use of the notion of transparency from an unpublished manuscript by Flores and Graves [5]. I am grateful to Flores for letting me read this ongoing work.

[3] I am thinking especially of Merleau-Ponty's Phenomenology of Perception as prime example and more recently of Leder [13].

nomena, that is intimately close to our ordinary experience: When we leave the realm of our lived human experience and shift our focus to animals the same kind of analysis applies as an *external* account. The extreme case is illustrative: Biologists have known for some time that invertebrates have a rather small repertoire of behavior patterns. For example, the locomotion of a cockroach has only a few fundamental modes: standing, slow walking, fast walking, and running. Nevertheless this basic behavioral repertoire makes it possible for these animals to navigate appropriately in *any* possible environment known on the planet, natural or artificial. The question for the biologist is then: How does the animal decide which motor action to take in a given circumstance? How does its behavioral selection operate so that the action is appropriate? How does the animal have the common sense to assess a given situation and interpret it as requiring running as opposed to slow walking?

In the two extreme cases, human experience during breakdowns, and animal behaviors at moments of behavioral transitions, we are confronted—in vastly different manners to be sure—with a common issue: At each such breakdown, the manner in which the cognitive agent will next be constituted is neither externally decided nor simply planned ahead. It is a matter of *commonsensical emergence*, of autonomous configurations of an appropriate stance. Once a behavioral stance is selected or a microworld is brought forth, we can more clearly analyze its mode of operation and its optimal strategy. In fact, the key to autonomy is that a living system, out of its own resources, finds its way into the next moment by acting appropriately. The breakdowns, the hinges that articulate microworlds, are the source of the autonomous and creative side of living cognition. Such common sense, then, needs to be examined at a microscale, at the moments where it actualizes *during breakdowns*, the birthplace of the concrete. This is, to be sure, also a central question for the design of autonomous robots [14], and it will be interesting to see to what extent similar solutions might not apply.

1.4 Knowledge as Enaction

Let me explain what I mean by the word *embodied*, highlighting two main points: (a) that cognition depends on the kinds of experience that come from having a body with various sensorimotor capacities; and (b) that these individual sensorimotor capacities are themselves embedded in a more encompassing biological and cultural *context*. These two points were already introduced when discussing breakdown and common sense, but here I explore further their corporeal specificity, to emphasize once again that sensory and motor processes, perception and action, are fundamentally inseparable in lived cognition, and not merely contingently linked in individuals.

In order to make my ideas more precise, let me give a preliminary formulation of what I mean by an *enactive approach to cognition* [19, 20]. In a nutshell, the enactive approach consists of two key points: (a) that perception consists in perceptually guided action; and (b) that cognitive structures emerge from the recurrent sensorimotor patterns that enable action to be perceptually guided. These two statements will become transparent as we proceed.

Let us begin with the notion of perceptually guided action. For the dominant computationalist tradition, the point of departure for understanding perception is typically abstract: the information processing problem of recovering predetermined properties of the world. In contrast, the point of departure for the enactive approach is the study of how the perceiver can guide its actions in its local situation. Because these local situations constantly change as a result of the perceiver's activity, the reference point for understanding perception is no longer a predetermined, perceiver-independent world, but rather the sensorimotor structure of the cognitive agent, the way in which the nervous system links sensory and motor surfaces. It is this structure—the manner in which the perceiver is embodied—rather than some predetermined world, that determines how the perceiver can act and be modulated by environmental events. Thus the overall concern of an enactive approach to perception is not to determine how some perceiver-independent world is to be recovered; it is, rather, to determine the common principles or lawful linkages between sensory and motor systems that explain how action can be *perceptually guided* in a *perceiver-dependent* world.[4]

In such an approach, then, perception is not simply embedded within and constrained by the surrounding world; it also contributes to the *enactment* of this surrounding world. Thus, the organism both initiates and is shaped by the environment. We must see the organism and environment as bound together in reciprocal specification and selection—a point to which we need to constantly remind ourselves, for it is contrary to views familiar to us from the Cartesian tradition.

A classical illustration of the perceptual guidance of action is the study of Held and Hein who raised kittens in the dark and exposed them to light only under controlled conditions [8]. A first group of animals was allowed to move around normally, but they were harnessed to a simple carriage and basket that contained the second group of animals. The two groups therefore shared the same visual experience, but the second group was entirely passive. When the animals were released after a few weeks of this treatment, the first group of kittens behaved normally, but those who had been carried around behaved as if they were blind: They bumped into objects and fell over edges. This beautiful study supports the enactive view that objects are not seen by the visual extraction of features, but rather by the visual guidance of action. Similar results have been obtained under

[4]For more on this approach, see [10].

other diverse circumstances and studied even at the single-cell level.

Lest the reader feel that this example is fine for cats, but removed from human experience, consider another example. Bach designed a video camera for blind persons that can stimulate multiple points in the skin by electrically activated vibration [1]. Using this technique, images formed with the camera were made to correspond to patterns of skin stimulation, thereby substituting for the visual loss. Patterns projected onto the skin have no visual content unless the individual is behaviorally active by directing the video camera using head, hand, or body movements. When the blind person does actively behave in this way, after a few hours of experience a remarkable emergence takes place: The person no longer interprets the skin sensations as body related, but rather as images projected into the space being explored by the bodily directed "gaze" of the video camera. Thus, in order to experience "real objects out there" the person must actively direct the camera (by head or hand).

1.5 The Fine Structure of the Present

I have now situated the emergence of the concrete within the enactive framework for cognition, where it can really make sense. We can now return to the problem we started with: How can emergent microworlds arise out of a turmoil of many cognitive agents and subnetworks? The answer I propose is that within the gap during a breakdown there is a rich *dynamics* involving the concurrent subidentities and agents. This rapid dialogue, invisible to introspection, seems to have been finally addressed directly in recent in brain studies.

The central idea was introduced by Freeman who, over many years of research, managed to insert an array of electrodes into the olfactory bulb of a rabbit so that a small portion of the global activity can be measured while the animal behaves freely [3]. He found that there is no clear pattern of global activity in the bulb unless the animal is exposed to one specific odor several times. Furthermore, he found for the first time that such emergent patterns of activity are created out of a background of incoherent or chaotic activity by fast oscillations (i.e., with periods of about 5–10 msec) until the cortex settles into pattern, which lasts until the end of the sniffing behavior and then dissolves back into the chaotic background [4]. Smell appears in this light not as a mapping of external features, but rather as a creative form of enacting significance on the basis of the animal's embodied history. What is most pertinent here is that this enaction happens at the hinge between one behavioral moment and the next, via fast oscillations between cell populations that can give rise to coherent patterns.

There is growing evidence that this kind of fast dynamics can underlie the configuration of neuronal ensembles. It has been reported in the cortex in cats and monkeys linked to visual stimulation; it has also been found in radically different neural structures such as a bird's brain, and even the ganglia of an invertebrate.[5] This universality is important, for it points to the fundamental nature of this mechanism for the enaction of sensorimotor couplings. Had it been a very species-specific process, typical, for example, of mammalian cortex, it would be far less convincing as a working hypothesis.

It is important to note here that this fast dynamics is not restricted to sensorial trigger: The oscillations appear and disappear quickly and quite spontaneously in various places of the brain. This suggests that such fast dynamics involve all of those subnetworks that give rise to the entire readiness-to-hand in the next moment. They don't only involve sensory interpretation and motor action, but also the entire gamut of cognitive expectations and emotional tonality that are central to the shaping of a microworld. Between breakdown, these oscillations are the symptoms of—very rapid—reciprocal cooperation and competition between distinct agents that are activated by the current situation, vying with each other for differing modes of interpretation for a coherent cognitive framework and readiness for action. On the basis of this fast dynamics, as in an evolutionary process, one neuronal ensemble (one cognitive subnetwork) finally becomes more prevalent and becomes the behavioral mode for the next cognitive moment. When I say "becomes prevalent", I do not mean to this is a process of optimization: It resembles more a consolidation out of a chaotic dynamics. It follows that such a cradle of autonomous action is forever lost to lived experience because by definition we can only inhabit a microidentity when it is already present, not in gestation. In other words, in the breakdown before the next microworld shows up, there is a myriad of possibilities available until, out of the constraints of the situation and the recurrence of history, a single one is selected.

This fast dynamics is a very good candidate for the neural correlate of the autonomous constitution of a cognitive agent. Future work will determine whether this is actually the case or whether we need an alternative mechanism. For our purposes, what is important is that it gives the moment of behavioral selection its rightful place.

1.6 From Temporal Fine Structure to Cognitive Action

It is important to sketch in this context how I envisage cognitive structures to emerge from the kinds of recurrent sensorimotor patterns that enable action to be perceptually guided. As stated, the fast dynamics of agent reciprocity provide the playground for the emergence of a microworld. What

[5] For a recent review, see [18]. The work of Gray and Singer [7] has been largely responsible for the wider acceptance of this hypothesis; for Hermissenda, see [6].

we need to examine now is some evidence as to how to link this sensorimotor coupling with other kinds of higher cognitive performance. Otherwise, we might be tempted to attribute no significance to the foregoing except for the low level event of sensing and acting, but not for the true higher cognitive levels. In fact, this basic idea is at the very core of the Piagetian program and has been argued for in various recent works, such as Johnson and Lakoff [9, 12]. I present the idea of embodied cognitive structures with special reference to their work. Once again we must move out of the abstract and emphasize an experientialist approach to cognition. As Lakoff said, the central claim of their approach is that meaningful conceptual structures arise from two sources: (a) from the structured nature of bodily and social experience; and (b) from our capacity to project imaginatively from certain well-structured aspects of bodily and interactional experience to conceptual structures.

Rational and abstract thought is the application of very general cognitive processes—focusing, scanning, superimposition, figure-ground reversal, etc.—to such structures. Eco [11] provided a concise overview of Lakoff and Johnson's experientialist approach. The basic ideas that embodied sensorimotor structures are the substance for experience, and that experiential structures motivate conceptual understanding and rational thought. Because I have emphasized that perception and action are embodied in sensorimotor processes that are self-organizing, it is natural to see how cognitive structures *emerge* from recurrent patterns of sensorimotor activity. In either case, the point is not, as Lakoff noted, that experience strictly determines conceptual structures and modes of thought; it is, rather, that experience both makes possible and constrains conceptual understanding across the multitude of cognitive domains.[6]

Lakoff and Johnson provided numerous examples of cognitive structures that are generated from experiential processes. To review all of these examples here would take us too far afield. Let me discuss briefly only one of the most significant kinds: basic-level categories. Consider most of the middle-sized things with which we continually interact: tables, chairs, dogs, cats, forks, knives, cups, and so on. These things belong to a level of categorization that is intermediate between lower (subordinate) and higher (superordinate) levels. If we take a chair, for example, at the lower level it might belong to the category *rocking chair*, whereas at the higher level it belongs to the category *furniture*. Rosch and others have showed that this intermediate level of categorization (table, chair, etc.) is psychologically the most fundamental or *basic* [17]. Among the reasons why these basic-level categories are considered to be psychologically the most fundamental are: (a) the basic level is the most general level where category members have similar overall *perceived shapes*; (b) it is the most general level where a person uses similar *motor actions* for interacting with category mem-

[6]Ibid., p. 120.

bers; and (c) it is the level where clusters of correlated attributes are most *apparent.* It would seem, therefore, that what determines whether a category belongs to the basic-level depends not on how things are arranged in some predetermined world, but rather on the sensorimotor structure of our bodies and the kinds of perceptually guided interactions this structure makes possible. Basic-level categories are both experiential and embodied. A similar argument can be made for image schemas emerging from certain basic forms of sensorimotor activities and interactions.

1.7 In Conclusion

Let me conclude by considering where the ideas sketched here have taken us. I have argued that perception does not consist in the recovery of a predetermined world, but rather in the perceptual guidance of action in a world that is inseparable from our sensorimotor capacities. I have also argued that cognitive structures emerge from recurrent patterns of perceptually guided action. We can summarize by saying that cognition consists not in representation, but in *embodied action.* Correlatively, the world we know is not pre-established; it is, rather, enacted through our history of structural coupling. Furthermore we have also seen that the hinge that articulates *enaction* consists of fast noncognitive dynamics wherein a number of alternative microworlds are activated. These hinges are the source of both common sense and creativity in cognition, the key ingredients for a tasty nouvelle cognitive science.

If there is something that is nouvelle in the enactive direction of cognitive science evoked in this gathering, it is that it points in a direction we can consider post-Cartesian in two important respects. First, knowledge appears more and more as being built from small domains, microworlds, and microidentities. Such basic modes of readiness-to-hand are variable throughout the animal kingdom. But what all living cognitive beings seem to have in common is that knowledge is always a knowhow constituted on the basis of the concrete; what we call the general and the abstract are aggregates of readiness-for-action.

The second post-Cartesian aspect is that such microworlds are not coherent or integrated into some enormous totality that regulates the veracity of the smaller pieces. It is more like an unruly conversational interaction. It is the very presence of this unruliness that allows for the constitution of a cognitive moment according to the system's constitution and history. The very heart of this autonomy, the fast time of the agent's behavior selection, is forever lost to the cognitive system itself. Thus, what we call traditionally the irrational and the nonconscious is not contradictory to what appears as rational and purposeful, but its very underpinning.

References

[1] Bach, R. (1962). *Brain mechanisms in sensory substitution.* New York: Academic Press.

[2] Fodor, J. (1983). *The modularity of mind.* Cambridge, MA: MIT Press, Bradford Books.

[3] Freeman, W. (1975). *Mass action in the nervous system.* New York: Academic Press.

[4] Freeman, W., & Skarda, C. (1985). Spatial EEG patterns, Nonlinear dynamics, and perception: The neo-Sherringtonian view. *Brain Research Reviews, 10*, 145–175.

[5] Flores, F., & Graves, M. (1990). Unpublished manuscript. Berkeley, CA: Logonet.

[6] Gelperin, A., & Tank, A. (1990). Odour-modulated collective network oscillations of olfactory interneurons in a terrestrial mollusc. *Nature, 345*, 437–439.

[7] Gray, C., & Singer, W. (1986). Stimulus-specific neuronal oscillations in orientation columns in cat visual cortex. *Proceedings National Academy of Sciences (USA), 86*, 1698–1702.

[8] Held, R., & Hein, A. (1958). Adaptation of disarranged hand–eye coordination contingent upon re-afferent Stimulation. *Perceptual Motor Skills, 8*, 87–90.

[9] Johnson, M. (1989). *The body in the mind.* Chicago: University of Chicago Press.

[10] Kelso, J., & Kay, B. (1987). Information and control: A macroscopic analysis of perception-action coupling. In H. Heuer & F. Andries Sanders (Eds.), *Perspectives on perception and action.* (pp. 3–32). Hillsdale, NJ: Lawrence Erlbaum Associates.

[11] Lakoff, G. (1988). Cognitive semantics. In U. Eco *Meaning and mental representations* (p. 121). Bloomington: Indiana University Press.

[12] Lakoff, G., & Johnson, M. (1989). *Women, fire and dangerous things.* Chicago: University of Chicago Press.

[13] Leder, M. (1990). *The absent body.* Chicago: Chicago University Press.

[14] Maes, P. (1989). How to do the right thing. *Connection Science, 1*, 291–323.

[15] Minsky, M. (1986). *The society of mind.* New York: Simon & Schuster.

[16] Neuenschwander, S., & Varela, F. (in press). Sensori-triggered and spontaneous oscillations in the avian brain. *European Journal of Neuroscience.*

[17] Rosch, E., Mervis, C. B., Gray, W. D., Johnson, D. M., & Boyes-Braem P. (1976). Basic objects in natural categories. *Cognitive Psychology, 8*, 382–439.

[18] Singer, W. (in press). Synchronization of cortical activity and its putative role in information processing and learning. *Annual Review of Physiology.*

[19] Varela, F. (1989). Connaitre: les sciences cognitives [The cognitive sciences]. Paris: Seuil.

[20] Varela, F., Thompson, E., & Rosch, E., (1991). *The embodied mind: cognitive science and human experience.* Cambridge, MA: MIT Press.

Part I

Research Programmes

2. Intelligence Without Reason

RODNEY A. BROOKS [1]
MIT Artificial Intelligence Laboratory

2.1 Introduction

Artificial Intelligence (AI) as a formal discipline has been around for a little over 30 years. The goals of individual practitioners vary and change over time. A reasonable characterization of the general field is that it is intended to make computers do things that when done by people are described as having indicated intelligence. Winston [142] characterized the goals of AI as both the construction of useful intelligent systems and the understanding of human intelligence.

There is a temptation, often succumbed to, to then go ahead and define *intelligence*, but that does not immediately give a clearly grounded meaning to the field. In fact, there is danger of deep philosophical regress with no recovery. Therefore I prefer to stay with a more informal notion of intelligence being the sort of stuff that humans do, pretty much all the time.

2.1.1 Approaches

Traditional AI has tried to tackle the problem of building artificially intelligent systems from the top down. It tackled intelligence through the notions of *thought* and *reason*. These are things we only know about through introspection. The field has adopted a certain *modus operandi* over the years,

[1] This is a revised version of the IJCAI-91 Computers and Thought Award Lecture.

which includes a particular set of conventions on how the inputs and outputs to thought and reasoning are to be handled (e.g., the subfield of knowledge representation), and the sorts of things that thought and reasoning do (e.g., planning, problem solving, etc.). I argue that these conventions cannot account for large aspects of what goes into intelligence. Furthermore, without those aspects validity of traditional AI approaches comes into question. I also argue that much of the landmark work on thought has been influenced by the technological constraints of the available computers, and thereafter these consequences have often mistakenly become enshrined as principles, long after the original impetus has disappeared.

From an evolutionary stance, human intelligence did not suddenly leap onto the scene. There were precursors and foundations throughout the lineage to humans. Much of this substrate is present in other animals today. The study of that substrate may well provide constraints on how higher level *thought* in humans could be organized.

Recently there has been a movement to study intelligence from the bottom up, concentrating on physical systems (e.g., mobile robots), situated in the world, autonomously carrying out tasks of various sorts. Some of this work is based on engineering from first principles, other parts of the work are firmly based on biological inspirations. The flavor of this work is quite different from that of traditional AI. In fact, it suggests that despite our best introspections, traditional AI offers solutions to intelligence that bear almost no resemblance at all to how biological systems work.

There are of course dangers in studying biological systems too closely. Their design was not highly optimized from a global systems point of view. Rather, they were patched together and adapted from previously working systems, in ways that most expeditiously met the latest environmental pressures. Perhaps the solutions found for much of intelligence are terribly suboptimal. Certainly there are many vestigial structures surviving within humans' and other animals' digestive, skeletal, and muscular systems. One should suppose then that there are many vestigial neurological structures, interactions, and side effects. Their emulation may be a distraction.

2.1.2 Outline

The body of this chapter is formed by five main sections: *Robots*, *Computers*, *Biology*, *Ideas* and *Thought*. Its theme is how computers and thought have been intimately intertwined in the development of AI, how those connections may have led the field astray, how biological examples of intelligence are quite different from the models used by AI, and how recent new approaches point to another path for both computers and thought.

The new approaches that have been developed recently for AI arose from work with mobile robots. Section 2.2 briefly outlines the context within which this work arose and discusses some key realizations made by the researchers involved.

Section 2.3 traces the development of the foundational ideas for AI, and how they were intimately linked to the technology available for computation. Neither situatedness nor embodiment were easy to include on the original agenda, although their importance was recognized by many early researchers. The early framework with its emphasis on search has remained dominant and has led to solutions that seem important within the closed world of AI, but which perhaps are not relevant to practical applications. The field of cybernetics, with a heritage of very different tools from the early digital computer, provides an interesting counterpoint, confirming the hypothesis that models of thought are intimately tied to the available models of computation.

Section 2.4 is a brief overview of recent developments in the understanding of biological intelligence. It covers material from ethology, psychology, and neuroscience. Of necessity it is not comprehensive, but it is sufficient to demonstrate that the intelligence of biological systems is organized in ways quite different from traditional views of AI.

Section 2.5 introduces the two cornerstones to the new approach to AI, *situatedness* and *embodiment*, and discusses both intelligence and emergence in these contexts.

Section 2.6 outlines some details of the approach of my group at MIT to building complete situated, embodied, artificially intelligent robots. This approach shares more heritage with biological systems than with what is usually called AI.

2.2 Robots

There has been a scattering of work with mobile robots within the AI community over the years. Shakey from the late 1960s at SRI (see [99] for a collection of original reports) is perhaps the best known, but other significant efforts include the CART [89] at Stanford and Hilare [48] in Toulouse.

All these systems used offboard computers (and thus they could be the largest, most powerful computers available at the time and place), and all operated in mostly static environments.[2] All of these robots operated in environments that at least to some degree had been specially engineered for them. They all sensed the world and tried to build two- or three-dimensional world models of it. Then, in each case, a planner could ignore

[2]In the case of Shakey, experiments included the existence of a gremlin who would secretly come and alter the environment by moving a block to a different location. However, this would usually happen only once, for instance, in a many-hour run, and the robot would not perceive the dynamic act, but rather might later notice a changed world if the change was directly relevant to the particular subtask it was executing. In the case of the CART, the only dynamic aspect of the world was the change in sun angle over long time periods, and this, in fact, caused the robot to fail, as its position estimation scheme was confused by the moving shadows.

the actual world and operate in the model to produce a plan of action for the robot to achieve whatever goal it had been given. In all three of these robots, the generated plans included at least a nominal path through the world model along which the robot was intended to move.

Despite the simplifications (static, engineered environments, and the most powerful available computers) all these robots operated excruciatingly slowly. Much of the processing time was consumed in the perceptual end of the systems and in building the world models. Relatively little computation was used in planning and acting.

An important effect of this work was to provide a framework within which other researchers could operate without testing their ideas on real robots and even without having any access to real robot data. I call this framework the *sense-model-plan-act* framework, or *SMPA* for short. See section 2.3.6 for more details of how the SMPA framework influenced the manner in which robots were built over the following years and how those robots in turn imposed restrictions on the ways in which intelligent control programs could be built for them.

An implicit assumption in this early work with mobile robots was that once the simpler case of operating in a static environment had been solved, then the more difficult case of an actively dynamic environment could be tackled. None of these early SMPA systems were ever extended in this way.

In 1984, a number of people started to worry about the more general problem of organizing intelligence. There was a requirement that intelligence be reactive to dynamic aspects of the environment, that a mobile robot operate on time scales similar to those of animals and humans, and that intelligence be able to generate robust behavior in the face of uncertain sensors, an unpredicted environment, and a changing world. Some of the key realizations about the organization of intelligence were as follows:

- Most of what people do in their day to day lives is not problem solving or planning, but rather it is routine activity in a relatively benign, but certainly dynamic, world. Furthermore, the representations an agent uses of objects in the world need not rely on a semantic correspondence with symbols that the agent possesses, but rather can be defined through interactions of the agent with the world. Agents based on these ideas have achieved interesting performance levels and were built from combinatorial circuits plus a little timing circuitry [3, 4].

- An observer can legitimately talk about an agent's beliefs and goals, even though the agent need not manipulate symbolic data structures at run time. A formal grounding in semantics used for the agent's design can be compiled away. Agents based on these ideas have achieved interesting performance levels and were built from combinatorial circuits plus a little timing circuitry [104, 61].

- In order to test ideas of intelligence, it is important to build complete agents that operate in dynamic environments using real sensors. Internal world models, which are complete representations of the external environment besides being impossible to obtain, are not at all necessary for agents to act in a competent manner. Many of the actions of an agent are quite separable; coherent intelligence can emerge from subcomponents interacting in the world. Agents based on these ideas have achieved interesting performance levels and were built from combinatorial circuits plus a little timing circuitry [21, 24, 26].

A large number of others have also contributed to this approach to organizing intelligence. [67] is the most representative collection.

There is no generally accepted term to describe this style of work. It has sometimes been characterized by the oxymoron *reactive planning.* I have variously used *robot beings* [28] and *artificial creatures* [24]. Related work on non mobile, but nevertheless active, systems has been called *active vision*, or *animate vision* [13]. Some workers refer to their beings or creatures as *agents*; unfortunately that term is also used by others to refer to somewhat independent components of intelligence within a single physical creature (e.g., the agencies of [16]). Sometimes the approach is called *behavior based* as the computational components tend to be direct behavior producing modules.[3] For the remainder of this chapter, I simply call the entities of discussion *robots* or *behavior-based robots.*

There are a number of key aspects characterizing this style of work.

- *Situatedness.* The robots are situated in the world—they do not deal with abstract descriptions, but with the here and now of the world directly influencing the behavior of the system.

- *Embodiment.* The robots have bodies and experience the world directly—their actions are part of a dynamic with the world and have immediate feedback on their own sensations.

- *Intelligence.* They are observed to be intelligent—but the source of intelligence is not limited to just the computational engine. It also comes from the situation in the world, the signal transformations within the sensors, and the physical coupling of the robot with the world.

- *Emergence.* The intelligence of the system emerges from the system's interactions with the world and from sometimes indirect interactions between its components—it is sometimes hard to point to one event or place within the system and say that is why some external action was manifested.

[3] Unfortunately this clashes a little with the meaning of *behavior* as used by ethologists as an observed interaction with the world, rather than as something explicitly generated.

Recently there has been a trend to try to integrate traditional symbolic reasoning, on top of a purely reactive system, both with real robots (e.g., [9, 87]) and in simulation (e.g, [44]). The idea is that the reactive system handles the real-time issues of being embedded in the world, whereas the deliberative system does the hard stuff traditionally imagined to be handled by an AI system. I think these approaches are suffering from the well-known horizon effect: They have bought a little better performance in their overall system with the reactive component, but they have simply pushed the limitations of the reasoning system a bit further into the future. I am not concerned with such systems for the remainder of this chapter.

Before examining this work in greater detail, I turn to the reasons why traditional AI adopted such a different approach.

2.3 Computers

In evolution there is a theory [50] of punctuated equilibria, where most of the time there is little change within a species, but at intervals a subpopulation branches off with a short burst of greatly accelerated changes. Likewise, I believe that in AI research over the last 40 or so years, there have been long periods of incremental work within established guidelines and occasionally a shift in orientation and assumptions causing a new subfield to branch off. The older work usually continues, sometimes remaining strong and sometimes dying off gradually. This description of the field also fits more general models of science, such as [64].

The point of this section is that all those steady-state bodies of work rely, sometimes implicitly, on certain philosophical and *technological* assumptions. The founders of the bodies of work are quite aware of these assumptions, but over time as new people come into the fields, these assumptions get lost, forgotten, or buried, and the work takes on a life of its own for its own sake.

In this section I am particularly concerned with how the architecture of our computers influences our choice of problems on which to work, our models of thought, and our algorithms, and how the problems on which we work, our models of thought, and our algorithm choices put pressure on the development of architectures of our computers.

Biological systems run on massively parallel, low-speed computation, within an essentially fixed topology network with bounded depth. Almost all AI research, and indeed almost all modern computation, runs on essentially Von Neumann architectures, with a large, inactive memory that can respond at very high speed over an extremely narrow channel to a very high speed central processing unit that contains very little state. When connections to sensors and actuators are also considered, the gap between biological systems and our artificial systems widens.

Besides putting architectural constraints on our programs, even our mathematical tools are strongly influenced by our computational architectures. Most algorithmic analysis is based on the RAM model of computation (essentially a Von Neumann model, shown to be polynomially equivalent to a Turing machine, e.g., [52]). Only in recent years have more general models gained prominence, but they have been in the direction of oracles, and other improbable devices for our robot beings. Are we doomed to work forever within the current architectural constraints?

Over the past few centuries computation technology has progressed from making marks on various surfaces (chiselling, writing, etc.), through a long evolutionary chain of purely mechanical systems, then electromechanical relay-based systems, through vacuum tube-based devices, followed by an evolutionary chain of silicon-based devices to the current state of the art.

It would be the height of arrogance and foolishness to assume that we are now using the ultimate technology for computation, namely silicon based integrated circuits, just as it would have been foolish, at least in retrospect, to assume in the 16th century that Napier's Bones were the ultimate computing technology [138]. Indeed the end of the exponential increase in computation speed for uniprocessors is in sight, forcing somewhat the large amount of research into parallel approaches to more computation for the dollar and per second. But there are other more radical possibilities for changes in computation infrastructure.[4] These include computation based on optical switching [47, 20], protein folding, gene expression and nonorganic atomic switching.

2.3.1 Prehistory

During the early 1940s even while the second world war was being waged, and the first electronic computers were being built for cryptanalysis and trajectory calculations, the idea of using computers to carry out intelligent activities was already on people's minds.

Turing, already famous for his work on computability [124], had discussions with Michie as early as 1943, and others less known to the modern AI world as early as 1941, about using a computer to play chess. He and others developed the idea of minimaxing a tree of moves and of static evaluation and carried out elaborate hand simulations against human opponents. Later, from 1945 to 1950 at least, he and Shannon communicated about these ideas.[5] Although there was already an established field of mathematics concerning a theory of games, pioneered by Von Neumann [129],

[4] Equally radical changes have occurred in the past, but admittedly they happened well before the current high levels of installed base of silicon-based computers.

[5] Wiener also outlined the idea of minimax in the final note of the original edition of [136]. However he restricted the idea to a depth of two or three plays—one assumes for practical reasons, as he did express the general notion for n plays. See Section 2.3.3 for more details on the ways in which cybernetic models of thought were restricted by the computational models at hand.

chess had such a large space of legal positions that even though everything about it is deterministic, the theories were not particularly applicable. Only heuristic and operational programs seemed plausible means of attack.

In a paper entitled *Intelligent Machinery*, written in 1948[6] but not published until long after his death [126], Turing outlined a more general view of making computers intelligent. In this rather short insightful paper he foresaw many modern developments and techniques. He argued (somewhat whimsically, to the annoyance of his employers [55]) for at least some fields of intelligence, and his particular example was the learning of languages, that the machine would have to be embodied, and claimed success "seems however to depend rather too much on sense organs and locomotion to be feasible"[126]p. 22.

Turing argued that it must be possible to build a thinking machine because it was possible to build imitations of "any small part of a man". He made the distinction between producing accurate electrical models of nerves and replacing them computationally with the available technology of vacuum tube circuits (this follows directly from his earlier paper [124]), based on the assumption that the nervous system can be modeled as a computational system. For other parts of the body he suggested that "television cameras, microphones, loudspeakers", for example, could be used to model the rest of the system. "This would be a tremendous undertaking of course". Even so, Turing noted that the so constructed machine "would still have no contact with food, sex, sport and many other things of interest to the human being"[126]p. 18. Turing concluded that the best domains in which to explore the mechanization of thought are various games, and cryptanalysis, "in that they require little contact with the outside world"[126]p. 18.[7]

Turing thus carefully considered the question of embodiment, and for technical reasons chose to pursue aspects of intelligence that could be viewed, at least in his opinion, as purely symbolic. Minimax search, augmented with the idea of pursuing chains of capture to quiescence, and clever static evaluation functions (the *Turochamp* system of Champernowne and Turing,[8], [112]) soon became the dominant approach to the problem. [93] compared all four known implemented chess playing programs of 1958 (with a total combined experience of six games played), including Turochamp, and they all followed this approach.

The basic approach of minimax with a good static evaluation function has not changed to this day. Programs of this ilk compete well with International Grand Masters. The best of them, *Deep Thought* [58], uses

[6]Different sources cite 1947 and 1948 as the time of writing.

[7]Interestingly, Turing did not completely abstract even a chess playing machine away from embodiment, commenting that "its only organs need be 'eyes' capable of distinguishing the various positions on a specially made board, and means for announcing its own moves"[126]p. 18.

[8]See *Personal Computing* (January 1980, p. 80–81), for a description of this hand simulation of a chess machine.

special purpose chips for massive search capabilities, along with a skillful evaluation scheme and selective deepening to direct that search better than in previous programs.

Although Turing had conceived of using chess as a vehicle for studying human thought processes, this notion has largely gotten lost along the way. (There are, of course, exceptions; for example, [137] describes a system that substitutes chess knowledge for search in the middle game—usually there are very few static evaluations, and tree search is mainly to confirm or deny the existence of a mate). Instead the driving force has always been performance, and the most successful program of the day has usually relied on technological advances. Brute force tree search has been the dominant method, itself dominated by the amount of brutishness available. This, in turn, has been a product of clever harnessing of the latest technology available. Over the years, the current champion program has capitalized on the available hardware. *MacHack-6* [51] made use of the largest available fast memory (256K 36 bits words—about a megabyte or so, or $45 by today's standards) and a new comprehensive architecture (the PDP-6) largely influenced by Minsky and McCarthy's requirements for Lisp and symbolic programming. *Chess 4.0* and its descendants [116] relied on running on the world's faster available computer. *Belle* [33] used a smaller central computer, but had a custom move generator, built from LSI circuits. Deep Thought, mentioned already as the most recent champion, relies on custom VLSI circuits to handle its move generation and tree search. It is clear that the success and progress in chess playing programs have been driven by technology enabling large tree searches. Few would argue that today's chess programs/hardware systems are very good models for general human thought processes.

There were some misgivings along the way, however. An early article [111] argued that better static evaluation is the key to playing chess, so that look-ahead can be limited to a single move except in situations close to mate (and one assumes he would include situations where there is capture, and perhaps exchanges, involved). But, he claimed that humans come to chess with a significant advantage over computers (the thrust of the paper is on learning, and in this instance on learning to play chess) as they have concepts such as value, double threat, the centre, and so on, already formed. Chess to Selfridge is not a disembodied exercise, but one where successful play is built upon a richness of experience in other, perhaps simpler, situations.

There is an interesting counterpoint to the history of computer chess, the game of Go. The search tree for Go is much larger than for chess, and a good static evaluation function is much harder to define. Go has never worked out well as a vehicle for research in computer game playing; any reasonable crack at it is much more likely to require techniques closer to those of human thought. Mere computer technology advances are not going to bring the minimax approach close to success in this domain (see

[29] for a brief overview).

Before leaving Turing entirely there is one other rather significant prescient contribution he made to the field. In [125] he posed the question "Can machines think?". To tease out an acceptable meaning for this question Turing presented what has come to be known as the *Turing test*, where a person communicates in English over a teletype with either another person or a computer. The goal is to guess whether it is a person or a computer at the other end. Over time this test has come to be an informal goal of AI[9]. Notice that it is a totally disembodied view of intelligence, although it is somewhat situated in that the machine has to respond in a timely fashion to its interrogator. Turing suggested that the machine should try to simulate a person by taking extra time and making mistakes with arithmetic problems. This is the version of the Turing test that is bandied around by current AI researchers.[10]

Turing advanced a number of strawman arguments against the case that a digital computer might one day be able to pass this test, but he did not consider the need that the machine be fully embodied. In principle, of course, he was right. But how a machine might then be programmed is a question. Turing provided an argument that programming the machine by hand would be impractical, so he suggested having it learn. At this point he brought up the need to embody the machine in some way. He rejected giving it limbs, but suspected that eyes would be good, although not entirely necessary. At the end of the paper he proposed two possible paths toward his goal of a thinking machine. The unembodied path is to concentrate on programming intellectual activities like chess, whereas the embodied approach is to equip a digital computer "with the best sense organs that money can buy, and then teach it to understand and speak English"(p.). Artificial Intelligence followed the former path, and has all but ignored the latter approach.[11]

2.3.2 Establishment

The establishment of AI as a discipline occurred during the period from the famous Dartmouth Conference of 1956 through the publication of *Computers and Thought* in 1963 [43].

Named and mostly organized by John McCarthy as "The Dartmouth Summer Research Project on Artificial Intelligence," the 6-week workshop brought together those who would establish and lead the major AI research

[9]Turing expressed his own belief that it would be possible for a machine with 10^9 bits of store to pass a five minute version of the test with 70% probability by about the year 2000.

[10]In fact there is a yearly competition with a $100,000 prize for a machine that can pass this version of the Turing test.

[11]An excerpt from Turing's paper is reprinted in [56], but the whole section on learning and embodiment is left out.

centers in North America for the next 20 years. McCarthy jointly established the MIT Artificial Intelligence Laboratory with Marvin Minsky and then went on to found the Stanford Artificial Intelligence Laboratory. Allen Newell and Herbert Simon shaped and lead the group that turned into the computer science department at Carnegie Mellon University. Even today a large number of the researchers in AI in North America had one of these four people on their doctoral committee or were advised by someone who did. The ideas expressed at the Dartmouth meeting have thus had a signal impact on the field first named there.

As can be seen from interviews of the participants published in [76] there is still some disagreement over the intellectual property that was brought to the conference and its relative significance. The key outcome was the acceptance and rise of search as the pre-eminent tool of AI. There was a general acceptance of the use of search to solve problems, and with this there was an essential abandonment of any notion of situatedness.

Minsky's earlier work had been involved with neural modeling. His PhD thesis at Princeton was concerned with a model for the brain [83]. Later, while at Harvard he was strongly influenced by McCulloch and Pitts (see [77]), but by the time of the Dartmouth meeting he had become more involved with symbolic search-based systems. In his collection [84] of versions of his students' PhD theses, all were concerned to some degree with defining and controlling an appropriate search space.

At the Dartmouth meeting, Simon and Newell presented their recent work on the *Logic Theorist* [92], a program that proved logic theorems by searching a tree of subgoals. The program made extensive use of heuristics to prune its search space. With this success, the idea of heuristic search soon became dominant within the still tiny AI community.

McCarthy was not so affected by the conference that he had organized and continues to this day to concentrate on epistemological issues rather than performance programs. However, he was soon to invent the Lisp programming language [74], which became the standard model of computation for AI. It had great influence on the models of thought that were popular however, as it made certain things such as search and representations based on individuals much easier to program.

At the time, most programs were written in assembly language. It was a tedious job to write search procedures, especially recursive procedures in the machine languages of the day, although some people such as Samuel [109] (another Dartmouth participant) were spectacularly successful. Newell and Simon owed much of their success in developing the Logic Theorist and their later General Problem Solver [94], to their use of an interpreted language (IPL-V—see [95]) that supported complex list structures and recursion. Many of their student's projects reported in [43] also used this language.

McCarthy's Lisp was much cleaner and simpler. It made processing lists of information and recursive tree searches trivial to program—often a dozen lines of code could replace many hundreds of lines of assembler code. Search procedures became even easier and more convenient to include in AI programs. Lisp also had an influence on the classes of representational systems used, as is described in section 2.3.5.

In [81], AI was broken into five key topics: search, pattern recognition, learning, planning, and induction. The second through fourth of these were characterized as ways of controlling search (respectively by better selection of tree expansion operators, by directing search through previous experience, and by replacing a given search with a smaller and more appropriate exploration). Again, most of the serious work in AI according to this breakdown was concerned with search.

Eventually, after much experimentation [80], search methods became well understood, formalized, and analyzed [62], and became celebrated as the primary method of AI [98].

At the end of the era of establishment, in 1963, Minsky generated an exhaustive annotated bibliography [82] of literature "directly concerned with construction of artificial problem-solving systems"[12] It contained 925 citations, 890 of which were to scientific papers and books, and 35 of which were to collections of such papers. There are two main points of interest here. First, although the title of the bibliography, *A Selected Descriptor-Indexed Bibliography to the Literature on Artificial Intelligence*, refers to AI, the introduction refers to the area of concern as "artificial problem-solving systems." Second, and somewhat paradoxically, the scope of the bibliography is much broader than one would expect from an AI bibliography today. It includes many items on cybernetics, neuroscience, bionics, information and communication theory, and first generation connectionism.

These two contrasting aspects of the bibliography highlight a trend in AI that continued for the next 25 years. Out of a soup of ideas on how to build intelligent machines, the disembodied and nonsituated approach of problem-solving search systems emerged as dominant, at least within the community that referred to its own work as AI.

With hindsight we can step back and look at what happened. Originally search was introduced as a mechanism for solving problems that arguably humans used some search in solving. Chess and logic theorem proving are two examples we have already discussed. In these domains one does not expect instantaneous responses from humans doing the same tasks. They are not tasks that are situated in the world.

One can debate whether even in these tasks it is wise to rely so heavily on search, as bigger problems will have exponentially bad effects on search time—in fact [93] argued just this, but produced a markedly slower chess program of the complexity of static evaluation and search control. Some, such as [109] with his checkers playing program, did worry about keeping things on a human timescale. Slage,[115], in his symbolic integration

[12] It also acted as the combined bibliography for the papers in [43].

program, was worried about being economically competitive with humans, but as he pointed out in the last two paragraphs of his paper, the explosive increase in price/performance ratio for computing was able to keep his programs ahead. In general, performance increases in computers were able to feed researchers with a steadily larger search space, enabling them to feel they were because making progress as the years went by. For any given technology level, a long-term freeze would soon show that programs relying on search had very serious problems, especially if there was any desire to situate them in a dynamic world.

In the last paragraph of [81] he did bring up the possibility of a situated agent, acting as a "thinking aid" to a person. But again he relied on a performance increase in standard computing methods (this time through the introduction of time sharing) to supply the necessary time relevant computations.

In the early days of the formal discipline of AI, search was adopted as a basic technology. It was easy to program on digital computers. It lead to reasoning systems that are not easy to shoehorn into situated agents.

2.3.3 Cybernetics

There was, especially in the 1940s and 1950s, another discipline that could be viewed as having the same goals as we have identified for AI—the construction of useful intelligent systems and the understanding of human intelligence. This work, known as *cybernetics*, had a fundamentally different flavor from traditional AI.

Cybernetics co-evolved with control theory and statistical information theory (e.g., see [136]). Cybernetics is the study of the mathematics of machines, not in terms of the functional components of a machine and how they are connected, nor in terms of what an individual machine can do here and now, but rather in terms of *all* the possible behaviors that an individual machine can produce. There was a strong emphasis on characterizing a machine in terms of its inputs and outputs, and treating it as a *black box* as far as its internal workings were unobservable. The tools of analysis were often differential or integral equations, and these tools inherently limited cybernetics to situations where the boundary conditions were not changing rapidly. In contrast, conditions do change rapidly in a system situated in a dynamically changing world; that complexity needs to go somewhere, either into discontinuous models or changed boundary conditions.

Cybernetics arose in the context of regulation of machinery and electronic circuits and was often characterized by the subtitle of Wiener's book as the study of "control and communication in the animal and the machine." The model of computation at the time of its original development was analog. The inputs to and outputs from the machine to be analyzed were usually thought of as almost everywhere continuous functions with reasonable derivatives, and the mechanisms for automated analysis and modeling were usually things that today would be characterized as analog components. As such there was no notion of symbolic search; any search was couched in terms of minimization of a function. There was also much less of a notion of representation as an abstract manipulable entity than was found in the AI approaches.

Much of the work in cybernetics was aimed at understanding animals and intelligence. Animals were modeled as machines, and from those models, cyberneticians hoped to glean how the animals changed their behavior through learning and how that lead to better adaptation to the environment for the whole organism. It was recognized rather early (e.g., [10] for an explicit statement) that an organism and its environment must be modeled together in order to understand the behavior produced by the organism—this is clearly an expression of situatedness. The tools of feedback analysis were used [11] to concentrate on such issues as stability of the system as the environment was perturbed, and in particular a system's *homeostasis* or ability to keep certain parameters within prescribed ranges, no matter what the uncontrolled variations within the environment.

With regard to embodiment there were some experiments along these lines. Many cybernetic models of organisms were rather abstract demonstrations of homeostasis, but some were concerned with physical robots. [130, 131, 132] [13] describe robots built on cybernetic principles that demonstrated goal-seeking behavior, homeostasis, and learning abilities.

The complexity and abilities of Walter's physically embodied machines rank with the purely imaginary ones in the first half dozen chapters of [18] three decades later.

The limiting factors in these experiments were twofold: (a) the technology of building small self-contained robots when the computational elements were miniature (a relative term) vacuum tubes, and (b) the lack of mechanisms for abstractly describing behavior at a level below the complete behavior, so that an implementation could reflect those simpler components. Thus, in the first instance the models of thought were limited by technological barriers to implementing those models, and in the second instance, the lack of certain critical components of a model (organization into submodules) restricted the ability to build better technological implementations.

Let us return to Wiener and analyze the ways in which the mechanisms of cybernetics and the mechanisms of computation were intimately interrelated in deep and self-limiting ways.

Wiener was certainly aware of digital machines[14] even in his earlier

[13] Much of the book [132] is concerned with early work on electroencephalography and hopes for its role in revealing the workings of the brain. Forty years later these hopes do not seem to have been borne out.

[14] In the introduction to [136] Wiener talked about embodying such machines with photoelectric cells, thermometers, strain gauges, and motors in the service of mechanical labor. But, in the text of the book he did not make such a connection with models of

edition of [136]. He compared them to analog machines such as the Bush differential analyzer, and declared that the digital (or *numerical*, as he called them) machines were superior for accurate numerical calculations. But in some deep sense Wiener did not see the flexibility of these machines. In an added chapter in [136], he discussed the problem of building a self-reproducing machine, and in the cybernetic tradition, reduced the problem to modeling the input/output characteristics of a black box, in particular a nonlinear transducer. He related methods for approximating observations of this function with a linear combination of basic nonlinear transducers and then showed that the whole problem could be done by summing and multiplying potentials and averaging over time. Rather than turn to a digital computer to do this, he stated that there were some interesting possibilities for multiplication devices using piezo-electric effects. We see then the intimate tying together between models of computation (i.e., analog computation, and models of the essentials of self-reproduction). It is impossible to tease apart cause and effect from this vantage point. The critical point is the way in which the mathematical proposal is tied to a technological implementation as a certification of the validity of the approach.[15]

By the mid 1960s, it was clear that if the study of intelligence was to succeed, even a study arising from the principles of cybernetics, needed to be more broad based in its levels of abstraction and tools of analysis. A good example is Arbib [7].[16]. Even so, he still harbored hope that cybernetic methods would turn out to give an understanding of the "overall coordinating and integrating principles" that interrelate the component subsystems of the human nervous system.

2.3.4 Abstraction

The years immediately following the Dartmouth conference shaped the field of AI in a way that has not significantly changed. The next few years, in the main, amplified the abstraction away from situatedness or connectedness to the world.[17] There were a number of demonstrations along the way

organisms. Rather, he noted that they are intended for many successive runs, with the memory being cleared out between runs and states that "the brain, under normal circumstances, is not the complete analogue of the computing machine but rather the analogue of a single run on such a machine" (p.). His models of digital computation and models of thought were too dissimilar to make the connection that we would today.

[15]With hindsight, an even wilder speculation is presented at the end of the later edition. Wiener suggested that the capital substances of genes and viruses may self-reproduce through such a spectral analysis of infrared emissions from the model molecules that then induce self-organization into the undifferentiated magma of amino and nucleic acids available to form the new biological material.

[16]Arbib included an elegant warning against being too committed to models, even mathematical models, which may turn out to be wrong. His statement that the "mere use of formulas gives no magical powers to a theory" is just as timely today as it was then.

[17]One exception was a computer-controlled hand built at MIT [40] and connected to the TX-0 computer. The hand was very much situated and embodied and relied heavily

that seemed to legitimize this abstraction. In this section I review some of those events and argue that there were fundamental flaws in the conclusions generally drawn.

At MIT, Roberts [102] demonstrated a vision program that could match prestored models to visual images of blocks and wedges. This program was the forerunner of all modern vision programs, and it was many years before its performance could be matched by others. It took a gray level image of the world and extracted a cartoonlike line drawing. It was this line drawing that was then fitted via an inverse perspective transform to the prestored models. To those who saw its results, this looked like a straightforward and natural way to process images and to build models (based on the prestored library) of the objective reality in front of the camera.

The unfortunate truth, however, is that it is extraordinarily difficult to extract reliable line drawings in any sort of realistic cases of images. In Roberts's case the lighting was carefully controlled, the blocks were well painted, and the background was chosen with care. The images of his blocks produced rather complete line drawings with very little clutter where there should, by human observer standards, be no line elements. Today, after almost 30 years of research on bottom-up, top-down, and middle-out line finders, there is still no line finder that gets such clean results on a single natural image. Real-world images are not at all the clean things that our personal introspection tells us they are. It is hard to appreciate this without working on an image yourself.[18]

The fallout of Roberts's program, which worked on a very controlled set of images, was that people thought that the line detection problem was doable and solved. Evans [41] cited Roberts in his discussion of how input could be obtained for his analogy program, which compared sets of line drawings of 2-D geometric figures.

During the late 1960s and early 1970s the Shakey project [99] at SRI reaffirmed the premises of abstract AI. Shakey, mentioned in section 2.2, was a mobile robot that inhabited a set of specially prepared rooms. It navigated from room to room, trying to satisfy a goal given to it on a teletype. It would, depending on the goal and circumstances, navigate around obstacles consisting of large painted blocks and wedges, push them out of the way, or push them to some desired location.

Shakey had an onboard black-and-white television camera as its primary sensor. An offboard computer analyzed the images and merged descriptions of what was seen into an existing first-order predicate calculus model of the world. A planning program, STRIPS, operated on those symbolic descriptions of the world to generate a sequence of actions for Shakey. These plans were translated through a series of refinements into calls to atomic actions in fairly tight feedback loops with atomic sensing operations

on the external world as a model, rather than using internal representations. This piece of work seems to have gotten lost, for reasons not clear to me.

[18] Try it! You'll be amazed at how bad it is.

using Shakey's other sensors such as a bump bar and odometry.

Shakey was considered a great success at the time, demonstrating an integrated system involving mobility, perception, representation, planning, execution, and error recovery. Shakey's success thus reaffirmed the idea of relying completely on internal models of an external objective reality. That is precisely the methodology it followed, and it appeared successful. However, it only worked because of very careful engineering of the environment. Twenty years later, no mobile robot has been demonstrated matching all aspects of Shakey's performance in a more general environment, such as an office environment.

The rooms in which Shakey operated were bare except for the large colored blocks and wedges. This made the class of objects that had to be represented very simple. The walls were of uniform color and carefully lighted, with dark rubber baseboards, making clear boundaries with the lighter colored floor. This meant that very simple and robust vision of trihedral corners between two walls and the floor could be used for relocalizing the robot in order to correct for drift in the robot's odometric measurements. The blocks and wedges were painted different colors on different planar surfaces. This ensured that it was relatively easy, especially in the good lighting provided, to find edges in the images separating the surfaces, thus making it easy to identify the shape of the polyhedron. Blocks and wedges were relatively rare in the environment, eliminating problems due to partial obscurations. The objective reality of the environment was thus quite simple and the mapping to an internal model of that reality was also quite plausible.

Around the same time, a major demonstration was mounted at MIT of a robot that could view a scene consisting of stacked blocks, then build a copy of the scene using a robot arm (see [141]—the program was known as the *copy-demo*). The programs to do this were very specific to the blocks world and would not have worked in the presence of simple curved objects, rough texture on the blocks, or without carefully controlled lighting. Nevertheless, it reinforced the idea that a complete three-dimensional description of the world could be extracted from a visual image. It legitimized the work of others, such as Winograd [139], whose programs worked in a make-believe world of blocks; if one program could be built that understood such a world completely and could also manipulate that world, then it was assumed that programs that assumed that abstraction could in fact be connected to the real world without great difficulty. The problem remained of the program's slowness due to the large search spaces, but as before, faster computers were always just around the corner.

The key problem I see with all this work, apart from the use of search, is that it relied on the assumption that a complete world model could be built internally and then manipulated. The examples from Roberts, Shakey, and the copy-demo all relied on very simple worlds and controlled situations. The programs were able to largely ignore unpleasant issues like sensor uncertainty and were never really stressed because of the carefully controlled perceptual conditions. No computer vision systems can produce world models of this fidelity for anything nearing the complexity of realistic world scenes; even object recognition is an active and difficult research area. There are two responses to this: (a) eventually computer vision will catch up and provide such world models, which I don't believe given the biological evidence presented next, or (b) complete objective models of reality are unrealistic, and hence the methods of AI that rely on such models are unrealistic.

With the rise in abstraction it is interesting to note that it was still quite technologically difficult to connect to the real world for most AI researchers.[19] For instance, Barrow and Salter [14] described efforts at Edinburgh, a major AI center, to connect sensing to action, and the results are extraordinarily primitive by today's standards; both MIT and SRI had major engineering efforts in support of their successful activities. Moravec [88] related a sad tale of frustration from the early 1970s of efforts at the Stanford Artificial Intelligence Laboratory to build a simple mobile robot with visual input.

Around the late 1960s and early 1970s there was a dramatic increase in the availability of computer processing power available to researchers at reasonably well-equipped laboratories. Not only was there a large increase in processing speed and physical memory, but time sharing systems became well established. An individual researcher was now able to work continuously and conveniently on a disembodied program designed to exhibit intelligence. However, connections to the real world were not only difficult and overly expensive, but the physical constraints of using them made development of the intelligent parts of the system slower by at least an order of magnitude, and probably two orders, as compared to the new-found power of time sharing. The computers clearly had a potential to influence the models of thought used, and certainly that hypothesis is not contradicted by the sort of microworld work that actually went on.

2.3.5 Knowledge

By this point in the history of AI, the trends, assumptions, and approaches had become well established. The last 15 years have seen the discipline thundering along on inertia more than anything else. Apart from a renewed flirtation with neural models (see section 2.3.8), there has been very little change in the underlying assumptions about the models of thought. This coincides with an era of very little technical innovation in our underlying models of computation.

[19] It is still fairly difficult even today. There are very few turnkey systems available for purchase that connect sensors to reasonable computers and reasonable computers to actuators. The situation does seem to be rapidly improving however; we may well be just about to step over a significant threshold.

For the remainder of section 2.3, I rather briefly review the progress made over the last 15 years and show how it relates to the fundamental issues of situatedness and embodiment brought up earlier.

One problem with microworlds is that they are somewhat uninteresting. The blocks world was the most popular microworld, and there is very little that can be done in it other than make stacks of blocks. After a flurry of early work where particularly difficult problems or puzzles were discovered and then solved (e.g., [120]), it became more and more difficult to do something new within that domain.

There were three classes of responses to this impoverished problem space:

- Move to other domains with equally simple semantics, but with more interesting print names than *block-a*, and so on. It was usually not the intent of the researchers to do this, but many in fact did fall into this trap. Winograd and Flores [140] exposed and criticized a number of such dressings up in the chapter on "Understanding Language."
- Build a more complex semantics into the blocks world and work on the new problems that arise. A rather heroic example of this is Fahlman [42] who included balance, multishaped blocks, friction, and the like. The problem with this approach is that the solutions to the puzzles become so domain specific that it is hard to see how they might generalize to other domains.
- Move to the wider world. In particular, represent knowledge about the everyday world, and then build problem solvers, learning systems, and so on, that operate in this semantically richer world.

The last of these approaches has spawned possibly the largest recognizable subfield of AI, known as knowledge representation. It has its own conferences, it has theoretical and practical camps, yet it is totally ungrounded. It concentrates much of its energies on anomalies within formal systems, which are never used for any practical tasks.

[19] is a collection of papers in the area. The knowledge representation systems described receive their input either in symbolic form or as the output of natural language systems. The goal of the papers seems to be to represent knowledge about the world. However, it is totally ungrounded. There is very little attempt to use the knowledge (save in the naive physics [53], or qualitative physics [36] areas—but note that these areas too are ungrounded). There is an implicit assumption that someday the inputs and outputs will be connected to something that will make use of them (see [26] for an earlier criticism of this approach).

In the meantime, the work proceeds with very little to steer it, and much of it concerns problems produced by rather simple-minded attempts at representing complex concepts. To take but one example, there have been many pages written on the problem of penguins being birds, even though they cannot fly. The reason that this is a problem is that the knowledge representation systems are built on top of a computational technology that makes convenient the use of very simple individuals (Lisp atoms) and placing links between them. As pointed out in [24], and much earlier in [26], such a simple approach does not work when the system is to be physically grounded through embodiment. It seems pointless to try to patch up a system that in the long run cannot possibly work. Dreyfus [39][20] provided a useful criticism of this style of work.

Perhaps the pinnacle of the knowledge-is-everything approach can be found in [65], which discusses the foundations of a 10-year project to encode knowledge having the scope of a simple encyclopedia. It is a totally unsituated and totally disembodied approach. Everything the system is to know is through hand-entered units of knowledge, although there is some hope expressed that later it will be able to learn itself by reading. [117] provides a commentary on this approach, and points out how the early years of the project have been devoted to finding a more primitive level of knowledge than was previously envisioned for grounding the higher levels of knowledge. It is my opinion, and also Smith's, that there is a fundamental problem still, and one can expect continued regress until the system has some form of embodiment.

2.3.6 Robotics

Section 2.2 outlined the early history of mobile robots. There have been some interesting developments over the last 10 years as attempts have been made to embody some theories from AI in mobile robots. In this section I briefly review some of the results.

In the early 1980s the Defense Advanced Research Projects Agency (DARPA) in the United States sponsored a major thrust in building an Autonomous Land Vehicle. The initial task for the vehicle was to run along a paved road in daylight using vision as the primary perceptual sense. The first attempts at this problem (e.g., [134]) followed the SMPA methodology. The idea was to build a three-dimensional world model of the road ahead, then plan a path along it, including steering and velocity control annotations. These approaches failed as it was not possible to recover accurate three-dimensional road models from the visual images. Even under fairly strong assumptions about the class of roads being followed, the programs produced ludicrously wrong results.

With the pressure of getting actual demonstrations of the vehicle running on roads and of having all the processing onboard, radical changes had to be made in the approaches taken. Two separate teams came up with similar approaches—[127] at Martin Marietta, the integrating contractor,

[20] Endorsement of some of Dreyfus' views should not be taken as a whole-hearted embrace of all his arguments.

and [122] at Carnegie Mellon University, the main academic participant in the project, both producing vision-based navigation systems. Both systems operated in picture coordinates rather than world coordinates, and both successfully drove vehicles along the roads. Neither system generated three-dimensional world models. Rather, both identified road regions in the images and servo-ed the vehicle to stay on the road. The systems can be characterized as reactive, situated, and embodied. Horswill and Brooks [57] described a system of similar vintage that operated an indoor mobile robot under visual navigation. The shift in approach taken on the outdoor vehicle was necessitated by the realities of the technology available and the need to get things operational.

Despite these lessons there is still a strong bias in following the traditional AI SMPA approach as can be seen in the work at CMU on the Ambler project. The same team that adopted a reactive approach to the road-following problem have reverted to a cumbersome, complex, and slow complete world modeling approach [113].

2.3.7 Vision

Inspired by the work of [102] and that on Shakey [99], the vision community has been content to work on scene description problems for many years. The implicit intent has been that when the reasoning systems of AI were ready, the vision systems would be ready to deliver world models as required, and the two could be hooked together to get a situated or embodied system.

There are numerous problems with this approach and too little room to treat them in this chapter. The fundamental issue is that AI and computer vision have made an assumption that the purpose of vision is to reconstruct the static external world (for dynamic worlds it is just supposed to do it often and quickly) as a three-dimensional world model. I do not believe that this is possible with the generality that is usually assumed. Furthermore, I do not think it is necessary, nor do I think that it is what human vision does. Section 2.4 discusses some of these issues.

2.3.8 Parallelism

Parallel computers are potentially quite different from Von Neumann machines. One might expect then that parallel models of computation would lead to fundamentally different models of thought. The story about parallelism, and the influence of parallel machines on models of thought, and the influence of models of thought on parallel machines are comprised of two and a half pieces. The first piece arose around the time of the early cybernetics work, the second piece exploded in the mid-1980s, and we have yet to see all the casualties. The last half piece has been pressured by the current models of thought to change the model of parallelism

There was a large flurry of work in the late 1950s and 1960s involving linear threshold devices, commonly known as perceptrons. The extremes in this work are represented by [103] and [86]. These devices were used in rough analogy to neurons and were to be wired into networks that learned to do some task, rather than having to be programmed. Adjusting the weights on the inputs of these devices was roughly equivalent in the model to adjusting the synaptic weights where axons connect to dendrites in real neurons; this is currently considered as the likely site of most learning within the brain.

The idea was that the network had specially distinguished inputs and outputs. Members of classes of patterns would be presented to the inputs, and the outputs would be given a correct classification. The difference between the correct response and the actual response of the network would then be used to update weights on the inputs of individual devices. The key driving force behind the blossoming of this field was the perceptron convergence theorem, which showed that a simple parameter adjustment technique would always let a single perceptron learn a discrimination if there existed a set of weights capable of making that discrimination.

To make things more manageable, the networks were often structured as layers of devices with connections only between adjacent layers. The directions of the connections were strictly controlled, so that there were no feedback loops in the network; at the same time, there was a natural progression from one single layer that would then be the input layer, and one layer would be the output layer. The problem with multilayer networks was that there was no obvious way to assign the credit or blame over the layers for a correct or incorrect pattern classification.

In the formal analyses that were carried out (e.g., [97] and [86]) only a single layer of devices that could learn or be adjusted were ever considered. [97] in the later chapters did consider multilayer machines, but in each case, all but one layer consisted of static unmodifiable devices. There was very little work on analyzing machines with feedback.

None of these machines was particularly situated or embodied. They were usually tested on problems set up by the researcher. There were many abuses of the scientific method in these tests; the results were not always as the researchers interpreted them.

After the publication of [86], which contained many negative results on the capabilities of single layer machines, the field seemed to die out for about 15 years.

Recently there has been a resurgence in the field starting with the publication of [106]. The new approaches were inspired by a new learning algorithm known as *back propagation* [105]. This algorithm gives a method for assigning credit and blame in fully connected multilayer machines without feedback loops. The individual devices within the layers have linearly weighted inputs and a differentiable output function, a sigmoid, which closely matches a step function or threshold function. Thus, they are only slight generalizations of the earlier perceptrons, but their continuous and differentiable outputs enable hill climbing to be performed, which lets the networks converge eventually to be able to classify inputs appropriately as trained.

Back propagation has a number of problems; it is slow to learn in general, and there is a learning rate that needs to be tuned by hand in most cases. The effect of a low learning rate is that the network might often get stuck in local minima. The effect of a higher learning rate is that the network may never really converge as it will be able to jump out of the correct minimum as well as it can jump out of an incorrect minimum. These problems combine to make back propagation, which is the cornerstone of modern neural network research, inconvenient for use in embodied or situated systems.

In fact, most of the examples in the new wave of neural networks have not been situated or embodied. There are a few counterexamples (e.g., [12, 110, 128] but in the main, they are not based on back propagation. The most successful recent learning techniques for situated, embodied, mobile robots have not been based on parallel algorithms at all; rather they use a reinforcement learning algorithm such as Q-learning [18], as for example, [7] and [70].

One problem for neural networks becoming situated or embodied is that it does not have a simple translation into time varying perception or action pattern systems. They need extensive front and back ends to equip them to interact with the world; all the cited examples mentioned here have had such features added to them.

Both waves of neural network research have been heralded by predictions of the demise of all other forms of computation. It has not happened in either case. Both times there has been a bandwagon effect where many people have tried to use the mechanisms that have become available to solve many classes of problems, often without regard to whether the problems could even be solved in principle by the methods used. In both cases the enthusiasm for the approach has been largely stimulated by a single piece of technology, first the perceptron training rule, and then the back propagation algorithm.

And now for the last half-piece of the parallel computation story. The primary hope for parallel computation helping AI has been the Connection Machine developed by Hillis [54]. This is a SIMD machine, and as such might be thought to have limited applicability for general intelligent activities. Hillis, however, made a convincing case that it could be used for many algorithms having to do with knowledge representation, and that it would speed them up, often to be constant time algorithms. The book describing the approach is exciting, and in fact, on pages 4 and 5 of [54] the author promised to break the Von Neumann bottleneck by making all the silicon in a machine actively compute all the time. The argument is presented that most of the silicon in a Von Neumann machine is devoted to memory, and most of that is inactive most of the time. This was a brave new approach, but it has not survived the market place. New models of the connection machine have large local memories (in the order of 64K bits) associated with each 1-bit processor (there can be up to 64K processors in a single Connection Machine). Once again, most of the silicon is inactive most of the time. Connection machines are used within AI laboratories mostly for computer vision where there is an obvious mapping from processors and their NEWS network to pixels of standard digital images. Traditional AI approaches are so tied to their traditional machine architectures that they have been hard to map to this new sort of architecture.

2.4 Biology

We have our own introspection to tell us how our minds work, and our own observations to tell us how the behavior of other people and of animals works. We have our own partial theories and methods of explanation.[21] Sometimes, when an observation, internal or external, does not fit our preconceptions, we are rather ready to dismiss it as something we do not understand and do not need to understand.

In this section, I skim over a scattering of recent work from ethology, psychology, and neuroscience in an effort to indicate how deficient our everyday understanding of behavior is. This is important to realize because traditional AI has relied at the very least implicitly, and sometimes quite explicitly, on these folk understandings of human and animal behavior. The most common example is the story about getting from Boston to California (or vice versa), which sets up an analogy between what a person does mentally in order to *plan* the trip, and the means–ends method of planning. See [2] for a more detailed analysis of the phenomenon.

2.4.1 Ethology

Ethology, the study of animal behavior, tries to explain the causation, development, survival value, and evolution of behavior patterns within animals. See [78] for an easy introduction to modern ethology.

Perhaps the most famous ethologist was Niko Tinbergen (closely followed by his co-Nobel winners Konrad Lorenz and Karl von Frisch). His hierarchical view of intelligence, described in [123], is often quoted by AI researchers in support of their own hierarchical theories. However, this approach was meant to be a neurobiologically plausible theory, but it was described in the absence of any evidence. Tinbergen's model has largely been replaced in modern ethology by theories of motivational competition, disinhibition, and dominant and subdominant behaviors.

[21] See [31] for a discussion of folk psychology.

There is no completely worked out theory of exactly how the decision is made as to which behavioral pattern (e.g., drinking or eating) should be active in an animal. A large number of experiments give evidence of complex internal and external feedback loops in determining an appropriate behavior. McFarland [79] presented a number of such experiments and demonstrated the challenges for the theories. The experimental data has ruled out the earlier hierarchical models of behavior selection, and current theories share many common properties with the behavior-based approach advocated in this chapter.

2.4.2 Psychology

The way in which our brains work is hidden from us. We have some introspection, we believe, to some aspects of our thought processes, but there are certainly perceptual and motor areas that we are quite confident we have no access to.[22] To tease out the mechanisms at work we can do at least two sorts of experiments: We can test the brain at limits of its operational envelope to see how it breaks down, and we can study damaged brains and get a glimpse at the operation of previously integrated components. In fact, some of these observations call into question the reliability of any of our own introspections.

There have been many psychophysical experiments to test the limits of human visual perception. We are all aware of so-called *optical illusions* where our visual apparatus seems to break down. *Perception* regularly publishes work that shows that what we perceive is not what we see (e.g., [101]). For instance, in visual images of a jumping leopard whose spots are made to artificially move about, we perceive them all as individually following the leopard. The straightforward model of human perception proposed by [71], and almost universally accepted by AI vision researchers, does not account for such results. Likewise it is now clear that the color pathway is separate from the intensity pathway in the human visual system, and our color vision is something of an illusion.[23] We are unaware of these deficiencies—most people are not aware that they have a blind spot in each eye the size of the image of the moon—because they are totally inaccessible to our consciousness. Even more surprising, our very notion of consciousness is full of inconsistencies: psychophysical experiments show that our experience of the flow of time as we observe things in the world is an illusion, as we can often consciously perceive things in a temporal order inconsistent with the world as constructed by an experimenter (see [38] for an overview).

We turn now to damaged brains to get a glimpse at how things might

[22] This contrasts with a popular fad in AI where all reasoning of a system is supposed to be available to a meta-reasoning system, or even introspectively to the system itself.

[23] See the techniques used in the current trend of colorization of black-and-white movie classics for a commercial capitalization on our visual deficiencies.

be organized. This work can better be termed *neuropsychology*. There is a large body of literature on this subject from which we pick out just a few instances here. The purpose is to highlight the fact that the approaches taken in traditional AI are vastly different from the way the human brain is organized.

The common view in AI, and particularly in the knowledge representation community, is that there is a central storage system that links together the information about concepts, individuals, categories, goals, intentions, desires, and whatever else might be needed by the system. In particular, there is a tendency to believe that the knowledge is stored in a way that is independent from the way or circumstances in which it was acquired.

McCarthy and Warrington [75] (and a series of earlier articles by them and their colleagues) gave cause to doubt this seemingly logical organization. They reported on a particular individual (identified as TOB), who at an advanced age developed a semantic deficit in knowledge of living things, but retained a reasonable knowledge of inanimate things. By itself, this sounds perfectly plausible—the semantic knowledge might just be stored in a category-specific way, and the animate part of the storage has been damaged. But, it happens that TOB is able to access the knowledge when, for example, he was shown a picture of a dolphin; he was able to form sentences using the word *dolphin* and talk about its habitat, its ability to be trained, and its role in the U.S. military. When verbally asked what a dolphin is, however, he thought it was either a fish or a bird. He had no such conflict in knowledge when the subject was a wheelbarrow, say. The authors argued that because the deficit was not complete but showed degradation, the hypothesis that there is a deficit in a particular type of sensory modality access to a particular category subclass in a single database was not valid. Through a series of further observations they argued to have shown evidence of modality-specific organization of meaning, besides a category-specific organization. Thus, knowledge may be duplicated in many places and may by no means be uniformly accessible. There are examples of where the knowledge is shown to be inconsistent. Our normal introspection does not reveal this organization and would seem to be at odds with these explanations. Next I call into question our normal introspection.

[91] presented a long discussion of visuospatial disorders in brain-damaged patients. Many of these severely tax the model of a person as an integrated rational agent. One simple example reported is finger agnosia, where a patient may be quite impaired in the way he can carry out conscious simple tasks using their fingers, but could still do things such as thread a needle or play the piano well. This example suggested the existence of multiple parallel channels of control, rather than some centralized finger control box, for instance.

[121] summarized work that shows that rat locomotion involves a number of reflexes. Drugs can be used to shut off many reflexes so that a rat

will appear to be unable to move. Almost all stimuli have no effect; the rat simply remains with its limbs in whatever configuration the experimenter has arranged them. However, certain specific stimuli can trigger a whole chain of complex motor interactions (e.g., tilting the surface on which the rat's feet are resting to the point where the rat starts to slide will cause the rat to leap). There has also been a recent popularization of the work of Sacks [108], which showed similar symptoms, in somewhat less understood detail, for humans. Again, it is hard to explain these results in terms of a centralized will; rather, an interpretation of multiple almost independent agencies such as hypothesized by [16] seems a better explanation.

Perhaps the most remarkable set of results is from split-brain patients. It has become common knowledge that we all possess a left brain and a right brain, but in patients whose *corpus callosum* has been severed, the brains become separate operationally [46].

Through careful experimentation, it is possible to communicate independently with the two brains, visually with both, and verbally with the left. By setting up experiments where one side does not have access to the information possessed by the other side, it is possible to push hard on the introspection mechanisms. It turns out that the ignorant half try to fabricate explanations for what is going on, rather than admitting ignorance. These are normal people (except for the severing of the corpus callosum), and it seems that they sincerely believe the lies they are telling, as a result of confabulations generated during introspection. One must question then the ordinary introspection that goes on when our brains are intact.

What is the point of all this? The traditional AI model of representation and organization along centralized lines does not reflect how people are built. Traditional AI methods are certainly not necessary for intelligence then, and so far they have not really been demonstrated to be sufficient in situated, embodied systems. The organization of humans is by definition sufficient; it is not known at all whether it will turn out to be necessary. The point is that we cannot make assumptions of necessity under either approach. The best we can expect to do for a while at least is to show that some approach is sufficient to produce interesting intelligence.

2.4.3 Neuroscience

The working understanding of the brain among AI researchers seems to be that it is an electrical machine with electrical inputs and outputs to the sensors and actuators of the body. One can see this assumption made explicit, for example, in the fiction and speculative writing of professional AI researchers such as [37] and [90]. This view, and further reduction, leads to the very simple models of brain used in connectionism [106].

In fact, however, the brain is embodied with a more serious coupling. The brain is situated in a soup of hormones that influences it in the strongest possible ways. It receives messages encoded hormonally and sends messages so encoded throughout the body. This electrocentrism, based on electronic models of computation, has lead us to ignore these aspects in informal models of neuroscience, but hormones play a strong, almost dominating role in determination of behavior in both simple [63] and higher animals [17].[24]

Real biological systems are not rational agents that take inputs, compute logically, and produce outputs. They are a mess of many mechanisms working in various ways, out of which emerges the behavior that we observe and rationalize. We can see this in detail by looking both at the individual computational level and at the organizational level of the brain.

We do not really know how computation is done at the lowest levels in the brain. There is debate over whether the neuron is the functional unit of the nervous system or whether a single neuron can act as many independent smaller units [32]. However, we do know that signals are propagated along axons and dendrites at very low speeds compared to electronic computers and that there are significant delays crossing synapses. The usual estimates for the computational speed of neuronal systems are no more than about 1 KHz. This implies that the computations that go on in humans to effect actions in the subsecond range must go through only a very limited number of processing steps; the network cannot be very deep in order to get meaningful results out on the timescales that routinely occur for much of human thought. On the other hand, the networks seem incredibly richly connected compared to the connection width of either our electronic systems or our connectionist models. For simple creatures, some motor neurons are connected to tenths of a percent of the other neurons in the animal. For mammals, motor neurons are typically connected to 5,000 other neurons, and some neurons in humans are connected to as many as 90,000 other neurons [31].

For one very simple animal *Caenorhabditis elegans*, a nematode, we have a complete wiring diagram of its nervous system, including its development stages [143]. In the hermaphrodite there are 302 neurons and 56 support cells out of the animal's total of 959 cells. In the male there are 381 neurons and 92 support cells out of a total of 1,031 cells. Even though the anatomy and behavior of this creature are well studied, and the neuronal activity is well probed, the way in which the circuits control the animal's behavior is not understood very well at all.

Given that even a simple animal is not yet understood, one cannot expect to gain complete insight into building AI by looking at the nervous systems of complex animals. We can, however, get insight into aspects of intelligent behavior, and some clues about sensory systems and motor systems.

[24] See [16] for a history of theories of the brain and how these theories were influenced by the current technologies available to provide explanatory power. Unfortunately, this book is marred by the author's lack of understanding of computation, which leads him to dismiss electrical activity of the brain as largely irrelevant to the process of thought.

[135], for instance, gives great insight into the way evolution has selected for sensor-neurological couplings with the environment, which can be very specialized. By choosing the right sensors, animals can often get by with very little neurological processing, in order to extract just the right information about the here and now around them for the task at hand. Complex world model building is not possible given the sensors' limitations and not needed when the creature is appropriately situated.

[35] and [49] give insight into how simple animals work, based on an understanding at a primitive level of their neurological circuits. These sorts of clues can help us as we try to build walking robots; for examples of such computational neuroethology see [22] and [15].

These clues can help us build better artificial systems, but by themselves they do not provide us with a full theory.

2.5 Ideas

Earlier we identified situatedness, embodiment, intelligence, and emergence, with a set of key ideas that have led to a new style of AI research we are calling behavior-based robots. In this section, I expound on these four topics in more detail.

2.5.1 Situatedness

Traditional AI has adopted a style of research in which the agents built to test theories in intelligence are essentially problem solvers that work in a symbolic abstracted domain. The symbols may have referents in the minds of the builders of the systems, but there is nothing to ground those referents in the real world. Furthermore, the agents are not situated in a world at all. Rather, they are given a problem, and they solve it. Then, they are given another problem, and they solve it. They are not participating in a world as agents would in the usual sense.

In these systems there is no external world per se, with continuity, surprises, or ongoing history. The programs deal only with a model world with its own built-in physics. There is a blurring between the knowledge of the agent and the world it is supposed to be operating in; indeed in many AI systems, there is no distinction between the two: The agent has access to direct and perfect perception, and direct and perfect action. When consideration is given to porting such agents or systems to operate in the world, the question arises of what sort of representation they need of the real world. Over the years within traditional AI, it has become accepted that they will need an objective model of the world with individuated entities, tracked, and identified over time; the models of knowledge representation that have been developed expect and require such a one-to-one correspondence between the world and the agent's representation of it.

The early robots such as Shakey and the Cart certainly followed this approach. They built models of the world, planned paths around obstacles, and updated their estimate of where objects were relative to themselves as they moved. We developed a different approach [21] where a mobile robot used the world as its own model—continuously referring to its sensors rather than to an internal world model. The problems of object class and identity disappeared. The perceptual processing became much simpler. And the performance of the robot was better in comparable tasks than that of the Cart,[25] and with much less computation, even allowing for the different sensing modalities.

[1] and [30] formalized these ideas in their arguments for *deictic* (or *indexical-functional* in an earlier incarnation) representations. Instead of having representations of individual entities in the world, the system has representations in terms of the relationship of the entities to the robot. These relationships are both spatial and functional. For instance, in Pengi [3], rather than refer to *Bee-27* the system refers to *the-bee-that-is-chasing-me-now*. The latter may or may not be the same bee that was chasing the robot 2 minutes previously; it doesn't matter for the particular tasks in which the robot is engaged.

When this style of representation is used, it is possible to build computational systems that trade off computational depth for computational width. The idea is that the computation can be represented by a network of gates, timers, and state elements. The network does not need long paths from inputs (sensors) to outputs (actuators). Any computation that is capable of being done is done in a very short time span. There have been other approaches that address a similar time-bounded computation issue, namely the *bounded rationality* approach [15]. Those approaches try to squeeze a traditional AI system into a bounded amount of computation. With the new approach we tend to come from the other direction: We start with very little computation and build up the amount, staying away from the boundary of computation that takes too long. As more computation needs to be added, there is a tendency to add it in breadth (thinking of the computation as being represented by a circuit whose depth is the longest path length in gates from input to output) rather than depth.

A situated agent must respond in a timely fashion to its inputs. Modeling the world completely under these conditions can be computationally challenging, but it provides some continuity to the agent. That continuity can be relied on, so that the agent can use its perception of the world instead of an objective world model. The representational primitives that are useful then change quite dramatically from those in traditional AI.

The key idea from situatedness is: *The world is its own best model.*

---

[25] The tasks carried out by this first robot, *Allen*, were of a different class than those attempted by Shakey. Shakey certainly could not have carried out the tasks that Allen did.

2.5.2 Embodiment

There are two reasons that embodiment of intelligent systems is critical. First, only an embodied intelligent agent is fully validated as one that can deal with the real world. Second, only through a physical grounding can any internal symbolic or other system find a place to bottom out, and give meaning to the processing going on within the system.

The physical grounding of a robot in the world forces its designer to deal with all the issues. If the intelligent agent has a body, sensors, and actuators, then all the details and issues of being in the world must be faced. It is no longer possible to argue in conference papers that the simulated perceptual system is realistic or that problems of uncertainty in action will not be significant. Instead, physical experiments can be done simply and repeatedly. There is no room for cheating.[26] When this is done it is usual to find that many of the problems that seemed significant are not so in the physical system (typically puzzle-like situations in which symbolic reasoning seemed necessary, tend not to arise in embodied systems), and many that seemed nonproblems become major hurdles (typically these concern aspects of perception and action).[27]

A deeper problem is to ask if there can be disembodied mind. Many believe that what distinguishes humans is directly related to our physical experiences. For instance, Johnson [59] argued that a large amount of our language is metaphorically related to our physical connections to the world. Our mental concepts are based on physically experienced exemplars. Smith [117] suggested that without physical grounding there can be no halt to the regress within a knowledge-based system as it tries to reason about real-world knowledge such as that contained in an encyclopedia (e.g., [65]).

Without an ongoing participation and perception of the world there is no meaning for an agent. Everything is random symbols. Arguments might be made that at some level of abstraction even the human mind operates in this solipsist position. However, biological evidence (see section 2.4) suggests that the human mind's connection to the world is so strong and many faceted that these philosophical abstractions may not be correct.

The key idea from embodiment is: *The world grounds regress.*

2.5.3 Intelligence

Brooks [26] argued that the sorts of activities we usually think of as demonstrating intelligence in humans have been taking place for only a small

---

[26] I mean this in the sense of causing self-delusion, not in the sense of wrongdoing with intent.

[27] In fact, there is some room for cheating as the physical environment can be specially simplified for the robot, and in fact, it may be very hard in some cases to identify such self-delusions. In some research projects it may be necessary to test a particular class of robot activities, and therefore it may be necessary to build a test environment for the robot. There is a fine and difficult to define line to be drawn here.

fraction of our evolutionary lineage. Furthermore, I argue that the simple things to do with perception and mobility in a dynamic environment took evolution much longer to perfect, and that all those capabilities are a necessary basis for higher level intellect.

Therefore, I propose looking at simpler animals as a bottom-up model for building intelligence. It is soon apparent, when reasoning is stripped away as the prime component of a robot's intellect, that the dynamics of the interaction of the robot and its environment are primary determinants of the structure of its intelligence.

Simon [114] discussed a similar point in terms of an ant walking along the beach. He pointed out that the complexity of the behavior of the ant is more a reflection of the complexity of its environment than its own internal complexity. He speculated that the same may be true of humans, but within two pages of text, he reduced studying human behavior to the domain of crypto-arithmetic problems.

It is hard to draw the line between what is intelligence, and what is environmental interaction. In a sense it does not really matter which is which, as all intelligent systems must be situated in some world or other if they are to be useful entities.

The key idea from intelligence is: *Intelligence is determined by the dynamics of interaction with the world.*

2.5.4 Emergence

In discussing where intelligence resides in an AI program Minsky [81] pointed out that "there is never any 'heart' in a program" and "we find senseless loops and sequences of trivial operations." It is hard to point at a single component as the seat of intelligence. There is no homunculus. Rather, intelligence emerges from the interaction of the components of the system. The way in which it emerges, however, is quite different for traditional and behavior-based AI systems.

In traditional AI the modules that are defined are information processing or functional. Typically these modules might be a perception module, a planner, a world modeler, a learner, and so on. The components directly participate in functions such as perceiving, planning, modeling, learning, and so on. Intelligent behavior of the system, such as avoiding obstacles, standing up, and controlling gaze, emerges from the interaction of the components.

In behavior-based AI the modules defined are behavior producing. Typically these modules might be an obstacle-avoidance behavior, a standing-up behavior, a gaze-control behavior, and so on. The components directly participate in producing behaviors such as avoiding obstacles, standing up, controlling gaze, and so on. Intelligent functionality of the system, such as perception, planning, modeling, learning, and so on, emerges from the interaction of the components.

Although this dualism between traditional and behavior-based systems is compelling, it is not completely accurate. Traditional systems have hardly ever been connected to the world, and so the emergence of intelligent behavior is something more of an expectation in most cases, rather than an established phenomenon. Conversely, because of the many behaviors present in a behavior-based system and their individual dynamics of interaction with the world, it is often hard to say that a particular series of actions was produced by a particular behavior. Sometimes many behaviors are operating simultaneously or are switching rapidly [57].

Over the years there has been a lot of work on emergence based on the theme of self-organization (e.g., [96]). Within behavior-based robots evolving work better characterizes emergent functionality, but it is still in its early stages, (e.g., [118]). Steels defined it as meaning that a function is achieved "indirectly by the interaction of more primitive components among themselves and with the world."

It is hard to identify the seat of intelligence within any system, as intelligence is produced by the interactions of many components. Intelligence can only be determined by the total behavior of the system and how that behavior appears in relation to the environment.

The key idea from emergence is: *Intelligence is in the eye of the observer.*

2.6 Thought

Since late 1984, I have been building autonomous mobile robots in the "Mobot Lab" at the MIT Artificial Intelligence Laboratory; [21] gives the original ideas, and [24] contains a recent summary of the capabilities of the robots developed in my laboratory over the years.

My work fits within the framework I have described in terms of situatedness, embodiment, intelligence, and emergence. In particular, I have advocated situatedness, embodiment, and highly reactive architectures with no reasoning systems, no manipulable representations, no symbols, and totally decentralized computation. This different model of computation has lead to radically different models of thought.

I have been accused of overstating the case that the new approach is all that is necessary to build truly intelligent systems. It has even been suggested that as an evangelist I have deliberately overstated my case to pull people toward the correct level of belief and that all along, I have known that a hybrid approach is necessary.

That is not what I believe. I think that the new approach can be extended to cover the whole story, both in regard to building intelligent systems and to understanding human intelligence—the two principal goals of AI identified at the beginning of this chapter.

Whether or not I am right is an empirical question. Multiple approaches to AI will continue to be pursued. At some point, we will be able to evaluate which approach has been more successful.

In this section I outline the philosophical underpinnings of my work and discuss why I believe this approach is the one that in the end will prove dominant.

2.6.1 Principles

All research goes on within the constraints of certain principles. Sometimes these are explicit, and sometimes they are implicit. The first set of principles define the domain for the work:

- The goal is to study complete, integrated, intelligent autonomous agents.
- The agents should be embodied as mobile robots, situated in unmodified worlds found around the laboratory.[28] This confronts the embodiment issue. The environments chosen are for convenience, although we strongly resist the temptation to change the environments in any way for the robots.
- The robots should operate equally well when visitors or cleaners walk through their workspace, when furniture is rearranged, when lighting or other environmental conditions change, and when their sensors and actuators drift in calibration. This confronts the situatedness issue.
- The robots should operate on time scales commensurate with the time scales used by humans. This too confronts the situatedness issue.

The specific model of computation used was not originally based on biological models, but was arrived at by continuously refining attempts to program a robot to reactively avoid collisions in a people-populated environment [21]. Now, however, in stating the principles used in the model of computation, it is clear that it shares certain properties with models of how neurological systems are arranged. It is important to emphasize that it only shares certain properties. Our model of computation is not intended as a realistic model of how neurological systems work. We call our computation model the *subsumption architecture*, and its purpose is to program intelligent, situated, embodied agents. Our principles of computation are:

- Computation is organized as an asynchronous network of active computational elements (they are *augmented finite state machines*—see

[28] This constraint has slipped a little recently as we are working on building prototype small-legged planetary rovers [6]. We have built a special purpose environment for the robots—a physically simulated lunar surface.

[22] for details[29]), with a fixed topology network of unidirectional connections.

- Messages sent over connections have no implicit semantics; they are small numbers (typically 8 or 16 bits, but on some robots just 1 bit) and their meanings are dependent on the dynamics designed into both the sender and receiver.

- Sensors and actuators are connected to this network, usually through asynchronous two-sided buffers.

These principles lead to certain consequences. In particular:

- The system can certainly have state; it is not at all constrained to be purely reactive.

- Pointers and manipulable data structures are very hard to implement (because the model is equivalent to Turing's, it is of course possible, but hardly within the spirit).

- Any search space must be quite bounded in size, as search nodes cannot be dynamically created and destroyed during the search process.

- There is no implicit separation of data and computation; they are both distributed over the same network of elements.

In considering the biological observations outlined in section 2.4, certain properties seem worth incorporating into the way robots are programmed within the given model of computation. In all the robots built in the mobot lab, the following principles of organization of intelligence have been observed:

- There is no central model maintained of the world. All data is distributed over many computational elements.

- There is no central locus of control.

- There is no separation into perceptual system, central system, and actuation system. Pieces of the network may perform more than one of these functions. More importantly, there is intimate intertwining of aspects of all three of them.

- The behavioral competence of the system is improved by adding a more behavior-specific network to the existing network. We call this

[29] For programming convenience we use a higher level abstraction known as the *Behavior Language*, documented in [25]. It compiles down to a network of machines as described earlier.

process *layering*. This is a simplistic and crude analogy to evolutionary development. As with evolution, at every stage of the development the systems are tested; unlike evolution, there is a gentle debugging process available. Each of the layers is a behavior-producing piece of network in its own right, although it may implicitly rely on the presence of earlier pieces of network.

- There is no hierarchical arrangement (i.e., there is no notion of one process calling on another as a subroutine). Rather, the networks are designed so that needed computations will simply be available on the appropriate input line when needed. There is no explicit synchronization between a producer and a consumer of messages. Message reception buffers can be overwritten by new messages before the consumer has looked at the old one. It is not atypical for a message producer to send 10 messages for every one that is examined by the receiver.

- The layers, or behaviors, all run in parallel. There may need to be a conflict resolution mechanism when different behaviors try to give different actuator commands.

- The world is often a good communication medium for processes, or behaviors, within a single robot.

It should be clear that these principles are quite different from the ones we have become accustomed to using in programming Von Neumann machines. Our model forces the programmer to use a different style of organization for his programs for intelligence.

There are also always influences on approaches to building thinking machines that lie outside the realm of purely logical or scientific thought. The following, perhaps arbitrary, principles have also had an influence on the organization of intelligence that has been used in Mobot Lab robots:

- A decision was made early on that all computation should be done onboard the robots. This was so that the robots could run tether free and without any communication link. The idea is to download programs over cables (although in the case of some of our earlier robots the technique was to plug in a newly written erasable ROM) into nonvolatile storage on the robots, then switch them on to interact with and be situated in the environment.

- In order to maintain a long-term goal of eventually being able to produce very tiny robots [45], the computational model has been restricted so that any specification within that model could be rather easily compiled into a silicon circuit. This has put an additional constraint on designers of agent software, in that they cannot use nonlinear numbers of connections between collections of computational elements, as that would lead to severe silicon compilation problems. Note that this general model of computation is such that a goal of silicon compilation is in general realistic.

The point of section 2.3 was to show how the technology of available computation had a major impact on the shape of the developing field of AI. Likewise, there have been a number of influences on my own work that are technological in nature. These include:

- Given the smallness in overall size of the robots, there is a very real limitation on the amount of onboard computation that can be carried, and by an earlier principle, all computation must be done onboard. The limiting factor on the amount of portable computation is not weight of the computers directly, but the electrical power that is available to run them. We have observed that the amount of electrical power available is proportional to the weight of the robot.[30]
- Because there are many single chip microprocessors available, including EEPROM and RAM, it is becoming possible to include large numbers of sensors that require interrupt servicing, local calibration, and data massaging. The microprocessors can significantly reduce the overall wiring complexity by servicing a local group of sensors (e.g., all those on a single leg of a robot) *in situ*, and packaging the data to run over a communication network to the behavior-producing network.

These principles have been used in the programming of a number of behavior-based robots. Next we point out the importance of some of these robot demonstrations in indicating how the subsumption architecture (or one like it in spirit) can be expected to scale up to intelligent applications. In what follows individual references are given to the most relevant piece of the literature. For a condensed description of what each of the robots is and how they are programmed, the reader should see [24]; it also included a number of robots not mentioned here.

2.6.2 Reactivity

The earliest demonstration of the subsumption architecture was on the robot *Allen* [21]. It was almost entirely reactive, using sonar readings to keep away from people and other moving obstacles, while not colliding with static obstacles. It also had a nonreactive higher level layer that would select a goal to head toward, and then proceed to that location as the lower level reactive layer took care of avoiding obstacles.

[30] Jon Connell, a former member of the Mobot Lab, plotted data from a large number of mobile robots and noted the empirical fact that there is roughly 1 watt of electrical power available for onboard computation for every pound of overall weight of the robot. We call this *Connell's Law*.

The very first subsumption robot thus combined nonreactive capabilities with reactive ones. But the important point is that it used exactly the same sorts of computational mechanism to do both. In looking at the network of the combined layers, there was no obvious partition into lower and higher level components based on the type of information flowing on the connections or the state machines that were the computational elements. To be sure, there was a difference in function between the two layers, but there was no need to introduce any centralization or explicit representations to achieve a higher level, or, process having useful and effective influence over a lower level.

The second robot, *Herbert* [34], pushed on the reactive approach. It used a laser scanner to find soda-canlike objects visually, infrared proximity sensors to navigate by following walls and going through doorways, a magnetic compass to maintain a global sense of orientation, and a host of sensors on an arm that were sufficient to pick up soda cans reliably. The task for Herbert was to wander around looking for soda cans, pick one up, and bring it back to Herbert's starting point. Herbert reliably found soda cans in rooms using its laser range finder (some tens of trials), picked up soda cans many times (over 100 instances), navigated (many hours of runs), and in one finale, executed all the tasks together to navigate, locate, pick up, and return with a soda can.[31]

In programming Herbert, it was decided that it should maintain no state longer than 3 seconds and that there would be no internal communication between behavior-generating modules. Each one was connected to sensors on the input side and a fixed priority arbitration network on the output side. The arbitration network drove the actuators.

In order to carry out its tasks, Herbert, in many instances, had to use the world as its own best model and as a communication medium. For instance, the laser-based soda can object finder drove the robot so that its arm was lined up in front of the soda can. But it did not tell the arm controller that there was now a soda can ready to be picked up. Rather, the arm behaviors monitored the shaft encoders on the wheels; when they noticed that there was no body motion, they initiated motions of the arm, which in turn triggered other behaviors, so that eventually the robot would pick up the soda can.

The advantage of this approach was that there was no need to set up internal expectations for what was going to happen next; that meant that the control system could both (a) be naturally opportunistic if fortuitous circumstances presented themselves, and (b) easily respond to changed circumstances, such as some other object approaching it on a collision course.

As one example of how the arm behaviors cascaded upon one another, consider actually grasping a soda can. The hand had a grasp reflex that

[31] The limiting factor on Herbert was the mechanical seating of its chips; its mean time between chip seating failure was no more than 15 minutes.

operated whenever something broke an infrared beam between the fingers. When the arm located a soda can with its local sensors, it simply drove the hand so that the two fingers lined up on either side of the can. The hand then independently grasped the can. Given this arrangement, it was possible for a human to hand a soda can to the robot. As soon as it was grasped, the arm retracted; it did not matter whether it was a soda can that was intentionally grasped or one that magically appeared. The same opportunism among behaviors let the arm adapt automatically to a wide variety of cluttered desktops and still successfully find the soda can.

In order to return to where it came from after picking up a soda can, Herbert used a trick. The navigation routines could carry rules of implementation such as: *When passing through a door southbound, turn left.* These rules were conditionalized on the separation of the fingers on the hand. When the robot was outbound with no can in its hand, it effectively executed one set of rules. After picking up a can, it would execute a different set. By carefully designing the rules, Herbert was guaranteed, with reasonable reliability, to retrace its path.

The point of Herbert is two-fold:

- It demonstrates complex, apparently goal-directed and intentional behavior in a system that has no long-term internal state and no internal communication.

- It is very easy for an observer of a system to attribute more complex internal structure than really exists. Herbert appeared to be doing things like path planning and map building even though it was not.

2.6.3 Representation

My earlier work [26] is often criticized for advocating absolutely no representation of the world within a behavior-based robot. This criticism is invalid. I have made it clear that I reject traditional AI representation schemes (see section 5). I also reject explicit representations of goals within the machine.

There can, however, be representations that are partial models of the world; in fact, I mentioned that "individual layers extract only those *aspects* of the world which they find relevant—projections of a representation into a simple subspace" [26]. The form these representations take, within the context of the computational model we are using, will depend on the particular task those representations are to be used for. For more general navigation than that demonstrated by Connell it may sometimes[32] need to build and maintain a map.

[32] Note that we are saying only *sometimes*, not *must*: There are many navigation tasks doable by mobile robots that appear intelligent, but that do not require map information at all.

Mataric [72] introduced *active-constructive representations* to subsumption in a sonar-based robot, *Toto*, which wandered around office environments building a map based on landmarks and then used that map to get from one location to another. Her representations were totally decentralized and nonmanipulable, and there is certainly no central control that builds, maintains, or uses the maps. Rather, the map itself is an active structure that does the computations necessary for any path planning the robot needs to do.

Primitive layers of control let Toto wander around, following boundaries (such as walls and furniture clutter) in an indoor environment. A layer that detects landmarks, such as flat clear walls, corridors, and so on, runs in parallel. It informs the map layer as its detection certainty exceeds a fixed threshold. The map is represented as a graph internally. The nodes of the graph are computational elements (they are identical little subnetworks of distinct, augmented, finite state machines). Free nodes arbitrate and allocate themselves in a purely local fashion to represent a new landmark and set up topological links to physically neighboring nodes (using a limited capacity switching network to keep the total virtual wire length between finite state machines to be linear in the map capacity). These nodes keep track of where the robot is physically by observing changes in the output of the landmark detector, by comparing that to predictions they have made by local message passing, and by referring to other more primitive (magnetic compass-based) coarse position estimation schemes.

When a higher layer wants the robot to go to some known landmark, it merely excites in some particular way the particular place in the map that it wants to go. The excitation is an abstraction programmed into the particular finite state machines used here; it is not a primitive. As such there could be many different types of excitation co-existing in the map, if other types of planning are required. The excitation is spread through the map following topological links, estimating total path link, and arriving at the *landmark-that-I'm-at-now* node (a deictic representation) with a recommendation of the direction to travel right now to follow the shortest path. As the robot moves, so too does its representation of where it is, and at that new node, the arriving excitation tells it where to go next. The map thus bears a similarity to the *internalized plans* of [100], but is represented by the same computational elements that use it; there is no distinction between data and process. Furthermore, Mataric's scheme can have multiple simultaneously active goals; the robot will simply head toward the nearest one.

This work demonstrates the following aspects of behavior-based or subsumption systems:

- Such systems can make predictions about what will happen in the world and have expectations.

- Such systems can make plans, but they are not the same as traditional

AI plans. See [4] for an analysis of this issue.

- Such systems can have goals. See [68] for another way to implement goals within the approach.
- All these things can be done without resorting to central representations.
- All these things can be done without resorting to manipulable representations.
- All these things can be done without resorting to symbolic representations.

2.6.4 Complexity

Can subsumptionlike approaches scale to arbitrarily complex systems? This is a question that cannot be answered affirmatively right now, just as it is totally unfounded to answer the same question affirmatively in the case of traditional symbolic AI methods. The best one can do is to point to precedents and trends.

There are a number of dimensions along which the scaling question can be asked:

- Can the approach work well as the environment becomes more complex?
- Can the approach handle larger numbers of sensors and actuators?
- Can the approach work smoothly as more and more layers or behaviors are added?

We answer each of these in turn in the following.

The approach taken at the Mobot Lab has been to always test the robot in the most complex environment for which it is ultimately destined. This forces even the simplest levels to handle the most complex environment expected. So for a given robot and intended environment, the scaling question is handled by the methodology chosen for implementation. But there is also the question of the complexity of the environments that are targeted with the current generation of robots. Almost all of our robots have been tested and operated in indoor environments with people unrelated to the research wandering through their work area at will. Thus, we have a certain degree of confidence that the same basic approach will work in outdoor environments (the sensory processing will have to change for some sensors) with other forms of dynamic action taking place.

The number of sensors and actuators possessed by today's robots are pitiful when compared to the numbers in even simple organisms such as insects. Our first robots had only a handful of identical sonar sensors and two motors. Later a six-legged walking robot was built [5]. It had 12 actuators and 20 sensors and was successfully programmed in subsumption [22] to walk adaptively over rough terrain. The key was to find the right factoring into sensor and actuator subsystems so that interactions between the subsystems could be minimized. A new six-legged robot, recently completed [6], is more challenging, but still nowhere near the complexity of insects. It has 23 actuators and over 150 sensors. With this level of sensing it is possible to start to develop some of the senses that animals and humans have, such as a kinesthetic sense that comes from the contributions of many sensor readings. Rather than feed into a geometric model, the sensors feed into a estimate of bodily motion. There is also the question of the types of sensors used. [57] generalized the subsumption architecture so that some of the connections between processing elements could be a *retina bus*, a cable that transmitted partially processed images from one site to another within the system. The robot so programmed was able to follow corridors and follow moving objects in real time.

As we add more layers, we find that the interactions can become more complex. [66] introduced the notion of switching whole pieces of the network on and off, using an *activation* scheme for behaviors. That idea is now incorporated into the subsumption methodology [25] and provides a way of implementing both competition and cooperation between behaviors. At a lower level, a hormonelike system has been introduced [27] that models the hormone system of the lobster [63] ([8] implemented a system with similar inspiration). With these additional control mechanisms, we have certainly bought ourselves breathing room to increase the performance of our systems markedly. The key point about these control systems is that they fit exactly into the existing structures and are totally distributed and local in their operations.

2.6.5 Learning

Evolution has decided that there is a trade-off between what we know through our genes and what we must find out for ourselves as we develop. We can expect to see a similar trade-off for our behavior-based robots. There are at least four classes of things that can be learned:

1. Representations of the world that help in some task;

2. Aspects of instances of sensors and actuators, which is sometimes called calibration;

3. Ways in which individual behaviors should interact; and

4. New behavioral modules

The robots in the Mobot Lab have been programmed to demonstrate the first three of these types of learning. The last one has not yet been successfully tackled.[33]

Learning representations of the world was already discussed with respect to the work of Mataric [72, 14]. The next step will be to generalize active-constructive representations to more classes of use.

Viola [128] demonstrated calibration of a complex head–eye system modeling the primate vestibulo-ocular system. In this system there is one fast channel between a gyroscope and a high-performance pan-tilt head holding the camera, and a slower channel using vision, which produces correction signals for the gyroscope channel. The same system was used to learn how to accurately have a saccade to moving stimuli.

Finally, [69] programmed an early six-legged robot to learn to walk using the subsumption architecture along with the behavior activation schemes of [66]. Independent behaviors on each leg monitored the activity of other behaviors and correlated that, their own activity state, and the results from a belly switch, which provided negative feedback as input to a local learning rule that learned under which conditions it was to operate the behavior. After about 20 trials per leg, spread over a total of a minute or two, the robot reliably learned the alternating tripod gait; it seemed to emerge out of initially chaotic flailing of the legs.

Learning within subsumption is in its early stages but it has been demonstrated in a number of different critical modes of development.

2.6.6 Vistas

The behavior-based approach has been demonstrated on situated, embodied systems doing things that traditional AI would have tackled in different ways. What are the key research areas that need to be addressed in order to push behavior-based robots toward more and more sophisticated capabilities?

In this section we outline research challenges in three categories or levels:[34]

- Understanding the dynamics of how an individual behavior couples with the environment via the robot's sensors and actuators. The primary concerns here are what forms of perception are necessary and what relationships exist between perception, internal state, and action (i.e., how behavior is specified or described).

- Understanding how many behaviors can be integrated into a single robot. The primary concerns here are how independent various perceptions and behaviors can be, how much they must rely on and

[33] We did have a failed attempt at this through simulated evolution; this is the approach taken by many in the Artificial Life movement.

[34] The reader is referred to [23] for a more complete discussion of these issues.

interfere with each other, how a competent complete robot can be built in such a way as to accommodate all the required individual behaviors, and to what extent apparently complex behaviors can emerge from simple reflexes.

- Understanding how multiple robots (either a homogeneous, or a heterogeneous group) can interact as they go about their business. The primary concerns here are the relationships between individuals' behaviors, the amount and type of communication between robots, the way the environment reacts to multiple individuals, and the resulting patterns of behavior and their impacts on the environment, which might not occur in the case of isolated individuals.

Just as research in AI is broken into subfields, these categories provide subfields of behavior-based robots within which it is possible to concentrate a particular research project. Some of these topics are theoretical in nature, contributing to a science of behavior-based systems. Others are engineering in nature, providing tools and mechanisms for successfully building and programming behavior-based robots. Some of these topics have already been touched upon by researchers in behavior-based approaches, but none of them are yet solved or completely understood.

At the individual-behavior level, some of the important issues are as follows:

Convergence: Demonstrate or prove that a specified behavior is such that the robot will indeed carry out the desired task successfully. For instance, we may want to give some set of initial conditions for a robot, some limitations on possible worlds in which it is placed, and show that under those conditions, the robot is guaranteed to follow a particular wall, rather than diverge and get lost.

Synthesis: Given a particular task, automatically derive a behavior specification for the creature so that it carries out that task in a way that has clearly demonstrable convergence. I do not expect progress in this topic on the near future.

Complexity: Deal with the complexity of real-world environments and sift out the relevant aspects of received sensations rather than being overwhelmed with a multitude of data.

Learning: Develop methods for the automatic acquisition of new behaviors and the modification and tuning of existing behaviors.

As multiple behaviors are built into a single robot, the following issues need to be addressed:

Coherence: Although many behaviors may be active at once, or are being actively switched on or off, the robot should still appear to an observer to have coherence of action and goals. It should not be rapidly switching between inconsistent behaviors, nor should two behaviors be active simultaneously, if they interfere with each other to the point that neither operates successfully.

Relevance: The behaviors that are active should be relevant to the situation the robot finds itself in (e.g., it should recharge itself when the batteries are low, not when they are full).

Adequacy: The robot's behavior selection mechanism must operate in such a way that the long-term goals of the robot designer are met (e.g., a floor cleaning robot should successfully clean the floor in normal circumstances, besides doing all the ancillary tasks that are necessary for it to be successful at that).

Representation: Multiple behaviors might want to share partial representations of the world; in fact, the representations of world aspects might generate multiple behaviors when activated appropriately.

Learning: The performance of a robot might be improved by adapting the ways in which behaviors interact, or are activated, as a result of experience.

When many behavior-based robots start to interact there are a whole new host of issues that arise. Many of these same issues would arise if the robots were built using traditional AI methods, but there has been very little published in these areas.

Emergence: Given a set of behaviors programmed into a set of robots, we predict what the global behavior of the system will be, and as a consequence, determine the differential effects of small changes to the individual robots on the global behavior.

Synthesis: As at single behavior level, given a particular task, automatically derive a program for the set of robots so that they carry out the task.

Communication: Performance may be increased by increasing the amount of explicit communication between robots, but the relationship between the amount of communication increase and performance increase needs to be understood.

Cooperation: In some circumstances, robots should be able to achieve more by cooperating; the form and specification of such possible cooperations need to be understood.

Interference: Robots may interfere with one another. Protocols for avoiding this when it is undesirable must be included in the design of the creatures' instructions.

Density dependence: The global behavior of the system may be dependent on the density of the creatures and the resources they consume within the world. A characterization of this dependence is desirable. At the two ends of the spectrum it may be the case that (a) a single robot given n units of time performs identically to n robots each given 1 unit of time, and (2) the global task might not be achieved at all if there are fewer than, for example, m robots.

Individuality: Robustness can be achieved if all robots are interchangeable. A fixed number of classes of robots, where all robots within a class are identical, is also robust, but somewhat less so. The issue then is to, given a task, decide how many classes of creatures are necessary.

Learning: The performance of the robots may increase in two ways through learning. At one level, when one robot learns some skill it might be able to transfer it to another. At another level, the robots might learn cooperative strategies.

These are a first cut at topics of interest within behavior-based approaches. As we explore more we will find more topics, and some that seem interesting now will turn out to be irrelevant.

2.6.7 Thinking

Can this approach lead to thought? How could it? It seems the antithesis of thought. But we must ask first, what is thought? Like intelligence, this is a very slippery concept.

We only know that thought exists in biological systems through our own introspection. At one level we identify thought with the product of our consciousness, but that too is a contentious subject, and one that has had little attention from AI.

My feeling is that thought and consciousness are epiphenomena of the process of being in the world. As the complexity of the world increases, and the complexity of processing to deal with that world rises, we will see the same evidence of thought and consciousness in our systems as we see in people other than ourselves now. Thought and consciousness will not need to be programmed in. They will emerge.

2.7 Conclusion

The title of this chapter is intentionally ambiguous. The following interpretations all encapsulate important points:

- An earlier article [26][35] was titled "Intelligence without Representation." Its thesis was that intelligent behavior could be generated without having explicit manipulable internal representations. "Intelligence without Reason" is thus complementary, stating that intelligent behavior can be generated without having explicit reasoning systems present.

- "Intelligence without Reason" can be read as a statement that intelligence is an emergent property of certain complex systems—it sometimes arises without an easily identifiable reason for arising.

- "Intelligence without Reason" can be viewed as a commentary on the bandwagon effect in research in general, and in particular in the case of AI research. Many lines of research have become goals of pursuit in their own right, with little recall of the reasons for pursuing those lines. A little grounding occasionally goes a long way toward helping keep things on track.

- "Intelligence without Reason" is also a commentary on the way evolution built intelligence; rather than reason about how to build intelligent systems, it used a generate-and-test strategy. This is in stark contrast to the way all human endeavors to build intelligent systems must inevitably proceed. Furthermore, we must be careful in emulating the results of evolution; there may be many structures and observable properties that are suboptimal or vestigial.

We are a long way from creating an AI that measures up the to the standards of early ambitions for the field. It is a complex endeavor, and we sometimes need to step back and question why we are proceeding in the direction we are going, and look around for other promising directions.

Acknowledgments

Maja Mataric reviewed numerous drafts of this chapter and gave helpful criticism at every stage of the process. Lynne Parker, Anita Flynn, Ian Horswill, and Pattie Maes gave me much constructive feedback on later drafts.

The research reported here was done at the MIT Artificial Intelligence Laboratory. Support for this research was provided in part by NATO CRG.900311, in part by the University Research Initiative under Office of Naval Research contract N00014–86–K–0685, and in part by the Advanced Research Projects Agency under Office of Naval Research contract N00014–85–K–0124.

[35]Despite the publication date, it was written in 1986 and 1987 and was complete in its published form in 1987.

References

[1] Agre, P. (1988a). *The dynamic structure of everyday life* (Tech. Rep. No. 1085). Cambridge, MA: MIT.

[2] Agre, P. (1988b). *The dynamic structure of everyday life.* Cambridge, UK: Cambridge University Press.

[3] Agre, P., & Chapman, D. (1987). Pengi: An implementation of a theory of activity. *AAAI-87*, 268–272.

[4] Agre, P., & Chapman, D. (1990). What are plans for? In: P. Maes (Ed.), *Designing autonomous agents,* (pp. 17–34). Cambridge, MA: MIT Press.

[5] Angle, C. (1989). *Genghis, a six legged autonomous walking robot.* Unpublished manuscript, MIT, Cambridge, MA.

[6] Angle, C., & Brooks, R. (1990). Small planetary rovers. *Proceedings of IEEE/RSJ International Workshop on Intelligent Robots and Systems*, 383–388.

[7] Arbib, M. (1964). *Brains, machines and mathematics* New York: McGraw-Hill.

[8] Arkin, R. (1989). Homeostatic control for a mobile robot: dynamic replanning in hazardous environments. In W. Wolfe (Ed.), *SPIE Proceedings 1007, Mobile Robots,* III. 407–413.

[9] Arkin, R. (1990). Integrating behavioral, perceptual and world knowledge in reactive navigation. In P. Maes (Ed.), *Designing autonomous agents,* (pp. 105–122). Cambridge, MA: MIT Press.

[10] Ashby, R. (1952). *Design for a brain.* London: Chapman & Hall.

[11] Ashby, R. (1956) *An Introduction to cybernetics.* London: Chapman & Hall.

[12] Atkeson, C. (1989). Using local models to control movement. In D. Touretzky (Ed.), *Neural Information Processing 2.* (pp. 316–324). Los Altos, CA: Morgan Kaufmann.

[13] Ballard, D. (1989) Reference frames for active vision. *Proceedings IJCAI-89*, 1635–1641.

[14] Barrow, H., & Salter, S. (1970). Design of low-cost equipment for cognitive robot research. In B. Meltzer & D. Michie (Eds.), *Machine intelligence 5*, (pp. 555–566). New York: Elsevier.

[15] Beer, R. (1990). *Intelligence as adaptive behavior.* San Diego: Academic Press.

[16] Bergland, R. (1985). *The fabric of mind.* New York: Viking.

[17] Bloom, F. (1976). Endorphins: Profound behavioral effects. *Science, 194,* 630–634.

[18] Braitenberg, V. (1984). *Vehicles: Experiments in synthetic psychology.* Cambridge, MA: MIT Press.

[19] Brachman, R., & Levesque, H. (Eds.).(1985). *Readings in knowledge representation.* Los Altos, CA: Morgan Kaufmann.

[20] Brady, D. (1990). Switching arrays make light work in a simple processor. *Nature, 344,* 486–487.

[21] Brooks, R. (1986). A robust layered control system for a mobile robot. *IEEE Journal of Robotics and Automation, RA-2,* 14–23.

[22] Brooks, R. (1989). A robot that walks: Emergent behavior from a carefully evolved network. *Neural Computation, 1*(2), 253–262.

[23] Brooks, R. (1990a). Challenges for complete creature architectures. In Meyer, J-A. and S. Wilson (1990) *Proceedings of First International Conference on Simulation of Adaptive Behavior.* (pp. 434-443) Cambridge, MA: MIT Press.

[24] Brooks, R. (1990b). Elephants don't play chess. In P. Maes (Ed.), *Designing autonomous agents,* (pp. 3–15). Cambridge, MA: MIT Press.

[25] Brooks, R. (1990c). The behavior language: User's guide (Memorandum No. 1227). Cambridge, MA: MIT, AI Lab.

[26] Brooks, R. (1991b). Intelligence without representation. *Artificial Intelligence, 47,* 139–160.

[27] Brooks, R. (1991a). Integrated systems based on behaviors. *Sigart,* 20(3) (Special issue on Integrated Intelligent Systems),

[28] Brooks, R., & Flynn, A. (1989). Robot beings. *Proceedings of IEEE/RSJ International Workshop on Intelligent Robots and Systems,* 2–10.

[29] Campbell, J. (1983). Go. In A. Bramer (Ed.) *Computer gameplaying: Theory and practice.* (pp.34–55) Chichester, UK: Ellis Horwood.

[30] Chapman, D. (1990). Vision, instruction and action (Tech. Rep. No. 1085). Cambridge, MA: MIT, AI Lab.

[31] Churchland, P.S. (1986). *Neurophilosophy.* Cambridge, MA: MIT Press.

[32] Cohen, L., & Wu, J. (1990). One neuron, many units? *Nature, 346,* 108–109.

[33] Condon, J., & Thompson, K. (1984). Belle. In P. Frey (Ed.), *Chess skill in man and machine* (pp.110–136) Berlin: Springer-Verlag.

[34] Connell, J. H. (1989). A colony architecture for an artificial creature. (Tech. Rep. No. 1151). Cambridge, MA: MIT, AI Lab.

[35] Curse, H. (1990). What mechanisms coordinate leg movement in walking arthropods? *Trends in Neurosciences, 13,* 1, 15–21.

[36] De Kleer, J., & Brown, J. S. (1984). A qualitative physics based on confluences. *Artificial Intelligence, 24,* 7–83.

[37] Dennett, D. C. (1981). Where am I? In D. R. Hofstadter & D. C. Dennett (Eds.), *The mind's I* (pp.310–323). New York: Bantam Books.

[38] Dennett, D. C., & Kinsbourne, M. (1990). Time and the observer: The where and when of consciousness in the brain. (Tech. Rep. No.). Center for Cognitive Studies: Tufts University.

[39] Dreyfus, H. L. (1981). From micro-worlds to knowledge representation: AI at an impasse. In J. Haugeland *Mind design* (pp. 161–204). Cambridge, MA: MIT Press.

[40] Ernst, H. A. (1961). MH-1. *A computer-operated mechanical hand.* Unpublished doctoral dissertation, MIT.

[41] Evans, T. G. (1968). A program for the solution of geometric-analogy intelligence test questions. In M. Minsky (Ed.), *Semantic information processing* (pp. 271–353). Cambridge, MA: MIT Press.

[42] Fahlman, S. E. (1974). A planning system for robot construction tasks. *Artificial Intelligence, 5,* 1–50.

[43] Feigenbaum, E. A., & Feldman, J. (Eds.).(1963). *Computers and thought.* New York: McGraw-Hill.

[44] Firby, J. (1989). *Adaptive execution in dynamic domains.* Unpublished doctoral dissertation, Yale.

[45] Flynn, A. M. (1987). Gnat robots (and how they will change robotics) *IEEE Micro Robots and Teleoperators Workshop,*

[46] Gazzaniga, M. S., & LeDoux, J. E. (1977). *The integrated mind.* New York: Plenum.

[47] Gibbs, H. M. (1985). *Optical bistability: controlling light with light.* New York: Academic Press.

[48] Giralt, G., Chatila, R., & Vaisset, M. (1984). An integrated navigation and motion control system for multisensory robots. In M. Brady & L. Paul, (Eds.) *Robotics Research, 1* (pp. 191-214). Cambridge, MA: MIT Press.

[49] Götz, K. G., & Wenking, H. (1973). Visual control of locomotion in the walking fruitfly *Drosophilia. Journal of Computational Physiology, 85*, 235–266.

[50] Gould, S. J., & Eldredge, N. (1977). Punctuated equilibria: The tempo and mode of evolution reconsidered. *Paleobiology, 3*, 115–151.

[51] Greenblatt, R., Eastlake, D. E., & Crocker, S. D. (1967). American Federation of Information Processing Societies Conference Proceedings, 31, 801–810.

[52] Hartmanis, J. (1971). Computational complexity of random access stored program machines. *Mathematical Systems Theory, 5*(3), 232–245.

[53] Hayes, P. J. (1985). The second naive physics manifesto. In J. R. Hobbs & R. C. Moore (Eds.), *Formal theories of the commonsense world.* (pp. 1–36). Norwood, NJ: Ablex.

[54] Hillis, W. D. (1985). *The connection machine.* Cambridge, MA: MIT Press.

[55] Hodges, A. (1983). *Alan Turing: The enigma.* New York: Simon & Schuster.

[56] Hofstadter, D. R., & Dennett, D. C. (1981).(Eds.). The Mind's I. New York: Bantam Books.

[57] Horswill, I. D., & Brooks, R. A. (1988). Situated vision in a dynamic world: chasing objects. In *Proceedings of AAAI-88*, 796–800.

[58] Hsu Feng-hsiung, F., Anantharaman, T., Campbell, M., & Nowatzyk, A. (1990). A grandmaster chess machine. *Scientific American, 263*(4), 44–50.

[59] Johnson, M. (1987). *The body in the mind.* Chicago: University of Chicago Press.

[60] Kaelbling, L. (1990). *Learning in embedded systems.* PhD Thesis, Stanford University.

[61] Kaelbling, L., & Rosenschein, S. (1990). Action and planning in embedded agents. In P. Maes (Ed.), *Designing autonomous agents,* (pp. 35–48). Cambridge, MA: MIT Press.

[62] Knuth, D., & Moore, R. (1975). An analysis of alpha-beta pruning. *Artificial Intelligence, 6*, 293–326.

[63] Kravitz, E. A. (1988). Hormonal control of behavior: Amines and the biasing of behavioral output in lobsters. *Science, 241*, 1775–1781.

[64] Kuhn, T. S. (1970). *The Structure of scientific revolutions* Chicago: University of Chicago Press.

[65] Lenat, D. B. & Feigenbaum, E. A. (1991). On the thresholds of knowledge. *Artificial Intelligence, 47*, 185–250.

[66] Maes, P. (1989). The dynamics of action selection. *Proceedings of IJCAI-89,* 991–997.

[67] Maes, P. (1990a). (Ed.) *Designing autonomous agents: Theory and practice from biology to engineering and back.* Cambridge, MA: MIT Press.

[68] Maes, P. (1990b). Situated agents can have goals. In P. Maes (Ed.), *Designing autonomous agents,* (pp. 49–70). Cambridge, MA: MIT Press.

[69] Maes, P., & Brooks, R. (1990). Learning to coordinate behaviors. *Proceedings of AAAI-90,* 796–802.

[70] Mahadevan, S., & Connell, J. (1990). Automatic programming of behavior-based robots using reinforcement learning. Yorktown, NY: IBM T. J. Watson Research Center.

[71] Marr, D. (1982). *Vision.* San Francisco: W. H. Freeman.

[72] Mataric, M. J. (1990). Navigation with a rat brain: A neurobiologically-inspired model for robot spatial representation. *Proceedings First International Conference on Simulation of Adaptive Behavior* (pp. 169–175). Cambridge, MA: MIT Press.

[73] Mataric, M. J. (1991) Behavioral synergy without explicit integration. *SIGART* [Special Issue on Integrated Intelligent Systems].

[74] McCarthy, J. (1960). Recursive functions of symbolic expressions. CACM, 3, 184–195.

[75] McCarthy, R. A., & Warrington, E. K. (1988). Evidence for modality-specific systems in the brain. *Nature, 334*, 428–430.

[76] McCorduck, P. (1979). *Machines who think.* New York: Freeman.

[77] McCulloch, W. S., & Pitts, W. (1943). A logical calculus of the ideas immanent in nervous activity. *Bulletin of Mathematical Biophysics, 5*, 115–137.

[78] McFarland, D. (1985). *Animal behavior.* Menlo Park, CA: Benjamin/Cummings.

[79] McFarland, D. (1988). *Problems of animal behavior* Harlow, UK: Longman.

[80] Michie, D., & Ross, R. (1970). Experiments with the adaptive graph traverser. In B. Meltzer & D. Michie (Eds.), *Machine intelligence, 5* (pp. 301–318). New York: Elsevier

[81] Minsky, M. (1961). Steps toward artificial intelligence. *Proceedings of IRE, 49*, 8–30.

[82] Minsky, M. (1963). A selected descriptor-indexed bibliography to the literature on artificial intelligence. In E. A. Feigenbaum & J. Feldman (Eds.), *Computers and thought* (pp. 453–523) New York: McGraw-Hill.

[83] Minsky, M. (1985). Neural nets and the brain model problem. Unpublished doctoral dissertation. Princeton University, Princeton, NJ.

[84] Minsky, M. (1988). *Semantic Information Processing.* Cambridge, MA: MIT Press.

[85] Minsky, M. (1986). *The society of mind.* New York: Simon & Schuster.

[86] Minsky, M., & Papert, S. (1969). *Perceptrons.* Cambridge, MA: MIT Press.

[87] Mitchell, T. M. (1990). Becoming increasingly reactive. *Proceedings of AAAI-90*, 1051–1058.

[88] Moravec, H. (1981). *Robot rover visual navigation* Ann Arbor, MI: UMI Research Press.

[89] Moravec, H. (1982). The Stanford cart and the CMU rover. *Proceedings of the IEEE, 71*(7), 872–884.

[90] Moravec, H. (1988). *Mind children.* Cambridge, MA: Harvard University Press.

[91] Newcombe, F., & Ratcliff, G. (1989). Disorders of visuspatial analysis. In *Handbook of Neuropsychology, Vol. 2* (pp.). New York: Elsevier.

[92] Newell, A., Shaw, J. C., & Simon, H. (1957b). Empirical explorations with the logic theory machine. In *Proceedings of Western Joint Computer Conference, 15,* 218–329.

[93] Newell, A., Shaw, J. C., & Simon, H. (1957a). Chess playing programs and the problem of complexity. *IBM Journal of Research and Development, 2,* 320–335.

[94] Newell, A., Shaw, J. C., & Simon H. (1959). A general problem-solving program for a computer. *Computers and Automation, 8*(7), 10–16.

[95] Newell, A., Shaw, J. C., & Simon, H. (1961). *Information processing language V manual.* Englewood Cliffs, NJ: Prentice-Hall.

[96] Nicolis, G., & Prigogine, I. (1977). *Self-organization in nonequilibrium systems.* New York: Wiley.

[97] Nilsson, N. J. (1965). *Learning Machines.* New York: McGraw-Hill.

[98] Nilsson, N. J. (1971). *Problem-solving methods in artificial intelligence.* New York: McGraw-Hill.

[99] Nilsson, N. J. (1984). Shakey the robot. (Tech. Rep. No. 323). SRI AI Center.

[100] Payton, D. W. (1990). Internalized plans: A representation for action resources. In P. Maes (Ed.), *Designing autonomous agents,* (pp. 89–103). Cambridge, MA: MIT Press.

[101] Ramachandran, V. S., & Anstis, S. M.(1985). Perceptual organization in multistable apparent motion. *Perception, 14,* 135–143.

[102] Roberts, L. G. (1963). Machine perception of three-dimensional solids. (Tech. Rep. No. 315). Cambridge, MA: MIT, Lincoln Labs.

[103] Rosenblatt, F. (1962). *Principles of neurodynamics.* New York: Spartan Books.

[104] Rosenschein, S. J., & Kaelbling, L. P. (1986). The synthesis of machines with provable epistemic properties. In J. Halpern (Ed.), *Proceedings of Conference on Theoretical Aspects of Reasoning about Knowledge* (pp. 83–98). Los Altos, CA: Morgan Kaufmann.

[105] Rumelhart, D. E., Hinton, G. E., & Williams, R. J. (1986). Learning internal representations by error propagation. In D. E. Rumelhart & J. L. McClelland (Eds.), *Parallel distributed processing* (pp. 318–364). Cambridge, MA: MIT Press.

[106] Rumelhart, D. E., & McClelland, J. L. (1986). *Parallel distributed processing.* Cambridge, MA: MIT Press.

[107] Russell, S. J. (1989). Execution architectures and compilation. *Proceedings of IJCAI-89,* 15–20.

[108] Sacks, O. W. (1974). *Awakenings.* New York: Doubleday.

[109] Samuel, A. L. (1959). Some studies in machine learning using the game of checkers. *IBM Journal of Research and Development, 3,* 211–229.

[110] Sejnowski, T. J., & Rosenberg, C. R. (1987). Parallel networks that learn to pronounce english text. *Complex Systems, 1,* 145–168.

[111] Selfridge, O. G. (1956). Pattern recognition and learning. In C. Cherry (Ed.) Proceedings of Third London Symposium on Information Theory (pp. 345–353). New York: Academic Press.

[112] Shannon, C. E. (1950). A chess-playing machine. *Scientific American, 182*(2).

[113] Simmons, R., & Krotkov, E. (1991). An integrated walking system for the ambler planetary rover. *Proceedings of IEEE Robotics and Automation* (pp. 2086 2091).

[114] Simon, H. A. (1969). *The sciences of the artificial.* Cambridge, MA: MIT Press.

[115] Slagle, J. R. (1963). A heuristic program that solves symbolic integration problems in freshman calculus. In E. A. Feigenbaum & J. Feldman (Eds.), *Computers and thought* (pp. 191–206). New York: McGraw-Hill.

[116] Slate, D. J., & Atkin, L. R. (1984). Chess 4.5-The Northwestern University Chess Program. In P. Frey (Ed.), *Chess skill in man and machine* (pp. 331–380). Berlin: Springer-Verlag.

[117] Smith, B. C. (1991). The owl and the electric encyclopedia. *Artificial Intelligence, 47,* 251–288.

[118] Steels, L. (1990a). Towards a theory of emergent functionality. *Proceedings of First International Conference on Simulation of Adaptive Behavior* (pp. 451–461). Cambridge, Ma: MIT Press.

[119] Steels, L. (1990b). Exploiting analogical representations. In P. Maes (Ed.), *Designing autonomous agents* (pp. 71–88). Cambridge, MA: MIT Press.

[120] Sussman, G. J. (1975). *A computer model of skill acquisition* New York: Elsevier.

[121] Teitelbaum, P., Pellis, V. C., & Pellis, S. M. (1990). Can allied reflexes promote the integration of a robot's behavior? In *Proceedings of First International Conference on Simulation of Adaptive Behavior* (pp. 97–104). Cambridge, MA: MIT Press.

[122] Thorpe, C., Hebert, M., Kanade, T., & Shafer, S. A. (1988). Vision and navigation for the Carnegie-Mellon NAVLAB. *IEEE Trans. PAMI, 10*(3), 362–373.

[123] Tinbergen, N. (1951). *The study of instinct.* Oxford, UK: Oxford University Press.

[124] Turing, A. M. (1937). On computable numbers with an application to the entscheidungsproblem. *Proceedings of London Mathematical Society, 42*, 230–65.

[125] Turing, A. M. (1950). Computing machinery and intelligence. *Mind, 59*, 433–460.

[126] Turing, A. M. (1970). Intelligent machinery. In B. Meltzer & D. Michie (Eds.), *Machine Intelligence, 5* (pp. 3–23). New York: Elsevier

[127] Turk, M. A., Morgenthaler, D. G., Gremban, K. D., & Marra, M. (1988) Experiments with autonomous land vehicles. *IEEE Trans. PAMI, 10*(3), 342–361.

[128] Viola, P. (1990). Adaptive gaze control. Unpublished master's thesis, MIT, Cambridge, MA.

[129] von Neumann, J., & Morgenstern, O. (1944). *Theory of games and economic behavior.* New York: Wiley.

[130] Grey, W. (1950). An imitation of life. *Scientific American, 182*(5), 42–45.

[131] Grey, W. (1951). A machine that learns. *Scientific American, 185*(2), 60–63.

[132] Grey, W. (1953). *The living brain.* London: Duckworth.

[133] Watkins, C. (1989). Learning from delayed rewards. Unpublished doctoral dissertation, King's College, Cambridge, UK.

[134] Waxman, A. M., Le Moigne, J., & Srinivasan, B. (1985). Visual navigation of roadways. *Proceedings of IEEE Robotics and Automation*, 862–867.

[135] Wehner, R. (1987). "Matched Filters"—Neural models of the external world. *Journal of comp. Physiol. A, 161*, 511–531.

[136] Wiener, N. (1961). *Cybernetics*. Cambridge, MA: MIT Press.

[137] Wilkins, D. A. (1979). Using patterns and plans to solve problems and control search. (Memorandum No. 329), Stanford University, Palo Alto, CA.

[138] Williams, M. (19). From Napier to Lucas. *Annals of the History of Computing, 5*(3), 279–296.

[139] Winograd, T. (1972). *Understanding natural language* New York: Academic Press.

[140] Winograd, T., & Flores, F. (1986). *Understanding computers and cognition*. Reading, MA: Addison-Wesley.

[141] Winston, P. (1972). The MIT robot. In B. Meltzer & D. Michie (Eds.). *Machine intelligence, 7* (pp. 431–463). New York: Wiley.

[142] Winston, P. (1984). *Artificial intelligence*. Reading, MA: Addison-Wesley.

[143] Wood, W. (1988) *The nematode Caenorhabditis Elegans*. Cold Spring Harbor, NY: Cold Spring Harbor Laboratory.

3. Building Agents out of Autonomous Behavior Systems

LUC STEELS
VUB AI Lab, Brussels, Belgium

3.1 Introduction

This chapter sets out the main principles and hypotheses that have been driving the intelligent autonomous agents research in our Brussels laboratory since 1986.[1] Our research strategy is to some extent shared by other groups working in this area. In particular, strong interactions with the MIT AI lab mobile robots group headed by Brooks have influenced our current emphasis on building physical autonomous agents.[2] The engineering of physical robots received even more emphasis when Tim Smithers, who formerly headed the Edinburgh mobile robots group, joined the laboratory in 1991.[3] Joint projects with the Laboratory for Nonlinear Phenomena of the Brussels Free University (ULB) have influenced our emphasis on complex dynamics.[4] The past few years we have also had more and more interactions with ethologists, particularly with David McFarland from Oxford

[1]The bulk of the the funding of our activities has come from a Belgian government IMPULS action (1986-1992), an EEC Cost action (1986-1989) and an ESPRIT basic research action SUBSYM (1989-1993).

[2]The cooperation between the VUB AI lab and the MIT AI lab in this area was financed by a NATO grant (1990–1992).

[3]This visit was sponsored by SWIFT.

[4]Cooperation on the complex dynamics of neural networks (with A. Babloyantz) was financed partly by an ESPRIT basic research project (SUBSYM) and on collective behavior (with J. L. Deneubourg and S. Goss) by a Belgian government IUAP action.

University.

This chapter has four sections. The first one defines the subject matter: intelligent autonomous agents. The second section focuses on methodological issues. It discusses the kind of theories being looked for, the approach, and the nature of the experimental settings. The third section formulates the major hypotheses that we are currently exploring. The fourth section gives some concrete examples.

3.2 Defining Intelligent Autonomous Agents.

The subject matter of our research is intelligent autonomous agents. This first section circumscribes the meaning of the terms *agent*, *autonomy*, and *intelligence.*

Agents

We are interested in studying a particular class of physical objects known as *agents.* An agent, because it is a physical object, is subject to the laws described by physics. What distinguishes an agent from other objects is that an agent can control to some extent its own destiny. A stone, for example, is simply subjected to physical laws, such as the law of gravity. A stone cannot decide that it will not fall or that it wants to move a bit forward. A simple animal, even a unicellular one, can go toward areas with more nutritients or avoid lethal areas. The independence from physical laws is of course relative. If a person is hit by a car, there is little that he can do about it.

One requirement for this relative independence is *automaticity.* The agent must have a way to sense aspects of the environment and a way to act on the environment—for example, change its own position or manipulate objects. All this must happen by automatic mechanisms—mechanisms that do not require the intervention of other agents to be executed. This implies that the agent has its own locus of control: It must be able to decide what to do and when. Automaticity is a property that we find in many machines today—for example, in systems that control the central heating in a house or in an airplane that flies in automatic mode.

Autonomy

The real world is infinitely rich and dynamically changing. An agent, to be viable, must therefore be more than automatic. Autonomy becomes an important additional requirement. Smithers characterised autonomy as follows:

> The central idea in the concept of autonomy is identified in the etymology of the term: *autos* (self) and *nomos* (rule or

> law). It was first applied to the Greek city states whose citizens made their own laws, as opposed to living according to those of an external governing power. It is useful to contrast autonomy with the concept of automatic systems. The meaning of automatic comes from the etymology of the term *cybernetic*, which derives from the Greek for *self-steering*. In other words, automatic systems are self-regulating, but they do not make the laws that their regulatory activities seek to satisfy. These are given to them or built into them. They steer themselves along a given path, correcting and compensating for the effects of external perturbation and disturbances as they go. Autonomous systems, on the other hand, are systems that develop, for themselves, the laws and strategies according to which they regulate their behaviour: They are *self-governing* as well as self-regulating. They determine the paths they follow as well as steer along them. (T. Smithers, personal communication, September, 1992)

This description captures the essential point. To be autonomous you must first be automatic. This means that you must be able to operate in an environment, sense this environment, and impact it in ways that are beneficial to yourself and to the tasks that you have come to view as important. But autonomy goes beyond automaticity, because it also supposes that the basis of self-steering originates (at least partly) from the agent's own capacity to form and adapt its principles of behavior. Moreover the process of building up or adapting competence is something that takes place *while the agent is operating in the environment.* It is not the case that the agent has the time to study a large number of examples or to think deeply about how it could cope with unforeseen circumstances. Instead, it must continuously act and respond in order to survive. As Smithers put it, "the problem of autonomous systems is to understand how they develop and modify the principles by which they regulate their behaviour while becoming and remaining viable as task achieving systems in complex dynamical environments." (T. Smithers, personal communication, September, 1992).

Another way to characterise autonomy takes the viewpoint of the observer. The ethologist David McFarland pointed out that an automatic system is something of which you can fully predict the behavior as soon as you know its internal basis of decision making. An autonomous system on the other hand is a system that makes up its own mind. It is not clear, not even to the original designer, how a system will respond because it has precisely been set up so that responses evolve and change to cope with novel situations. Consequently autonomous systems cannot be controlled the same way that automatic systems can be controlled:

> Autonomous agents are *self controlling* as opposed to being under the control of an outside agent. To be self-controlling, the

> agent must have relevant self-knowledge and motivation, since they are the prerequisites of a controller. In other words, an autonomous agent must *know* what to do to exercise control, and must *want* to exercise control in one way and not in another way. ([15], p. 4).

AI systems built using the classical approach are not autonomous, although they may be automatic. Knowledge has been extracted from experts and put into the system explicitly. But the extraction and formalisation has been done by analysts. Current robotic systems are also automatic, but so far not autonomous. For example, algorithms for visual processing have been identified *in advance* by designers and explicitly coded in the computer. Control programs have been invented based on a prior analysis of the possible situations that could be encountered. The resulting systems can solve an infinite set of problems, just like a numerical computer program can solve an infinite number of calculation problems. But these systems can never step outside the boundaries of what was foreseen by the designers because they cannot change their own behavior in a fundamental way.

Intelligence

Intelligence continues to enhance the independence of agents from physical forces, for example, by having the ability to predict an event before it will happen and act on the basis of that prediction, to plan before acting, to pursue a target even if there is no direct sensory contact with it. It is common in the literature on intelligence to make a distinction between two different qualities of skill: action-centered and intellective (see e.g., [24]). Action-centered skills are exhibited in sensorimotor activities like walking around in the house, driving a car, playing piano, and carving a statue out of a piece of wood. Intellective skills are needed for designing and implementing computer programs, playing chess, or formulating a mathematical proof. Zuboff ([24], p. 61) identified four distinguishing characteristics:

> "*Sentience.* Action-centered skill is based upon sentient information derived from physical cues." Intellective skills are based on abstractions expressed as descriptions. It can operate in the absence of direct physical cues.
>
> "*Action-dependence.* Action-centered skill is developed in physical performance. Although in principle it may be made explicit in language, it typically remains unexplicated—implicit in action." Intellective skills are developed based on verbal or written communication or on theorizing while performing actions. It is or can be made explicit.
>
> "*Context-dependence.* Action-centered skill only has meaning within the context in which its associated physical activities can occur."

Intellective skill is context independent because it works on the basis of abstractions. The link between the descriptions and the skill needs to be established explicitly.

"*Personalism.* It is the individual body that takes in the situation and an individual's actions that display the required competence. There is a felt linkage between the knower and the known." Intellective skills are based on disembodied knowledge, which can be more easily shared, for example by writing it down. It is in many cases cultural knowledge, transmitted by books and explicit education.

It is obvious that AI research so far has focused on intellective skills. Elaborate symbol structures have been proposed and studied for representing models of the world, and very complex and elaborate operations over symbolic structures have been researched for replicating inference. The resulting theories and technologies have gone very far in explicating the nature of intellective skills. The stream of sophisticated and effective computer-based support tools for areas like scheduling, diagnosis, or design would otherwise not have been possible (an overview of recent research in this area is contained in [20]).

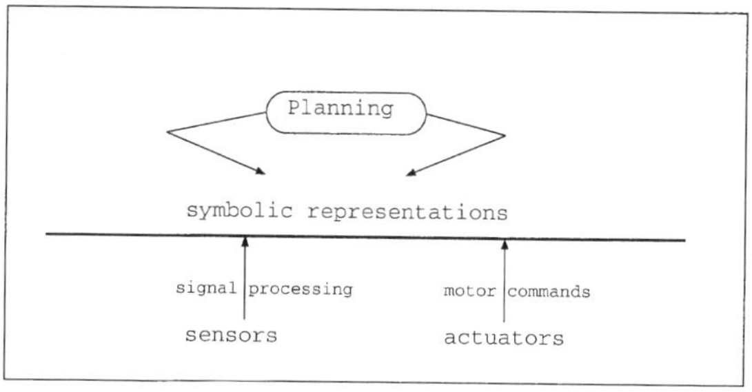

Fig. 3.1: Architecture of traditional AI-style robotics, which assumes that action-centered skill is of the same nature as intellective skill, except for the coupling to sensors and actuators.

On the other hand, much less progress has been made inside AI on action-centered skills, although it is clear that an agent that has to be viable in the world needs both, as well as a strong interaction between the two. If the subject of action-centered skills has been approached in AI at all, it has usually been by using the techniques of intellective skill. For example, traditional AI-style robotics, such as those underlying Shakey [8], assumed an architecture as in Fig. 3.1 where sensory inputs are translated via signal processing and pattern recognition routines into symbolic descriptions. These symbols are used to formulate a description of the world upon which planning—as a symbolic reasoning process—can take place.

The actions proposed by the planner are translated into concrete actions on the robot. This approach is known as the *top-down approach* because it assumes that intellective skills are the basis of action-centered skills.

There is a growing consensus that this approach does not work very well because:

- It is very difficult to construct signal processing and pattern recognition routines that can deliver the required symbols accurately and within the severe time constraints imposed by the real world. For example, an infrared sensor that emits and recaptures infrared light as it bounces back from obstacles is not a reliable obstacle detector. For instance, some objects reflect more infrared than others; there is background infrared that may cause the sensors to measure additional infrared, which is not due to reflection; an obstacle further away from the sensor may reflect more quickly than an obstacle closer to it, and so on. In many cases the signal itself does not contain all the information that is needed to unambiguously parse it without context. For example, not all phonemes show up in the effective speech signal because they may be blurred or left out by the speaker.

- The commands sent to actuators do not always yield the intended action. If we tell a robot to go forward a certain distance d in direction p, then there may be a slight deviation both in distance and direction because of friction on the wheels, an uneven surface, irregular power supply, small obstacles on the floor, and so on.

- The conceptual frameworks needed at the symbolic level are now constructed by the designer, explicitly put in, and then linked to the sensory inputs and motor commands. As a consequence the system cannot step outside the boundaries of its own framework. There has been substantial progress in machine learning, but the algorithms discovered so far (for example, inductive learning) operate within a designer-defined conceptual framework. Putting in fixed conceptual frameworks a priori would work if the world and the goals of an agent in that world could remain stable. But the world is highly dynamic and evolving constantly. This requires adapting the conceptual frameworks with which the world is approached.

- The rules that underly the inferences are now put in explicitly by the designer after analysis of the possible situations that the system may encounter, but an agent operating in a dynamically changing world may always encounter unforeseen circumstances and unusual situations. Putting in all the rules in advance therefore works only in closed worlds and highly controlled environments.

Outside of AI research, particularly in the cybernetics, control theory, and neural network areas, researchers have focused on action-centered skills but without using the symbolic machinery underlying intellective skills. This has lead to a large body of theories, techniques, and technologies. These results could be integrated in a more complete theory of intelligent behavior that explains both action-centered and intellective skills and the interaction between the two. This is precisely the goal of our research. We want to understand action-centered skills, but in the context of complete agents operating in real-world environments. This approach is known as the *bottom-up approach* to AI because action-centered skills are seen as a basis on which intellective skills will ultimately have to be built.

3.3 Methodological Issues

3.3.1 Types of Theories

Almost in any field of study there are three types of questions that one can ask: what, how, and why questions.

Observational Theories

The what question is concerned with what the phenomena are. The main result is a catalog classifying the phenomena and possibly a set of laws that capture the regularities in the phenomena. A law is of the form: In these circumstances you will see these phenomena because in similar circumstances in the past these phenomena could be observed. Newtonian mechanics results from asking such questions. Behaviorism, as practiced in the beginning of this century by Skinner, among others, sought an observational theory for behavior. Input—output behavior pairs were investigated systematically and objectively and the generalisations were expressed as laws. No assumptions were allowed to be made about the internals of the system.

Mechanistic Theories

The how question is concerned with the structures and processes giving rise to the observed phenomena. A collection of such structures and processes constitutes a mechanistic theory. An example of such a theory for behavior is neurobiology. A mechanistic theory requires that one descends one observational level below the phenomena of interest and makes (observational) theories at that level. Artificial intelligence clearly seeks a mechanistic theory of behavior. It wants to understand the mechanisms (structures and processes) that give rise to behavior, although the proposed mechanisms are not necessarily the ones that nature uses. As long as it can be proven that there is the same functionality, the mechanism is acceptable. This way AI can work at a more abstract level without loosing contact with the problem of physical realisation.

Explanatory Theories

The why question is concerned with finding an explanation of a particular phenomenon (i.e., why it is there in the first place). An example of such a theory for behavior is evolutionary biology. For example, one might not only observe that a certain bird species removes broken eggshells from their nest (the what question), but also try to identify the mechanisms responsible for it such as the motor programs and innate release mechanisms (the how question), and then try to find the reason why these birds do that (the why question). The explanation in this case comes from the higher risk of predation, and the principle of evolution by natural selection. Birds that remove eggshells from the nest are less exposed to predation, therefore have more offspring, and will gradually dominate the population ([4], pp. 38—39). Formulating explanatory theories means that a larger context is taken into account (not only the agent executing behavior but also the environment) and/or that the origin of the phenomenon is considered.

Until recently AI was not interested in explanatory theories. Structures and processes thought to be necessary for intelligent behavior were proposed, but no explanations were sought for why these structures are the way they are, nor why a specific behavior is necessary. An explanatory theory may, however, be unavoidable when the structures and processes underlying behavior need to change, for example, because of changes in the environment. It would then be impossible to build artificial systems without taking contextual influence and evolution strongly into account.

3.3.2 The Synthetic Method

AI distinguishes itself from the other cognitive sciences not by its subject matter (intelligent behavior) but by its methodology. This methodology is derived from the inductive method used in most scientific research today.

The inductive method illustrated in Fig 3.2 starts from observed facts about the behavior of the system under study. What counts as a fact is somewhat dependent on the theory because the formulation of a fact implies that the scientist has focused on certain aspects of the system and left out others. It also implies that concepts have been introduced to describe the behavior, concepts like mass, speed, acceleration, force, and so on.

A theory is a generalised description of the behavior of a system. It captures the dependencies between facts describing a particular state of a system—for example, that the speed of a falling object increases with time. The step from observed facts to theories takes place by an inductive process, which tries to generalise as much as possible. Because of this generalisation, a theory can be used to make predictions about instances of system behavior that have not been observed yet. For numerically formulated theories, the prediction is made using techniques of mathematics. Often the computer assists in making the necessary calculations to accu-

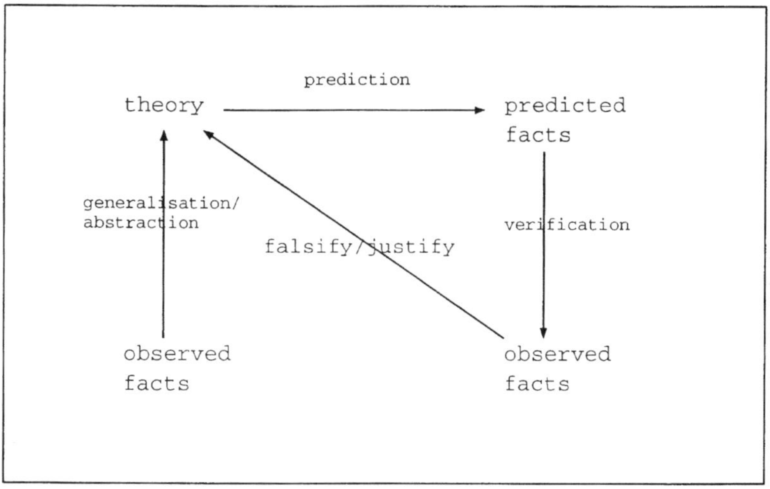

Fig. 3.2: The inductive method tests a theory of a system by matching predicted facts against observed facts.

rately perform the predictions particularly with more complex theories.

The test of the theory takes place by confronting the predictions with reality. This step is known as the verification of the theory. In the simplest case, it is a simple matching process: The predicted facts are compared with the observed facts. Either the predicted facts match, in which case the theory is confirmed, or the predicted facts do not match, in which case the theory, or at least a small aspect of it, is falsified and needs to be changed. Usually the nature of the mismatch provides some indication of how the theory should be changed, and often it is necessary to go back to the facts and review them or take more facts into consideration.

The *synthetic method* underlying AI research is complementary to the inductive method and seems particularly appropriate for studying complex systems as described in Fig. 3.3.

The initial steps in this method are the same as for the inductive method: A theory is constructed by abstraction and generalisation from observed facts of the system. But the next step is different. Instead of gen-

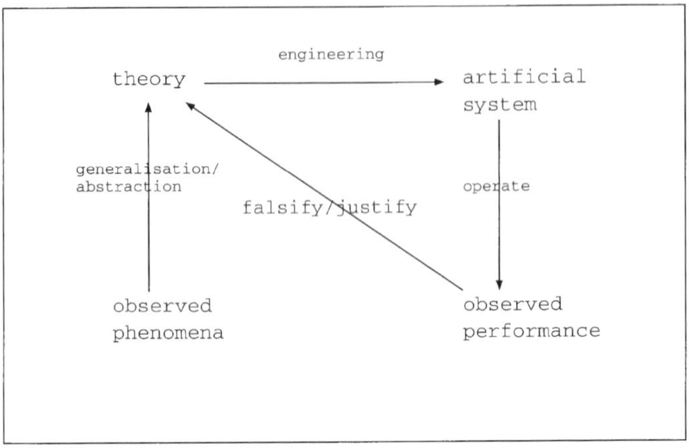

Fig. 3.3: The synthetic method builds up theories of a system by attempting to construct an artificial system that exhibits the same capabilities as the natural system.

erating predictions using mathematics or other deductive approaches, the theory is used as a basis for constructing an artificial system. The artificial system must be able to establish the same functionality in the same context setting as the natural system under investigation. An artificial kidney is a good example of an artificial system. Building it requires (a) knowing what the (natural) kidney does, (b) understanding how this function can be achieved, namely through a particular chemical process, (c) mastering the technology to replicate the processes used by the natural system, and (d) setting up the appropriate interfaces between the real world and the artificial system. The replication does not need to be identical to the process used by nature, as long as it is possible to establish the appropriate interfaces between it and the original context.

In a synthetic method, the test of the theory comes from a confrontation of the artificial system with reality. The artificial system is put in the same context setting as the natural system, and differences in performance with respect to specific functionalities are carefully measured. Two things may happen:

- The performance deviates dramatically (usually this means that the artificial system is not at all able to achieve the same functionality as the natural system). This means that there is something wrong along the chain between observed facts and artificial system. The theory could be wrong. But, of course, there could also have been errors in the engineering. In any case revisions are in order.

- The artificial system is able to function with similar performance in the same context setting. Then the whole framework has been confirmed and partially justified.

The strength of the synthetic method is two-fold. The challenge of building an artificial system is a powerful creative stimulus that triggers our engineering intuitions. Second, the testing of the theory is done in a rigorous and objective way, simply by putting the artificial system in the appropriate setting and observing whether it is able to perform in the same way as the natural system. There are two extra bonuses: (a) Using the artificial system, it is possible to explore systematic variations; (b) There is a useful practical side-effect because we have alternative systems that can take over the function of the original, if needed. For example, if a kidney does not function well the patient could use an artificial kidney.

The synthetic method goes further than a computer simulation. If we make a computer simulation, then we use a formal model of a phenomenon and let the predictions that this model generates be made automatically by the computer. For example, we can make a computer simulation of rain based on a system of differential equations. This simulation predicts properties of rain given certain parameters and initial conditions. But the relationship to the real world is absent. There is no real rain coming out of the computer. The result of the simulation could not water plants. In contrast, the artificial kidney is fully embedded in the world and interacts physically with a patient to alleviate problems with his kidney. An airplane interacts physically with the surrounding environment. It is not simulating this interaction. Simulation is part of the tools supporting the inductive method because it helps to generate predictions. It may also be used as part of the engineering methodology to find out how an artificial system should be built. But a simulation is not an artificial system.

Many mental functions, like scheduling, for example, can be viewed as information processing, and because the computer is an information processor, the distinction between the computer simulation of a scheduler and an artificial scheduler built with a computer is small. The only thing that needs to be added are the appropriate interfaces to the real world, and these interfaces could possibly be computer-based interfaces interacting with other human beings. This contrasts with the artificial kidney, which requires chemical processing and the exchange of physical materials. For perception and action, the distinction between computer simulation and artificial system is much bigger because building the interfaces is a nontrivial problem. This is why the construction of robots is so important from a methodological point of view. A robot, like an airplane, is physically embedded in the world. By building robots we address not only what the internal (information processing) mechanisms are for an intelligent agent but also what the mechanisms are that constitute the interfaces to the real world. When we are building robots we are clearly no longer simulating intelligence or making computational models of intelligence, we are building artificial intelligence.

Critics of AI are often unaware of the distinction between simulation and building artificial systems. The philosopher Searle [12] stated for example,

> "Nobody supposes that the computer simulation is actually the real thing; no one supposes that a computer simulation of a storm will leave us all wet, or a computer simulation of a fire is likely to burn the house down. Why on earth would anyone in his right mind suppose a computer simulation of mental processes actually had mental processes?" (p. 38)

Yes indeed, there is a distinction between simulation and the real thing. But what we do is not merely simulate mental processes. The goal is to build an artificial system that can function *instead of* the natural system in the same context setting—the same way an airplane that engages in artificial flight is really flying; it is not merely simulating flight.

3.3.3 Experiments

Because testing of theories takes place by putting integrated artificial systems in a natural context, it is very important, from a methodological point of view, to determine what the contexts are. A context is sometimes called a microworld. The most famous example is the blocksworld formulated by researchers at the MIT AI laboratory in the beginning of the 1970s. It consisted of an environment with a robot arm, a camera, and a scene with various stylised objects (cubes, pyramides, balls, etc.) as illustrated in Fig. 3.4. Within this microworld different aspects of intelligence were studied: vision [21], knowledge representation and planning [5], natural language [22], learning [23]. All of these aspects were to some extent integrated. The natural language system produced internal representations that could be used by the planning system to plan a series of actions executable by the arm. The learning system produced definitions of concepts that could be used by the vision system to categorize the scene. In retrospect, it is amazing how many fundamentally new concepts and techniques emerged from this integrated focus.

The idea of a microworld as complete experimental testbed has been less prominent lately as AI researchers focus more and more on separate components: a mechanism for maintaining truth, an algorithm for edge detection, a representation for time, a method for inducing decision trees. We insist on this practice again although the microworlds that we use are different from the blocksworld.

> The blocksworld is static. It does not change except through actions of the robot arm. No actions can take place by other agents that might interfere with the execution of a plan. This makes it possible to adopt a closed world assumption or to assume that planning can be strictly separated from action.

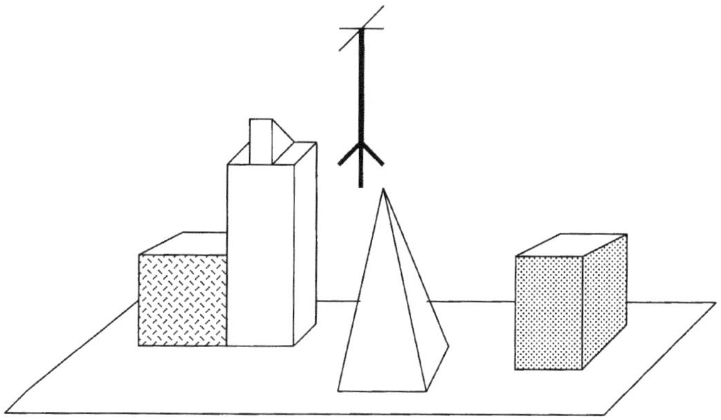

Fig. 3.4: Microworld in the form of a blocksworld. There is a physical world with blocks, a camera and an arm that can be instructed to make changes in the world.

The objects are stylised and can only be recognized under strict light conditions. This makes it possible to use algorithms for edge detection, shape from shading, computational geometry, and so on. Many of these algorithms break down when the world is dynamically changing or when the sensors give very weak information (as is indeed the case for infrared sensors, for example).

There is no time constraint, either for the vision modules or for the planning modules. Each of these modules can work as long as it wants to. This implies that certain solutions are possible that are excluded when the real-time aspect is taken into account.

Learning takes place through a carefully constructed series of examples. The agent does not have to remain operational while it learns and can strongly rely on the availability of a teacher. This makes it possible for certain algorithms to work but reduces the utility for real-world agents.

Instead of such closed and static microworlds, we are using dynamic physical environments we call *robot ecosystems.* A robot ecosystem is first and foremost a physical environment. It contains robotic agents. The ecosystem also contains various objects that have their own dynamical behavior. Some objects are mere obstacles. Others are in themselves agents that have their own dynamics. Some objects are dangerous and need to be avoided. Other objects may provide resources. The ecosystem may contain additional elements such as varying climatic elements likes changes in light conditions or changes in temperature.

The ecosystem is set up in such a way that the agents operate in an

Fig. 3.5: Example of robotic agent used in the experiments. The robot has a cylinder-shaped physical body (50 cm high), about 30 different sensors (infrared, sonar, pyro, touch, sound), batteries, a mobile base, and on board microprocessors.

unpredictable, dynamic, and often hostile, real-world environment. Decisions must be made in quasi-real time, in any case fast enough to cope with the dynamically changing world. The agents are responsible to a large extent for building up and maintaining the knowledge that they need. They can move about in the environment and perform various actions. These actions are (at least at this point) mostly carried out to ensure their own survival—for example, gathering new energy that may involve foraging to find sources of energy, discriminating between good and bad energy sources, cooperating and communicating with other agents to find and exploit energy, avoiding dangerous situations that may physically damage the agent, and so on.

The creation and study of robot ecosystems is motivated as follows: By considering real physical agents (as opposed to simulated agents or agents that interact with the world through human intermediaries), we make sure to address the problems of how sensors and actuators relate to the structures inside the system and to subject the agents properly to the real constraints of the world, such as limited time and resources to make decisions. By considering a complete ecosystem, we shift focus from the agent in isolation to the complete environment of which the agent is only a part. There are two motivations for this: first, the belief that the agent cannot be understood without taking the environment into account, particularly not if we are developing an explanatory theory; second, an attempt to take the designer out of the loop as much as possible. The latter means that we do not put in all the conceptual representations a priori as is now done in AI systems. The agent must develop at least some of its own representations starting from signals coming from sensors and consequences of actions carried out by the actuators. It also means that we do not put in all the action patterns and their relation to specific situations that the agent encounters. The agent must—by exploring the environment—partly develop its own repertoire of actions and representations. Similarly we do not supply tasks in the form of goals to the agent. The agent must formulate its own goals and manage them.

Computer simulations of robots, even if the environment is simulated alongside with the behavior of the robot in that environment, are not sufficient because the designer has still decided what features of the environment are important, (i.e., what may count as information to the agent). Moreover no computer simulation can ever be expected to cope with the time–space complexity of the real world, and it is precisely in the infinite richness of the world that the developing agent must find its way. A computer simulation would not even make this problem visible. Computer simulations are still an extremely valuable tool, of course, to explore the properties of certain proposed mechanisms, for example, to get an understanding of the behavior of a mechanism given certain parameters. Computer simulations are in this sense complementary to mathematical investigations of the equations describing the behavioral dynamics. But, because autonomy (and ipso facto intelligence) is a property of the relation between an agent and an environment, it can only be observed when a real physical agent interacts with the world. We therefore need both the physical agent and the real world to make any plausible claims about the validity of our experiments.

3.3.4 Conclusions

The following major points summarise the methodological discussion in this section:

- There is a consensus on distinguishing intellective and action-centered skills. But the top-down approach of classical AI emphasised intellective skills and hopes to treat action-centered skills using intellective mechanisms. We are pursuing a bottom-up approach where action-centered skills are seen as the foundation for intellective skills. Both need to be available and integrated if we ever want to have viable artificial agents.

- Not only a mechanistic theory is sought but an explanatory theory as well. This means that the context (interaction between agent and environment) and the evolution of skill (driven by forces in the ecosystem) are to be investigated as much as the internal mechanisms of the agent.

- We follow the synthetic methodology practised in AI, which means that theories are tested by using them to build artificial systems that are validated by being put in a concrete environmental setting. The setting we use takes the form of robot ecosystems in which robotic agents have to function under environmental pressure, which lead them to evolve structure and function.

3.4 Hypotheses

This section discusses the hypotheses underlying our current work: We pursue a behavior-oriented as opposed to function-oriented decomposition, and dynamics as opposed to symbol processing as the basis for a behavior unit. We hypothesise that the process networks defining the dynamics show recurring patterns; one of the most powerful ones is the pattern; of emergent functionality. Finally we hypothesize that selectionist mechanisms play a very large role in the formation of new behavior systems. Each of these hypotheses is now briefly introduced.

3.4.1 Behavior-Oriented Decomposition

When we observe humans, or even extremely simple animals for that matter, we can (subjectively) divide their activities into different behaviors—for example, obstacle avoidance, going around a corner, seeking energy, avoiding dangerous situations. Each behavior involves the following aspects:

- Sensory data must be collected through external or internal sensors.

- The data must be interpreted.

- An action must be determined in response to the perceived situation. Determining the action may be based on knowledge and inference. The action could be a communication to another agent.

- The action must be translated to motor commands. Because there can be many possible behaviors, there is a further problem: A selection must be made which behavior will be pursued.

And because we are interested in autonomous agents that can adapt and learn, there is another aspect:

- The agent must learn (i.e., change some of its processes and structures to do any of these actions: change its processes for interpreting data, for determining the action, for selecting the most appropriate behavior, and so on).

There are two ways to organise the internals of an agent: a function-oriented and a behavior-oriented way. The *function-oriented* approach, which dominates classical AI and cognitive science, assumes that each aspect is performed in a separate module:

- There is a vision module responsible for interpreting visual data. The module is assumed to deliver a detailed and accurate symbolic description of the situation. An example of such a module has been proposed by Marr [6].
- There is a module deciding about the most appropriate action. This module is usually split up into a knowledge representation module that contains case-specific or general domain knowledge and an inference module that is responsible for using this knowledge to decide on the most appropriate action.
- There is a communication module entirely responsible for formulating and transmitting a communication if that is the action that was decided.
- There is a motor command module responsible for translating actions into concrete commands.
- There is a control module (the planner) that decides which action pattern is the most appropriate to pursue.
- There is a separate learning module that tries to expand the structures and processes available to the agent.

Splitting things up this way makes sense because everything related to one aspect can be grouped together and thus optimised. There will be no duplication of effort with respect to different behaviors. For example, the vision module supplies information to all possible behaviors. It is also easier to see how a language faculty could work because it would receive conceptual structures about what needs to be said and then produce the communication regardless of its content. A function-oriented organisation seems therefore the natural choice for intellective skills. On the other hand, there is necessarily a lack of swiftness in response to the world because information needs to travel through all the different (possibly very complicated) modules before sensing is related to acting.

There is an alternative *behavior-oriented* approach, which brings everything needed for one behavior together in one unit. Let us call such a unit a *behavior system*. A behavior system contains all the necessary structures and processes for linking sensing with acting: mechanisms for interpretation, structures representing knowledge, mechanisms for deciding on the most appropriate action and translating it to motor commands, mechanisms for adaption and learning. Each behavior system sees the world from its particular point of view and extracts only information from the sensors that is immediately relevant to establish the behavior it is responsible for. The behavior system is also its own control locus. It decides by itself when to become active and it has all the resources to do so. For example, there could be a behavior system for obstacle avoidance that has access to sensory data and is able to control the motors moving forward. This behavior system becomes active as soon as the sensors detect the presence of an obstacle. The obstacle avoidance behavior system could itself be made up of different subsystems, which themselves also establish direct links between sensors and actuators—for example, a behavior subsystem that performs obstacle avoidance based on the touch sensors and another subsystem that works based on the infrared sensors.

A behavior-oriented organisation is much more reactive because everything is immediately available to establish an efficient link between sensing and effecting. It seems therefore more appropriate for action-centered skills. This is probably why researchers pursuing the bottom-up approach quickly reached a consensus that an alternative behavior-oriented decomposition is more appropriate. [5] The fact that representations and decision making are distributed among different behavior systems immediately explains why it is so difficult to make such skills explicit using language and why there is this apparent gap between intellective and action-centered skills.

But what about the decision of which behavior to pursue? The function-oriented organisation assumes a central control module. A behavior-oriented organisation, if pursued to its logical consequence, assumes instead a completely distributed system (see Fig. 3.6). Behavior selection must still take place. But there are various possibilities:

- In some cases, the behaviors are orthogonal and simply take place in parallel. For example, we are walking forward and turn our head toward the source of a sound at the same time.

- The constraints imposed by the external and internal world situation are unique enough to determine which behavior system will have a dominating influence on the motor commands.

- In those cases where there is a genuine potential conflict between different behavior systems, motivational variables are introduced that can be influenced by other behavior systems.

This architecture differs from the subsumption architecture [4]. The subsumption architecture also assumes a behavior-oriented organisation. But one behavior system can turn on or off the sensory inflow and motor control outflow of another behavior system, and there are timers available for the finite state machines defining each behavior unit.

[5] See Brooks [4]. The term *behavior-based AI* was coined to emphasise this point of view [15]. The term was intended to contrast with *knowledge-based AI*.

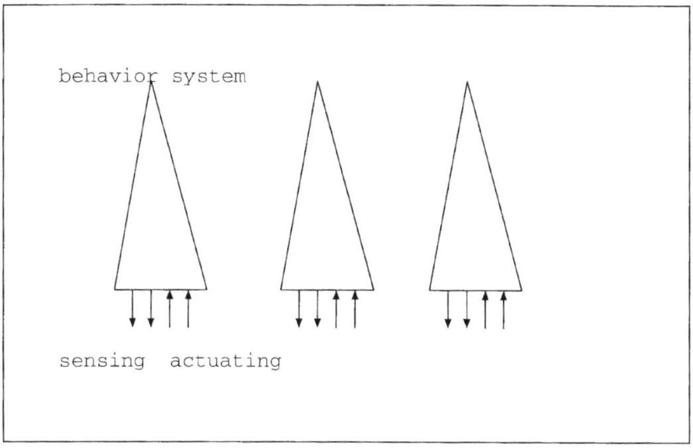

Fig. 3.6: Different behavior systems operate all in parallel. Each has their own interaction with the environment. In a limited number of cases there are explicit control influences between them.

3.4.2 The Dynamical Basis of Behavior Systems

The modules proposed by the classical AI architecture are not only function oriented, they also have an important internal characteristic; namely they consist of symbol processing mechanisms. Knowledge is represented in symbolic structures; the inference machinery manipulates these symbolic structures in order to develop models of the world or the internal state; learning takes place by manipulating symbolic representations of knowledge; communication is seen as transforming symbolic representations of the content of what needs to be communicated into semantic, syntactic, and morphophonological structures; overall planning and control is done by symbolic reasoning. The only exception are the modules that perform the translation from sensory data to symbolic representations and from symbolic representations to motor commands.

A symbolic description requires that the world, which is by nature continuous, is discrete and categorised. For example, temperature may be made discrete in time and categorised to be medium, low, or high. But it is not really necesary to perform this "discretisation". For example, a furnace can be controlled by directly linking temperature (a continuously varying quantity) to the opening of a valve. This is the approach followed by control theory, and it has been shown to be highly successful, for example, for automatic pilots.

Following these observations, we have adopted the hypothesis that a behavior system should similarly be based on relating dynamically varying quantities with each other—without going to the effort of discretising and categorising their states. This means that the internals of a behavior system consist of a set of processes linking continuously varying quantities. We call this set a *process network*. A process can increase or decrease a quantity as a function of the evolution of other quantities. There may still be discrete thresholds (subject to adaptive processes), but the general framework becomes that of dynamics instead of symbol processing. Because a neural network can be seen as a dynamic process, results from neural network research can easily be integrated.

Each process can play a role in different behavior systems. For example, a process causing retraction when the bumper sensors give a positive signal may be needed in obstacle avoidance as well as wall following. So, the process network that implements one behavior system is a dynamical structure established by the operation of the different processes. The behavior of the network is an emergent property of the interaction between the processes and the environment. The notion of behavior system remains useful from the viewpoint of design or from the viewpoint of an observer. But in practice all processes of all behavior systems run in parallel, and there is no additional control structure inside each behavior system. We have often encountered difficulties in categorising collections of processes in terms of behavior systems.

3.4.3 Recurrent Patterns

There is a bewildering complexity of possible process networks, so we have sought further constraints to make the design of behavior systems manageable. These constraints take the form of recurrent patterns that we expect to see as (or design into) process networks. One of the most basic patterns is the one depicted in Fig. 3.7. We call this the stabiliser-disturber pattern or simply SD-pattern. There is a quantity called the *controlled quantity*. This quantity is typically an action quantity, (i.e., a quantity directly related to an action by the robot). There is a process that acts as a *stabiliser*, bringing the controlled quantity to a default value. There is a process that acts as a (temporary) *disturber*, for example, pulling the controlled quantity up or down. The disturber process is directly triggered by sensory inputs.

Here is a concrete example. Consider the problem of performing wall following and assume that there is already a behavior system that keeps track of the infrared sensors and steers the robot toward (or away) from the wall. There is a second behavior system that is capable of handling corners. However if the corner is too sharp, there is a risk that the turning is too slow and contact with the wall is lost Fig. 3.8. The problem is resolved by increasing the turning angle, which means increasing the speed of the rotation motors, depending on the sharpness of the angle.

A process network achieving this functionality is given in Fig. 3.9. The controlled quantity is the turning of the rotation motor. The stabiliser is a

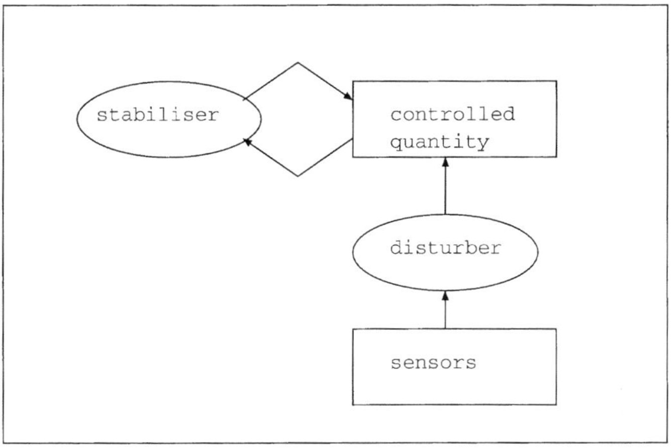

Fig. 3.7: Recurrent pattern in process networks based on a stabiliser and a disturber.

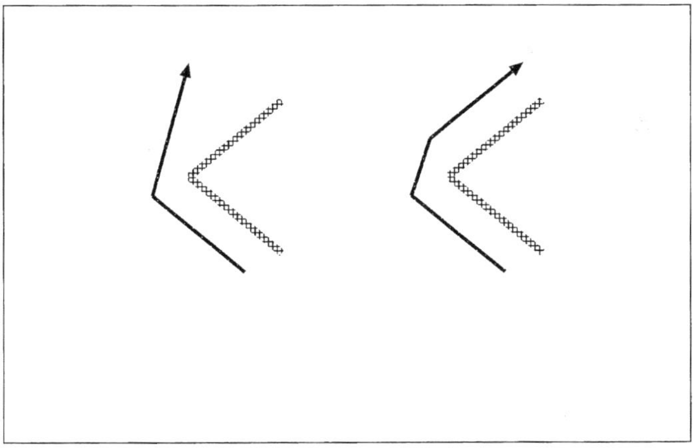

Fig. 3.8: The problem of corner handling. When the angle is too sharp, contact may be lost. The solution is to rotate faster.

process that brings this quantity down to its default value. The disturber temporarily increases the controlled quantity. It is linked to the infrared sensors that measure contact with the wall.

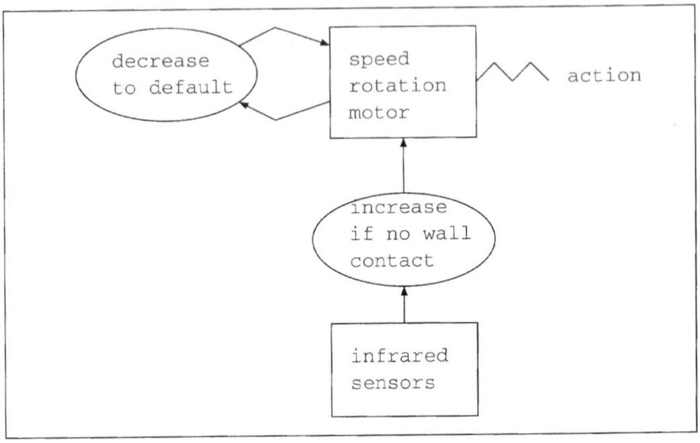

Fig. 3.9: Process network based on the stabiliser-disturber pattern. The network causes the turning angle to be increased (temporarily) when there is a risk that contact is lost.

Stabiliser-disturber-patterns can be chained. Consider for example left-wall-following behavior. This can be realised with two chained SD-patterns (Fig. 3.10). The top-level SD-pattern controls the turning quantity. There is a default value (equal to 0) that is temporarily overruled when another quantity (contact-with-left-wall) is very low. The latter quantity acts as the controlled quantity of a second SD-pattern. There is a process (the stabiliser) bringing contact-with-left-wall gradually to its default value (which is also 0). When contact is made with the wall (detected by the sensors), the contact-with-left-wall is suddenly made high.

A further variant of an SD-pattern occurs where there is both a positive and a negative force and when there are self-enforcing loops through the environment. This means that because of the action, the disturbing process will happen even stronger (or faster), and the whole process thus feeds on itself. We call this the pattern of emergent functionality. It was first identified in Steels [62] (Fig. 3.11). An example of this will be given later.

We believe that there are other patterns. Each pattern can be systematically studied, also from a mathematical point of view, and a catalog of patterns forms the beginning of a systematic design practice for constructing process networks.

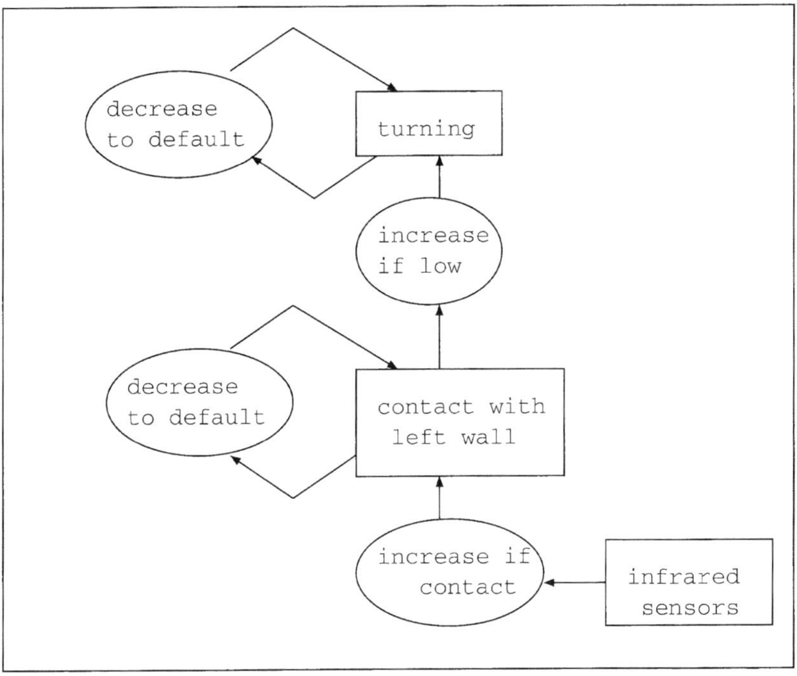

Fig. 3.10: Chain of two SD-patterns that give rise to left-wall following.

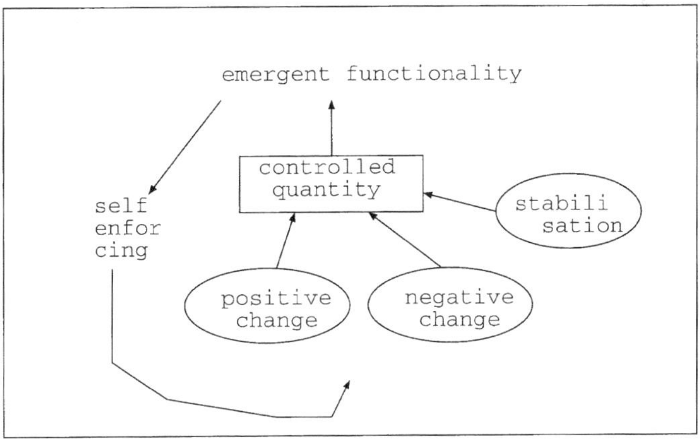

Fig. 3.11: Emergent functionality pattern observed in process networks. There are two opposing forces, possibly stabilised. The processes impact a controlled quantity that indirectly gives rise to emergent functionality. The positive process feeds on itself.

3.5 Selectionism

A final hypothesis concerns the formation of new behavior systems. Here we follow the selectionist principle, which is accepted as dominating explanatory principle in the formation of the bodily characteristics of animals and even in their behavior pattern, but which is rarely used for the formation of the structure inside a single agent. Edelman's theory of neural Darwinism is an exception [3].

We hypothesize that there are mechanisms that generate new copies of behavior systems inside the agent. The copies can have small variants like slightly different parameter settings, transformations of structures, additional sensors linked in, and so on. Because we have an additive nonhierarchical combination of behavior systems, these new copies can be added in a straightforward manner to the pool of existing behavior systems and will operate whenever the conditions in the environment match with their sensory requirements. A behavior system that is effectively used (i.e., that triggers and has an impact on the motor actions) becomes stronger. Strength means both survival in the pool of competing behavior systems and a higher probability that new offspring can be generated. Notice that there is no external evaluation criterion that assigns credit to one or the other system as is the case for genetic algorithms.

Here is an example of how this mechanism could operate: Assume there is a behavior system for obstacle avoidance (see later for more details). The decision as to whether there is an obstacle is based on the weighted impact on active infrared sensors. Assume also that the behavior system remains adaptive to variations in the environment, in the sense that the weights change to take environmental variations into account. (This is also illustrated in more detail later.) Copies could then be made of this behavior system, possibly linking in an additional light sensor. A copy could have slight variations in the weights for the infrareds and therefore trigger in different environmental circumstances. The copies that are used often would survive and may again lead to new copies. Those that are used less are discarded. This way there is a gradual build up of a population of behavior systems that are each specialised in specific different niches from the viewpoint of obstacle avoidance.

The exploitation of selective mechanisms is in itself a big subject that cannot be treated fully in this chapter. The aforementioned is intended to illustrate the directions we are exploring.

3.6 Conclusions

The previous section reviewed the major hypotheses underlying our work:

- We follow a behavior-oriented decomposition instead of a function-oriented decomposition for design. The major unit is a behavior system that establishes itself autonomously as a link between sensing and acting.

- A behavior system consists of a set of dynamical processes that operate in parallel. A process influences the continuous evolution of quantities as a function of other quantities. A collection of interconnected processes is called a *process network*.
- There are patterns in process networks that act as building blocks to make the engineering easier. One prominent pattern is emergent functionality.
- The formation of new behavior systems is based on selectionist principles.

3.7 An Example

We have been working the past 5 years toward an exploration and validation of these various hypotheses. We have built many different types of robots in order to explore different types of microprocessors, control and communications circuitry, and body shape. We have also developed tools to design behavior systems. One tool is a language called PDL (Process Description Language) [64], which makes it easier to implement process networks, either in simulation (LISP-based) or on real robots (C-based). We now have a complete data-recording facility with a camera that is mounted on the ceiling and records continuous behavior. Despite of all this, we feel that we are still in the beginning of our research, and many experiments still need to be carried out, particularly to validate the symbolic–subsymbolic hypothesis and the selectionist hypothesis. It is not possible to review in a single chapter what we have done so far. Instead I concentrate on one simple example, which should help to make the hypotheses more concrete, particularly the first three hypotheses.

Experimental Setup

We assume an ecosystem known as the plant world. It contains a collection of plants which have a particular physical shape and various associated dynamic properties including light or sound emission. The robot moves around in the plant world and is able to have an impact on the physical properties of the plants. The experimenter can introduce challenging conditions, which all put pressure on the robot to develop structure and function—for example, to develop a map of the plant world in order to quickly navigate back to plants associated with a source of energy for the agent.

For the purposes of this experiment, we assume that there is a beacon located at a particular position in the plant world. The beacon emits infrared light, and the robot has a right and a left infrared sensor to detect the plant. The robot also has touch sensors (bumpers) to detect when it has hit an obstacle.

Task Decomposition

The first step in the design of the agent is usually a decomposition into the major tasks (or functionalities) and subtasks. This decomposition is not the basis of the design of the internals of the agent—as it would be in a hierarchical system—but a design-oriented decomposition that helps to identify the behavior systems that need to be present. The top-level decomposition for this experiment is in terms of two tasks: explore (which includes obstacle avoidance) and go towards target.

The Explore Task

The explore behavior system is established by a number of (subcognitive) processes. It explores the twelve bumper sensors located in a ring on the robot base in Fig. 3.12.

There are four processes:

- retraction, if the front bumpers are touched,
- move a bit forward, if the back bumpers are touched,
- turn away left, if the left bumpers are touched, and
- turn away right, if the right bumpers are touched.

Here is C-code for the retract process, which links positive values for the front bumper sensors to a command for retraction and a change in translation speed.

```
void retract_reflex (void)
{
 if ((bumper_mapping[0] > 0) || (bumper_mapping[11] > 0) ||
     (bumper_mapping[10] > 0) ||
     (bumper_mapping[1] > 0) || (bumper_mapping[2] > 0)){
  do_Tless(retract_distance); /* go back some distance */
  do_change_TV(retract_speed);/* increase speed to retract quickly */
   }
}
```

When the robot is standing still, and some obstacle hits the front, there is a retract movement. Because the turn-away and retract reflexes operate in parallel, there is also a translatory movement.

The forward movement behavior subsystem is a collection of subcognitive processes as shown in Fig. 3.12. It follows the pattern outlined earlier: There is a stabiliser and a disturber both controlling an action quantity, called go_forward. When this quantity is at a particular value (in this case 10), the action of moving forward is executed.

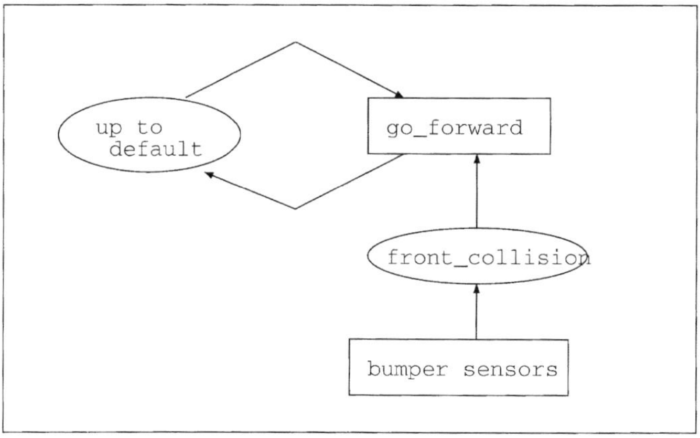

Fig. 3.12: Process network for forward movement behavior. The network has a stabiliser-disturber pattern.

The stabiliser is implemented as a process that brings the quantity toward its normal value (10). The C-code defining it is as follows:

```
void up_to_default_forward_tend (void)
{
   if (value(go_forward) < 10)
         add_value(go_forward,1);
}
```

This is an example where a value is not set (as in imperative sequential programming), but a stabiliser is introduced, which progressively causes the value to reach the target. Next there is the disturber, which is a process that will suddenly bring the value to a negative value (in this case -80) to avoid moving forward right after the bumper sensors have hit an object:

```
void front_collision (void)
{
   if ((value(bumper0) > 0) || (value(bumper1) > 0) ||
       (value(bumper11) > 0) || (value(bumper2) > 0) ||
       (value(bumper10) > 0))
     add_value(go_forward,-80);
}
```

When the processes operate together in interaction with the environment they exhibit emergent behaviors:

Obstacle avoidance: When the agent hits an obstacle, it will retract and turn away. The tendency to move forward is still there, so immediately after retraction the agent starts to move again. Because the agent has turned, it will approach the object now from another angle.

Explore: Because of the forward tendency, the agent is going around in the environment and will turn toward new directions when it hits either an obstacle or one of the sides of the plant world arena.

The next figure gives a trace of the robot through the arena, illustrating exploration while avoiding obstacles behavior. The trace is obtained by filtering the light from a light bulb on top of the robot.

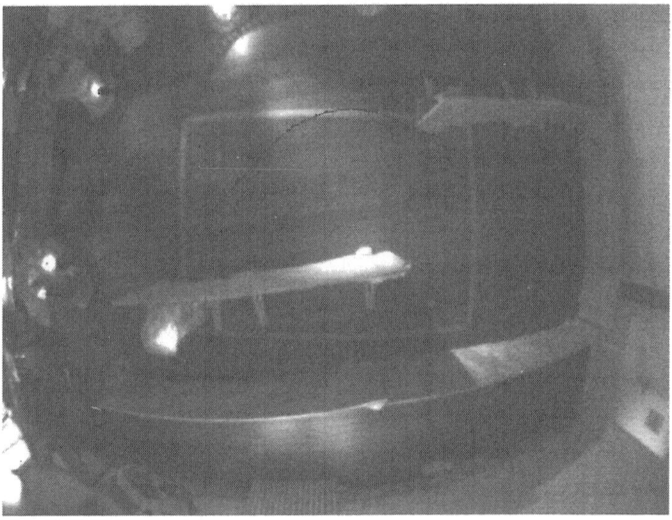

Fig. 3.13: Trace of the robot showing explore and obstacle avoidance. The behavior of the robot is achieved by putting together the four basic processes above and the go "forward" subsystem.

There is no central control, nor explicit subsumption relations between the different processes (reflexes and subcognitive processes). The processes work in parallel, and there are no imposed timing constraints. There is a potential conflict between the behavior subsystems, which means that there is an (apparent) control problem. The retract reflex implies a backward movement, whereas the forward movement tendency implies a forward movement. The way this conflict is resolved is not by a central agency but by the natural speed of the processes. Because the retract behavior is based on a reflex, it will happen faster than the forward movement behavior.

The Navigation Task (using taxis)

The navigation task consists of two behavior subsystems:

> *Maintain right contact*: This behavior system tries to maintain a contact between the right infrared sensor and the target. It proposes a rotational movement when there is no contact or a weak contact. The movement is always in a left direction.
>
> *Maintain left contact*: This behavior system tries to maintain a contact between the left infrared sensor and the target. It is a mirror of the "maintain right contact" behavior system. The movement is in a right direction.

Each behavior subsystem consists of a stabiliser and a disturber. The action quantity is called turn–direction and linked to the translation motors. This value is by default equal to 0, and so there is a process (the stabiliser) to bring the value down to the default when it is higher. For the maintain left contact subsystem, this process is defined as follows:

```
void down_to_default_turn_dir (void)
{
   if (value(turn_direction) > 0)
         add_value(turn_direction,-1);
}
```

The value is increased by the disturber when the left-IR sensors (in the case of the maintain left contact subsystem) no longer have contact:

```
void maintain_left_contact (void)
{
   if ((value(IR_2) < 150) && (value(IR_3) < 150))
      /*the left IR lost contact; impose turning right */
         add_value(turn_direction,100);
}
```

The maintain right contact subsystem is a mirror of this. The value of tendency to turn is brought to a negative value (which means turn left) by the disturber:

```
void maintain_right_contact (void)
{
   if ((value(IR_9) < 150) && (value(IR_10) < 150))
         /*the right IR lost contact; impose turning left */
         add_value(turn_direction,-100);
}
```

There is a process (part of the stabiliser) that will bring it back to the default again (which is 0).

```
void up_to_default_turn_dir (void)
{
   if (value(turn_direction) < 0)
         add_value(turn_direction,1);
}
```

The maintain right and left contact behavior subsystems are depicted in Fig. 3.14

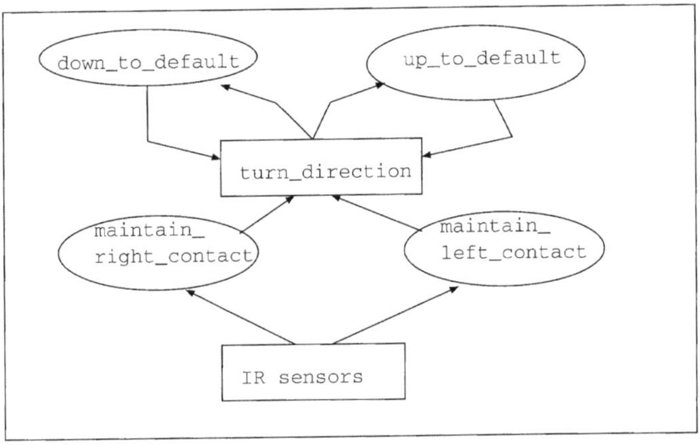

Fig. 3.14: The maintain right and left contact system consists of stabilisers to bring the action quantity turn_direction to its normal value (which is 0) and two disturbers, in a positive direction (for turning right) and a negative direction (for turning left).

Each of these behavior systems works independently of the others. The global taxis behavior is achieved by putting both of them together without any extra control or any extra processes influencing quantities or actions. When all processes and reflexes are working together, a zig-zag behavior emerges. This is therefore a good illustration of nonhierarchical behavior system combination. Other behaviors are observed when some of the behavior systems are left out. For example, when there is no forward movement, the agent will turn toward the beacon but not move toward it. When either the maintain left or right contact system falls out (for example, because the infrared sensors fail or give an insufficient reading), the other one is still sufficient to get taxis, although the agent sometimes must make a complete turn before making contact with the beacon again.

Fig. 3.16 shows the impact on a pair of right and left IR sensors during a 15-second time frame with all reflexes and processes active. Fig. 3.17

Fig. 3.15: Illustration of zig-zag behavior obtained by putting together the explore (while avoiding obstacles) and the maintain right and left contact behavior subsystems.

shows the movement of the rotational motor as influenced by these right and left infrared readings, for the same time frame.

The behavior system for taxis is of a striking simplicity and is computation-poor. There is, for example, no triangulation taking place. Instead some strong interaction loops have been set up between the agent and the environment, and it is through the simultaneous operation of these loops that the overall behavior emerges. At the same time there is a surprising robustness. Experiments have been performed in which the infrared sensors were temporarily shut off, one IR sensor was made more sensitive than another one, less energy was made available (because of low batteries) making the IR emission poorer, the speed increased or decreased, the turn angle increased or decreased, and so on. A solid performance remains observable.

Enhancing the Forward Movement Competence

Obviously both tasks can be improved. One way to improve obstacle avoidance is to perform additional sensing of the environment so that an obstacle can be avoided before it is hit. To achieve this, an additional behavior subsystem is added to the already existing components. Let us call this the

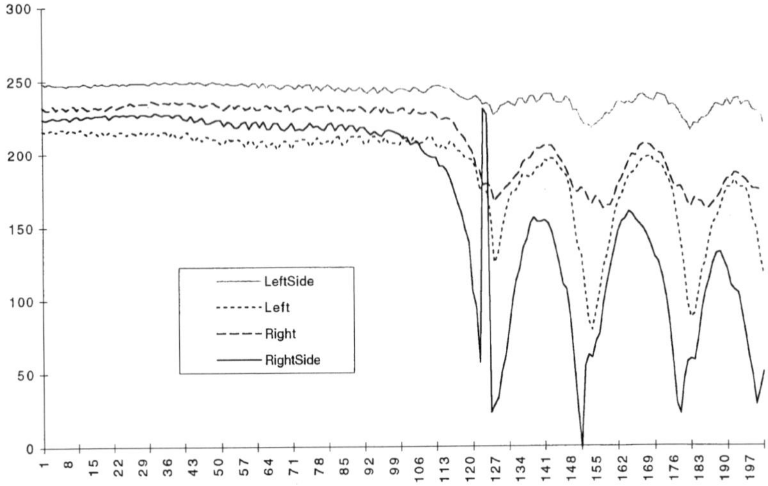

Fig. 3.16: Evolution on right and left IR sensors. These data have been taken from a run with the physical robot during a 15-second time frame.

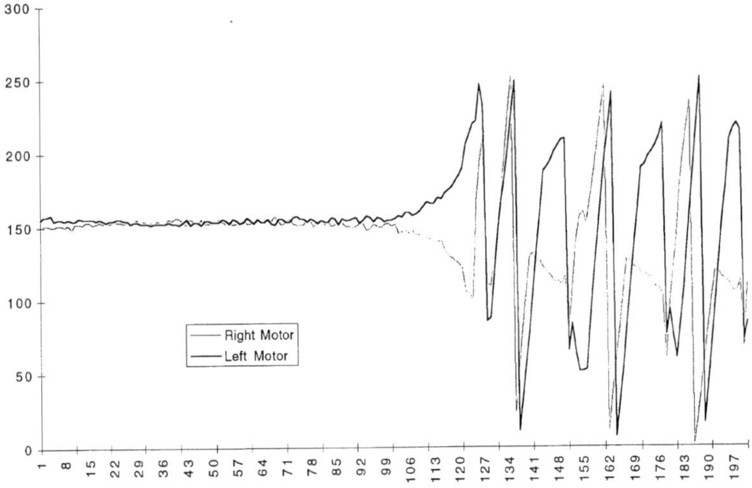

Fig. 3.17: Recording of the variation in the turn_direction quantity during the same time frame as in the previous figure.

anticipated turn-away subsystem.[6] Anticipated turn-away contains as part of its processes a perceptron-like network [11] as in Fig. 3.18. Each infrared input value is multiplied with a weight, and the sum is compared with a threshold. When the resulting value is greater than zero, a rotation is enacted that will cause the agent to steer away from the obstacle.

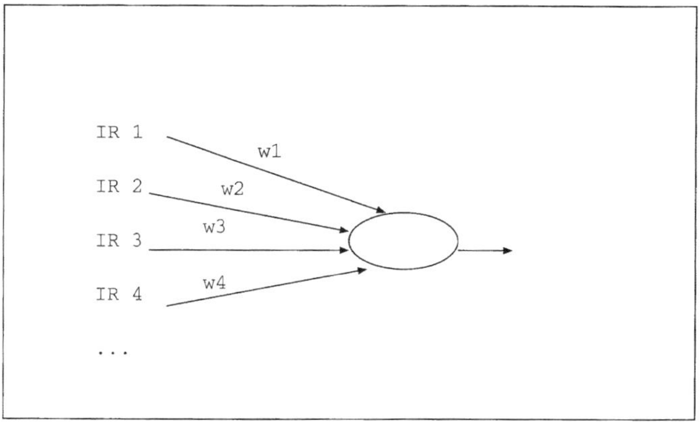

Fig. 3.18: Perceptronlike network implementing the combination of infrared measurements into a decision whether an obstacle is present.

The weights are formed using Hebbian learning. Hebbian learning means that co-occurrence of active nodes enforces the associations between the nodes. The two nodes here are activation signals on the infrareds and the action of turning away that is caused independently by the reflex. The action is initially due to the touch-sensor based turn-away reflex. Because the weights progressively become higher, there is a natural tendency of the network to generalise. To avoid unbounded increases and adaptation, a process causing a continuous decrease of the weights is added. This process can be viewed as forgetting. Temporary blocking of the weights acts as a stabilising force. A typical example of the evolution of weights is seen in Fig 3.19.

Our experiments demonstrate that, after a learning phase, the anticipated turn-away behavior system has fully and reliably developed and is routinely used by the agent to move around obstacles.

Some of the advantages of weighted decision networks have been observed. For example, on one occasion one infrared sensor failed. Progressively this was compensated for by an increase in the weights of the surrounding infrared sensors. No significant change in behavior could be seen by an external observer. We have also observed new adaptation. When

[6] This work was done by Sinnaeve and Van Aeken, originally inspired by simulation experiments conducted by Pfeifer and Verschuere [10].

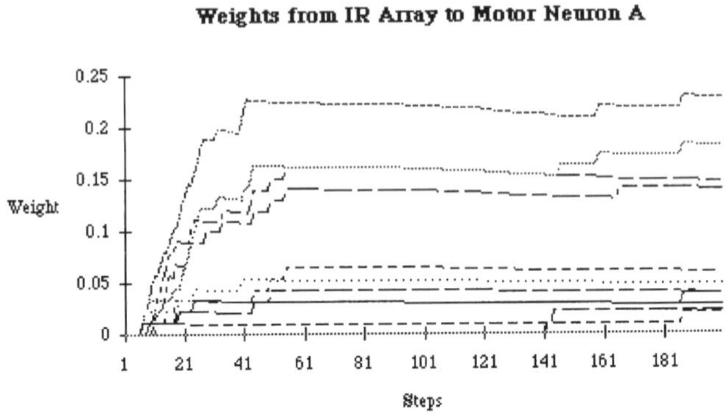

Fig. 3.19: Evolution of the weights in a network connecting infrared sensors with a quantity reflecting that an obstacle is present.

the agent was transferred from an infrared-poor to an infrared-rich environment, there was for a time a constant confusion between obstacles and nonobstacles. The turn-away action was triggered prematurely by the strong background infrared. Because of the forgetting process, the weights have a natural tendency to decrease, which eventually causes the weights to adapt to the new environment.

This example illustrates a number of important aspects of the hypotheses outlined earlier:

- No additional control structure was needed to add more effective obstacle avoidance behavior. The anticipated turn-away system works alongside the touch-sensor-based turn-away reflex. The anticipated turn-away system simply gets there first, most of the time because it has longer range sensors (namely infrared sensors). This illustrates an important advantage of the nonhierarchical parallel combination of behavior systems because improvements can simply be added without revising previous behavior systems.

- The example illlustrates in which way a behavior system (in this case obstacle avoidance) can be autonomous in the sense of forming and adapting its own structures and processes. The anticipated turn-away process improves itself while acting in the environment. All the time the total obstacle avoidance system remains viable because there is always touch-based sensing to fall back on. The representations that are developed (such as detecting whether there is an obstacle) are agent-centered and grounded in sensorimotor experience. More concretely, the notion of obstacle is related to turning away from

Fig. 3.20: Example of how the anticipated turn-away behavior system is built up gradually. Initially the robot bumps against the wall and reacts with the turn-away reflexes. After learning no more bumping against the walls takes place.

it. Without encountering obstacles and turning away from them, the representation would never develop and would not be able to maintain itself.

- The weighted decision network follows the pattern of emergent functionality. The enforcing mechanism pulls the weights up, and the forgetting mechanism pulls the weights down. These two mechanisms act therefore as the disturbers. The controlled quantity in this case are the weights, which indirectly determine the obstacle avoidance functionality based on infrared sensors. The blocking mechanism acts as stabiliser because it will dampen the influence of the disturbers as shown in Fig. 3.21. There is now a clear self-enforcing process through the environments. When the weights become higher there is a tendency to react faster (i.e., from a further distance) to the presence of an obstacle, which makes the weights even higher. This build-up is limited by the forgetting factor and by the range of the infrareds.

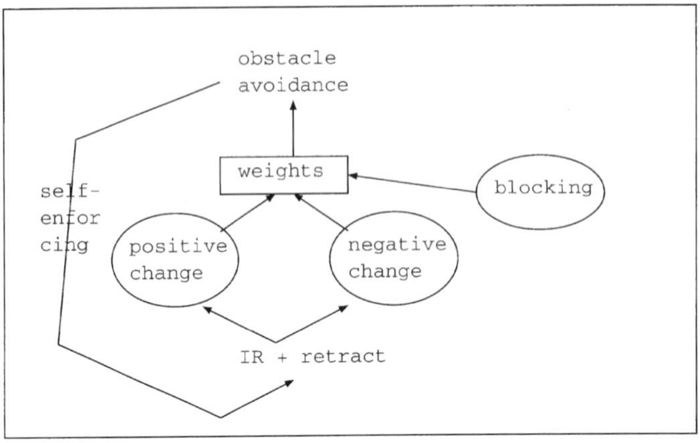

Fig. 3.21: Pattern of emergent functionality observed in the learning mechanism that builds up the anticipated turn-away behavior system.

3.8 Conclusions

This chapter surveyed the research strategy we are pursuing at our Brussels laboratory in order to investigate the phenomenon of intelligence. This strategy emphasises a bottom-up approach, which means that we focus on action-centered skills first and view intellective skills based on reasoning and planning to be embedded completely in action-centered skills. The construction of physical robots and robot ecosystems appears to be an experimental prerequisite to study action-centered skills. Five hypotheses were put forward: We pursue a behavior-oriented as opposed to function-oriented decomposition, and dynamics as opposed to symbol processing as the basis for a behavior unit. We hypothesise that the process networks defining the dynamics show recurring patterns; one of the most powerful is the pattern of emergent functionality. We propose a three-layered architecture with a layer for reflexes, a layer for (subcognitive) processes, and a layer for symbolic processes. Finally we hypothesize that selectionist mechanisms play a very large role in the formation of new behavior systems. An example was given to illustrate in more detail how some of the hypotheses translate to technical solutions.

We feel that there is still a large amount of research that needs to be done to elucidate and test the hypotheses, particularly in the area of the interaction between the symbolic and subsymbolic and the exploitation of selectionist mechanisms for building up new behavior systems. On the other hand, we have reached a theoretical and technical plateau from which these exciting explorations have become feasible.

3.9 Acknowledgment

This chapter has been stimulated by many of the researchers currently associated with the VUB AI laboratory. It took shape during the 1991 workshops in Corsendonck (Belgium) and Brussels on intelligent autonomous agents and at the"From Artificial Intelligence to Artificial Life" debate in Paris with Wielinga, Sloman, and Smithers, which was broadcast by the EUROPACE satellite network. Additional discussions with Brooks, McFarland, and Smithers have helped to clarify the ideas. Anne Sjostrom had a large impact on the current shape of the text. Her comments have proven to be extremely helpful in many respects. I am very much indebted to the current team of "robot ecologists" at the VUB AI laboratory, which is working with great enthusiasm toward the creation and investigation of the robot ecosystems along the lines advocated in this chapter: Franky Keppens, Giorgio Pappas, Miles Pebody, Ugo Piazzalunge, Ian Porter, Piet Ruyssinck, Geert Sinnaeve, Anne Sjostrom, Tim Smithers, Peter Stuer, Francis Van Aeken, Peter Van den Bossche, Danny Vereertbrugghen, Filip Vertommen. In particular, Filip Vertommen has been instrumental in some of the research results described in the example section of this chapter. Funding from ESPRIT Basic Research (the SUBSYM project) and the Belgian Government (IUAP and Impuls actions) is gratefully acknowledged.

References

[1] Brooks, R. (1986). A robust layered control system for a mobile robot. *IEEE Journal of Robotics and Autonomation, 2*, 14–23.

[2] Brooks, R. (1991). Intelligence without reason. *Proceedings of the IJCAI.* Los Angeles: Morgan Kaufmann.

[3] Edelman, G. (1990). *Neural Darwinism.* New York: Basic Books.

[4] Gould, S. (1982). *Animal Behaviour.* Cambridge, MA: Harvard University Press.

[5] Hewitt, C. (1969). PLANNER: A language for proving theorems in robots. *Proceedings of the International Joint Conference on Artificial Intelligence* (pp. 295–301). Bedford, MA: Mitre Corporation.

[6] Marr, D. (1982). *Vision.* San Francisco: W. H. Freeman.

[7] McFarland, D. (1992). *Autonomy and self-sufficiency in robots.* (Memorandum No. 92–3). Brussels: VUB AI Lab.

[8] Nilson, N. (1974). *Shakey the robot.* (Tech. Rep. No. 323). Stanford, CA: Stanford University, Stanford Research Institute.

[9] Pebody, M. (1991). *Getting a lego vehicle to do the right thing.* Unpublished master's thesis, University of Edinburgh, AI Department.

[10] Pfeifer, R., & Verschuere, P. (1991). Distributed adaptive control: A paradigm for designing autonomous agents. In: Bourgine, J. and Varela, F. (Eds.), *First European ALife Conference Proceedings.* Cambridge, MA: MIT Press.

[11] Rosenblatt, F. (1962) A comparison of several perceptron models. Washington: Spartan Books.

[12] Searle, J. (1984). *Minds, brains and science.* Cambridge, MA: Harvard University Press.

[13] Steels, L. (1989). Connectionist problem solving—An AI perspective. In R. Pfeifer, Z. Schreter, F. Folgeman-Soulie, & L. Steels (Eds.), *Connectionism in perspective* (pp. 215–229). Amsterdam: North-Holland.

[14] Steels, L. (1990a) Artificial intelligence and complex dynamics. In M. Tokoro & A. Yonezawa (Eds.), *Concepts and techniques for knowledge-based systems* (pp. 369–401). Amsterdam: North-Holland.

[15] Steels, L. (1990b) Cooperation between distributed agents through self organisation. In Y. Demazeau (Ed.), *Distributed AI* (pp. 450–468). Amsterdam: North-Holland.

[16] Steels, L. (1990c). Exploiting analogical representations. *Journal of Robotics and Autonomous Systems, 6*(1,2).

[17] Steels, L. (1991). Towards a theory of emergent functionality. In J. A. Meyer & S. W. Wilson (Eds.), *From animals to animats* (pp. 451–461). Cambridge, MA: MIT Press.

[18] Steels, L. (1992a). The PDL reference manual. (Memorandum No. 92–5). Brussels: VUB AI Lab.

[19] Steels, L. (1992b) Reusability and knowledge sharing. In L. Steels & B. Lepape (Eds.), *Enhancing the knowledge engineering process* (pp. 240–271). Amsterdam: Elsevier.

[20] Steels, L., & Lepape, B. (Eds.), (1992). *Enhancing the knowledge engineering process: contributions from ESPRIT.* Amsterdam: Elsevier.

[21] Waltz, D. L. (1975). Understanding line drawings of scenes with shadows. In P. Winston (Ed.), *The psychology of computer vision.* New York: McGraw-Hill.

[22] Winograd, T. (1972). Understanding natural language. *Cognitive Psychology, 3*(1).

[23] Winston, P. (1975). Learning structural descriptions from examples. In P. Winston (Ed.), *The psychology of computer vision.* New York: McGraw-Hill.

[24] Zuboff, S. (1988). *In the age of the smart machine.* New York: Basic Books.

4. Are Autonomous Agents Information Processing Systems?

TIM SMITHERS
VUB AI Lab, Brussels

When criticising the philosophy of an epoch, do not chiefly direct your attention to those intellectual positions which its exponents feel it necessary explicitly to defend. There will be some fundamental assumptions which adherents of all the variant systems within the epoch unconsciously presuppose. Such assumptions appear so obvious that people do not know what they are assuming because no other way of putting things has ever occurred to them.

— A. N. Whitehead, [72, p. 61]

4.1 Introduction

An agent is autonomous if it is able to cope with all the consequences of its actions to which it is subjected while remaining viable as a task-achieving agent in the world it operates in[1]. For any particular agent acting to achieve

[1] For a related, but more limited, characterisation of autonomy see [14], and for a rather different characterisation, but one which it is also argued underlies intelligent

some particular task or tasks in some particular environment its autonomy will be bounded: It will not be able to cope with all possible consequences of its actions. Autonomy is thus a matter of degree. It is, however, a necessary prerequisite for intelligent behaviour: The more or less autonomous an agent, the more or less its potential for intelligent behaviour. The questions of how autonomous an agent is, how it behaves intelligently, and what the bounds are on its intelligent behaviour, are therefore all closely related. I see the investigation of autonomous behaviour by building robots as properly a part of AI. [2]

In AI, as in the related disciplines of cognitive psychology, cybernetics, ethology, and neuroscience, it is a well entrenched dogma that *intelligent systems are information processing systems*: that the environment of an intelligently behaving agent can be abstractly characterised in all its essential detail as a world of information, and that the agent's interaction with this environment is to be properly understood as involving the picking up and processing (typically in some complex way) of this information to produce appropriate decisions about further actions.

In AI, the information processing view of an agent is embodied in the Physical Symbol System Hypothesis of Newell and Simon [47], and Newell's *Knowledge Level* characterization of an intelligent agent [45]. See also [38] for a recent restatement of this doctrine. According to this *classical* kind of AI, symbol processing is the way to do the necessary information processing, and provides a way to engender the knowledgeable, goal-oriented, rational-action selecting behaviour of an intelligent (autonomous) agent. Classical AI's main rival today, connectionism [56, 57], rejects explicit symbol manipulation as the basis for intelligent behaviour but still embodies the concept of information processing: Here it is the collective behaviour of large numbers of simple computational elements that count, rather than explicit symbols and their manipulation. In cognitive psychology the concept of information and its internal representation and application was offered as the common ground between its various founding disciplines [44, 53, 48], and now plays an unquestioned fundamental role in all its talk and descriptions. Although putting less stress on the role or representation, Gibson's ecological approach to perception [20, 16], is still essentially an information processing approach. In cybernetics [73, 6], the concept of information processing is central to its analysis of autonomous systems. Indeed, it was Wiener and Shannon [58] who first introduced a formal notion of information. Using these ideas and those of negative feedback control (the servomechanism), cybernetics has tried to characterise both natural and artificial autonomous systems as necessarily being a particular kind of information processing systems. Examples of attempts to develop architec-

---

behaviour, see [13].

[2] I take Artificial Intelligence to be the science which seeks to develop a theoretical understanding of intelligent behaviour in all its aspects by attempting to replicate it, or aspects of it, in the artificial.

tures of complete agents based on hierarchies of servomechanisms can be seen in the work of Albus [1], and Powers [51]. In ethology, the study of animal behaviour, the information processing concept is wrapped up within various kinds of control-theoretic and decision-theoretic schemes, which are employed as abstract descriptions of observed behaviour (see [33], for example). In neuroscience, the workings of the brain or individual neurons are often presented in terms of the information processing they are supposed to perform or the computations they are said to implement (see [31] and [26], for example).

In this chapter I present some difficulties with the characterisation of autonomous agents as information processing systems arising from my work on real autonomous mobile robots. Furthermore, I argue that the modern fashion for *situatedness* also fails to address the real problem of autonomous agent, and I argue that the so-called *symbol grounding* problem is an inappropriate response to those who have pointed out that the world of an autonomous agent does not come ready categorized and neatly labeled. I end with some speculations on what might be a more satisfactory characterisation, which has much in common with some ideas of Humberto Maturana and Francisco Varela.

I start by noting that, despite its widespread use, the concept of information continues to have a somewhat precarious existence as a scientific concept.

4.2 What is Information Processing?

Almost everywhere you look you can see autonomous agents, biological or artificial, described in some way or other as information processing systems. Slugs and thermostats are commonly used (simple) examples found in many an illustration. That humans are complex versions of information processing systems is taken for granted. But, what is *information*? Despite its almost universal employment in characterizing autonomous systems, and intelligent systems in general, there is no clear, widespread agreement about what information is and what information processing means. As Robert Rosen said, [55]:

> Ever since Shannon began talking of information theory (by which he meant a probablistic analysis of the deleterious effects of propagating signals through channels [see [58]]), the concept has been relentlessly analyzed and reanalyzed. The time and effort expended on these analyses must surely rank as one of the most unprofitable investments in modern scientific history; not only has there been no profit, but also the currency itself has been debased to worthlessness.

This has not prevented its widespread and unquestioned use in describing the workings of biological and artificial autonomous systems in abstraction from their implementational details and particulars. In the chapter just quoted, Rosen went on to question whether the concept of information has any real scientific relevance. He asked if it might not be a temporary anthropomorphic expedient, which merely reflects the immaturity of our science (of intelligent systems), and that perhaps it should be replaced at the earliest possible opportunity by more rigorous concepts (such as force, energy, and potential, etc.), which are the province of more mature sciences, like physics, for example, in which information is never mentioned. Or is our current, albeit ill-defined concept of information a precursor to something fundamental to an understanding of autonomous systems? Is it a prescientific concept waiting to be properly established in a true science of intelligent autonomous systems? Is it the concept that properly distinguishes autonomous agents from other kinds of systems and phenomena, such as swinging pendulums, waterfalls, and sunflowers, for example?

Rosen pursued this latter viewpoint. In doing so he offered a useful definition of information, which I borrow for some of the subsequent discussion. He defined information as *anything which is or can be the answer to a question.* [3] Before that, however, I briefly review what standard information theory (i.e., the Shannon and Wiener theory) offers us.

4.2.1 Standard Information Theory

Information theory, at least according to Shannon, can be presented as being the study of one theorem, the so-called *fundamental theorem of information theory*, which states that it is possible to transmit information through a noisy channel at any rate less than the channel capacity with an arbitrarily small probability of error. The kind of system it is therefore concerned with is shown in Fig. 4.1 and is called a *communication systems.*

In this type of system, information is communicated between two components by sending of messages via a channel that may be subject to externally induced noise, thus resulting in some degradation in the quality of the messages being communicated. According to information theory, by selecting appropriate encodings (and decodings) the amount of degradation can be made arbitrarily small at the cost of reducing the rate at which

[3] Though opposed to the general stance of the position I present here Rosen presents a novel and persuasive argument for why our current informational terms bespeak something fundamental missing from physics as we now understand it. In doing so he makes the striking observation that interrogation, the asking of questions, what he suggests information provides the answers to, does not form a part of formal logic (and mathematics in general). He points out that the symbol "?" is not a logical symbol, as, for example, are "$\vee$", "$\wedge$", "$\exists$", and "$\forall$"; nor is it a mathematical symbol. Rosen further concludes that if information is connected with interrogation, then it is not surprising that it has not yet been formally characterised.

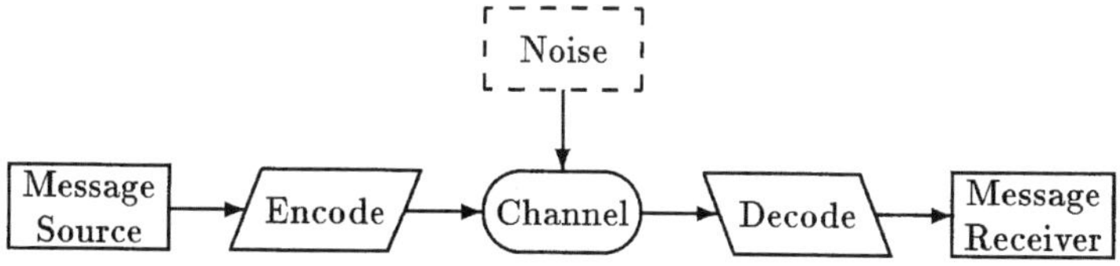

Fig. 4.1: The type of communication system studied by standard information theory.

messages, and thus information, can be successfully communicated. An important result of information theory is that to achieve arbitrarily high reliability of communication, it is not necessary to reduce the transmission rate to zero, but only to a number called the channel capacity.

The other important concept introduced by information theory is that of the information *content* of the message, sometimes also called the *selection content.* This is not a measure of the meaning of the message, but a measure of the uncertainty reducing effect on the state of the message receiver about the state of the sender. For example, suppose that a random variable X in the message source (see Fig. 4.1) can take the values $1, 2, 3, 4, 5$, with equal probability. We can then ask how much information is communicated by a message sent to the receiver that states that $1 \leq X \leq 2$. If the receiver tried to guess the value of X, before receiving this message, it would have the probability of $\frac{1}{5}$ of being correct. After it has received the message that X is either 1 or 2, it has a higher probability $(\frac{1}{2})$ of being correct. In other words, the receiver has less uncertainty about the value of X having received the message.

We can see from this simple example that for information transmission to be possible it must be the case that there is a finite number of states about which messages will be sent, and a finite (but possibly different number) of states in the receiver that are to be set in a correspondence relation to those of the sender, which it must also know about. If, in our example, the message receiver did not already know that the value of X could only take one of the values $1, 2, 3, 4, 5$, then the transmitted message would not have the uncertainty reducing effect described already. In other words, the message would not have any information content for the receiver. Thus, messages that cannot be decoded into uncertainty reducing states in the receiver about the state of the message source contain no information.

In general then, the information content measures the statistical unexpectedness of the states (or events) in question. The detailed nature of the state or states involved is not important, except as it may affect their prior probabilities. The more improbable a state, the larger the information content of any message specifying it. As long as the receiver knows this probability, that is. For a formal treatment of these properties see [5], for example.

4.2.2 Abstracted Information Processing

The kind of information communicating system described here is not the kind of system usually envisaged when we see systems described as information processing systems. In AI, and the cognitive sciences in general, it is presumed that what is of interest is the way in which the information received by a system is subsequently processed into decisions about further actions, for example. This is what Newell and Simon's Physical Symbol System Hypothesis was about, [47]. It states that a physical symbol system is necessary and sufficient for general intelligent action. Although, as Newell and Simon made clear, this is not meant to suggest that there is no need for appropriate sensorimotor connections of the agents to its world, to support the *designation* and *interpretation* of the symbols, it does significantly underplay what this must involve. In other words, the study of such information processing systems is abstracted away from the details of how information is communicated to it, or how it comes to possess the information it processes. A consequence of this abstraction, and one which has exercised various people in AI, is the question of where the meaning of the information being processed by an agent comes from—this, over and above the question of how the messages channelled to it by its sensors about its environment have uncertainty reducing content for it.

Dretske [18] has, for example, attempted to deal with this question by putting forward the idea that the semantic content of an informational state within an agent—its proper propositional interpretation—is fixed by the flow of information into the system that causes the system to be in that state. Dretske first presented a development of standard information theory, which he used to show how an agent's state can have a specific propositional content over and above representing a measure of the agent's uncertainty about some other system state that it has received information about. A different attempt to explain how the internal states processed by an agent can have meaning was presented by Cummins [14] and a clear analysis of the relationship between meaning and representation was presented in [15]. See also [39] for a relevant discussion.

This concern about the origin of meaning, its involvement with information, and how intelligent behaviour can be brought about by the computation-based schemes of symbol processing or artificial neural networks, has obscured any concern for where all this information comes from in the first place. If, as Rosen suggested, information is anything that is or can be an answer to a question, who or what is providing these answers? Or, in the words of J. Z. Young, "where is the sender of the message" [77, p. 82]? For Young this paradox was solved by pointing out that it is the senses of an organism that "provide the information for life, which depends upon the maintenance of *order*" (p.82). For him, "perception was the active search for the ordered features that we call 'information' ." What the senses search for is given by the needs of of the organism, which define the questions that need answering. The features selected by the senses thus become the information transmitted by the organism's environment, and received by its senses, in answer to these questions.

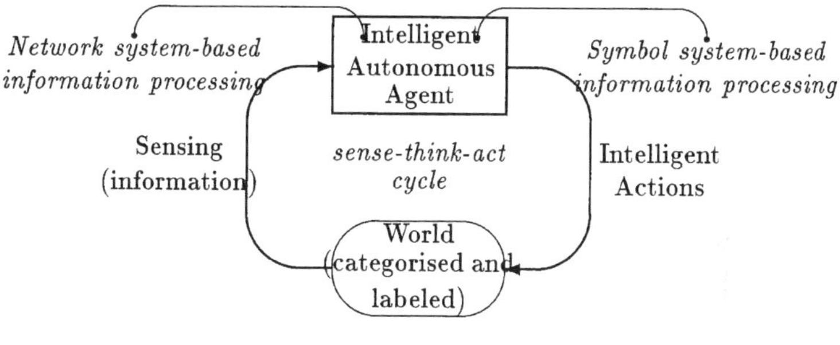

Fig. 4.2: An autonomous agent abstracted from its environment and characterised as a network or symbols system-based information processing system.

Although developed by a neuroscientist, I think this idea of an agent's environment sending messages that contain answers to questions raised by its ongoing needs captures the position that underlies all the various kinds of information processing characterisations of autonomous agents. It supports the idea implied by many of the abstract information processing approaches maintaining that an agent somehow reads the messages offered it by its environment. See [67] for a good representative example of this kind of abstracted information processing approach to autonomous agents. This presumed information-based relationship between an autonomous agent and its environment is depicted in Fig. 4.2. Agents get the information they process by going around reading the labels on the objects and states of the world. The problem of how an agent's sensors are to read all these labels is typically assumed to be a problem for the engineers, and not one that impinges on the problem of how the information so received is to be processed to produce intelligent autonomous behaviour. For an analysis of this classical approach in intelligent robotics, and an identification of some of the problems that arise, see [35] and [49].

4.2.3 Information Processing and Computation

With the development of AI as a scientific discipline has come the strong association of information processing with computation, Turing computation: To compute is to process information. This reflects the essentially logical or formal nature of information processing as it is generally understood. This equating of information processing with digital computation is more a historical development than it is a recognition of a fundamental relationship. This can be seen from the fact that we usually call analogue systems signal processing systems, not information processing systems. But with the trend to replace older analogue technologies with more modern digital technologies we do not start calling such systems information processing systems—compact disc players are not called information processing systems—although the older, record playing systems remain as signal processing systems. The question that all this general usage hides is when is a digital (computational) system an information processing system, rather than a digital signal processing system. The irony of all this is that record playing and compact disc playing systems can much more easily be identified with the communication systems, which are the subject of information theory and depicted in Fig. 4.1, than can the kinds of systems typically built and investigated in AI and related disciplines.

What we can identify from the associating of computation and information processing is the essentially syntactic nature of information and its processing. It is a syntactic matter dependent on the form and organisation of logical operations, not on the physical behaviour of the implementational devices used, as analogue signal processing is. Where the "meaning" of all this information processing comes from is, as we have said, an extra question. We come back to this aspect later.

4.3 Autonomous Agents in Practice

I am interested in understanding the behaviour of autonomous systems: the nature of the processes and their interactions that produce it, and the kinds of mechanisms that can be used to realise such *interaction processes*, and thus engender the autonomous behaviour we observe. I take autonomous behaviour to be a necessary (but possibly not a sufficient) condition for intelligent behaviour. An understanding of autonomous behaviour is therefore a necessary prerequisite to an understanding of intelligent behaviour.

I believe that the problem of autonomous behaviour is essentially a dynamic one, not a structural one, that it is the temporal constraints on the interaction processes constituting an agent that fundamentally govern the behaviour we observe. Furthermore, I believe that it is the material constraints that directly affect the underlying dynamics and that these material aspects cannot easily be abstracted away using information processing concepts. It therefore follows that I believe the proper way to investigate autonomous behaviour is in terms of complete real agent–environment systems, natural or artificial. In my case, I am investigating autonomous behaviour by attempting to build artificial autonomous agents, robots, thus making this work properly a part of AI. See [65] for some of the philosoph-

Fig. 4.3: An autonomous Lego vehicle. This mobile robot uses a Rockwell 6502 8-bit microprocessor with 32K of memory and is run at a 1MHz clock rate. It has: two whisker sensors, each using two microswitches; a front bumper sensor, also using two microswitches; left and right side bumper sensors, each using a single microswitch; three active infrared sensors, front-right, front-centre, and front-left; and a set of four light dependent resistor sensors mounted on the front (not used in the experiments described in the text). It has independent motor control of the two drive motors giving forward and reverse at full and half speeds, and it is programmed using a specially designed language that makes use of a time-slicing, real-time kernel running on the microprocessor to give psuedo-concurrent execution of control programs. See [17] for more details.

ical arguments for this position.

In this section I present a series of three sketches based on my experience of trying to build real autonomous systems: simple mobile robots. In each sketch I identify some problems with characterising these robots as information processing systems. The first sketch concerns getting a mobile robot to run around a real environment without getting stuck. The second sketch involves the implementation of a simple map-building and map-using competence. For the third sketch I return to the robot used in the first one to consider the relationship between its morphology and its control program in producing effective "don't get stuck" behaviour, and the role of computation in specifying control.

4.3.1 Sketch 1: Really Not Getting Stuck

To build the robot for this experiment I used a Lego vehicle kit [17]. This provides plenty of structural Lego Technic^{TM} components to build a light stiff chasis containing two drive wheels at the back plus a third free running wheel at the front (whose direction is fixed, but which can slide sideways over the floor to allow turn and rotation actions); a programmable Brain brick to run the control program; a motor control brick giving full and half speeds in each direction for each drive wheel; rechargeable batteries giving about 30 minutes of running time; microswitches with which to build contact sensors (bumpers and whiskers), and three active infrared (IR) sensor devices, which produce a binary output and have a hand-adjustable threshold setting, which can be set to register IR reflections at a distance of up to 300 millimeters. By using a tricycle configuration with the two powered wheels at the back and carefully distributing the weight of the other components, we can build a compact vehicle, which can turn on the spot, weighs about 1.5 kilograms, and moves quite fast, up to about 1.5 meters a second (see Fig. 4.3).

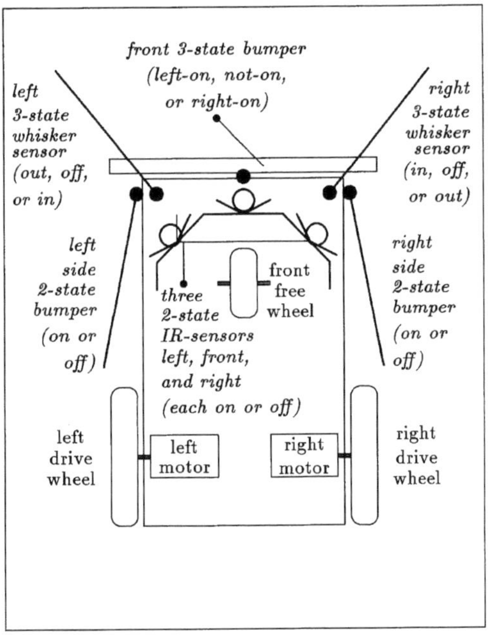

Fig. 4.4: Sensor-motor configuration of Lego vehicle.

The task is apparently straightforward; at least it is quite simply specified: to get this Lego vehicle to move anywhere around the floor of my office and the laboratory without becoming trapped (this includes continuously bouncing around within the legs of a chair without getting away, for example) or damaged (losing bits of Lego, etc.) [4]. My office and the laboratory floor are occupied by the usual kinds of things: desks, tables, chairs, including some typists chairs—the ones with 5 radial spokes with caster wheels on the ends—filing cabinets, waste bins (cylindrical and rectangular), boxes (cardboard A4 printer paper boxes, some empty, some with heavy things in them), papers, books, and power cables, to name the majority of the kinds of items [5].

This kind of competence in a mobile robot might seem simple, but it is a necessary prerequisite for any kind of mobile agent that is to do anything else. The measure of performance used during this experiment was the ratio of the total run time (which is usually set to be 1 or 5 minutes for a particular run) to the amount of time spent moving forward (i.e., the amount of time both motors are set in their full forward state). This ratio is never likely to be one—unless the environment is a very big open space or long wide corridor. But the nearer to one it is, the more able the vehicle is at getting away and at keeping away from obstacles in its environment; it will have spent less time reversing and turning away from obstacles.

The Lego vehicle used has three different kinds of sensors: bumper sensors, whisker sensors, and IR sensors. It has one (three-state) front

[4]This task and environment is not chosen arbitrarily. Some years ago I read Russell Anderson's book about his Ping-Pong playing robot, [2], and became interested in the question of whether it really needs as much computing power has his system uses (about seven Sun-3s worth) to make a robot play Ping-Pong? So far I have not made much progress in investigating this question, but early on I recognised that any experimenting with a Ping-Pong playing robot would result in lots of Ping-Pong balls being lost on the floor. I therefore decided that what was needed was a small mobile robot which can go around a laboratory floor finding and collecting Ping-Pong balls. To be a successful Ping-Pong ball collector requires a robot that can first get around such an environment without becoming trapped and without suffering any debilitating damage. This task and environment has subsequently become my main experimental domain for investigating the processes and mechanims necessary for just getting about, a prerequisite ability for any kind of autonomous mobile robot, and a problem that is proving to be much more difficult than I at first imagined.

[5]During this experiment my office has had two instantiations, first in the Department of Artificial intelligence, Edinburgh, and now at the AI Lab at the VUB, Brussels. The description offered in the main text applies to both versions, though there are some detailed differences between Scottish and Belgium office furniture that have had to be adjusted for in the design of the Lego vehicle. It nonetheless constitutes a complex environment for the Lego vehicle; much more complex than the environments to which most other autonomous robots are subjected to, either in simulation or in reality. This is because the geometry and variability of this environment at floor level, the level at which the Lego vehicle operates, is typically a lot more complex than it is at about desk top level, the level at which most mobile robots interact with their environments, see [8], [4], [3], [24], [36], for example, with [12] being a good counter example of two small robots (Tom and Jerry) designed to run around the floor.

bumper, two (two-state) side bumpers, two (three-state) whisker sensors one on each front corner, and three (two-state) IR sensors, left-front facing, front facing, and right-front facing, see Fig. 4.4. All this gives a sensor input space of 864 different possible configurations. The two motors (one per drive wheel) each have full and half speeds in each direction, plus stop, giving a motor space of 25 possible configurations.

The problem, according to the information processing story, is to map the sensor space into the motor space in such a way that all the relevant situations the vehicle can get into in its world are distinguished and related to appropriate motor states or sequences of motor states. In other words, the problem is to arrange for the sensor states to be properly interpreted as messages about (as answers to questions about) the world without the agent. To simplify the problem I introduced some decomposition into the sensor space and specified some motor actions: continuous full forward, right turn, left turn, right veer, left veer [6], and reverse. Except for continuous forward, each of these motor actions is done by putting the motors into appropriate states for fixed amounts of time.

The control program for the vehicle treats each kind of sensor set separately, and it uses turn and reverse actions for bumper and whiskers modalities, and turn, veer, and reverse actions for the IR modality. This gives three sensor-to-motor action mappings to get right: one of 12 sensor states to 3 actions (forward, reverse+right-turn, and reverse+left-turn) for the bumper sensors; one of 9 sensor states to 3 actions (forward, reverse+right-turn, and reverse+left-turn) for the whisker sensors; and one of 8 sensor states to 7 actions (forward, right-turn, left-turn, right-veer, left-veer, reverse+right-turn, and reverse+left-turn) for the IR sensors to motor actions, see Fig. 4.5. A semaphor mechanism operates between these three different sensor-to-motor mappings in the control program to prevent more than one of them setting the motor states at any one time.

The program that implements all this makes the vehicle behave quite well (having previously configured, by trial and error, the vehicle's morphology—its shape and sensor arrangement—to be well matched to its environment. It fails badly if this is not done properly), but it doesn't work well enough. The vehicle does get trapped sometimes, and it does knock bits of Lego off occasionally. By messing around with both the details of the mappings and the fixed amounts of time used by the turn, veer, and reverse actions, the vehicle's performance can be improved a bit, but mostly this sort of thing results in it doing better in some situations and worse in others with no overall improvement.

So, how is the performace to be improved? Or, is it the case that the vehicle works as well as it can? If this latter case were true it would

---

[6] A *veer* action is a less severe turn action. Turns are achieved by setting the motors in opposite directions at full speed. Veer actions are achieved by stopping one motor while leaving the other in the full forward state.

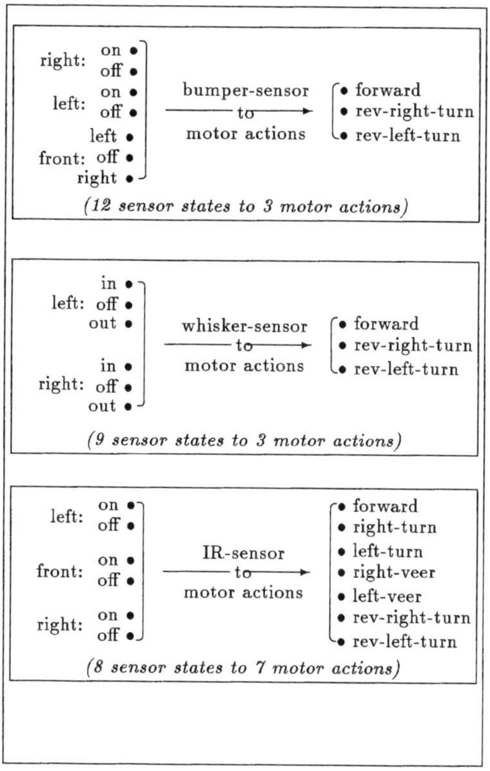

Fig. 4.5: Decomposed sensor-motor space mapping used to simplify programming.

mean that the vehicle doesn't have the sensors necessary to detect certain important situations it can get into or the motor actions required to get it out of them, or both. This seems unlikely. Adding other kinds of sensors, like light sensitive devices, for example, or adding new motor actions may well help, but it is difficult to believe that the present vehicle cannot be made to do better without such extensions [7]. So, back to the first question,

[7] In discussions with other people about this problem it has been suggested that it is the resolution of the sensors that is not good enough. The argument is that binary sensors cannot be expected to distinguish between all the different situations that require different motor actions, or different combinations of motor actions. The problem with this kind of argument, what I call the technological fix argument, is that as we demand sensors with more and more resolution in the face of continuing inadequate performance, so increasingly we face a new problem, that of the accuracy of the sensors. If we need sensors of higher resolution which can be used to pick out more different situations in order to select the appropriate actions, then these sensors must reliably do this picking

how to make it perform better with the sensors and motor actions it has.

One way might be to remove the sensor modality division I have introduced. Perhaps the decomposition I used is not able to deal with the variety of sensor-to-action mappings required. I think this might be a way, at least in principle, to improve things, but in practice it's hard. It could take a very long time to discover all the details of the mapping from the full sensor space to the full motor space. (This is, however, what I think some insect nervous systems do, but they have evolutionary time to get it sorted out.) Another thing to do along the same lines is to increase the number of actions available, but again, discovering all that might be required is not easy. The question is, is it more structural complexity that is required in the control program to pick out the required information from the world and process it into appropriate motor actions?

An alternative approach I have been attempting is to modify each of the sensor-to-motor action mappings dynamically in some way. At first, I thought that perhaps quite simple dynamic changes might be enough—like increasing the turn and reverse times after a certain amount of bumper, whisker, or IR signals have been received within a certain period of time. In fact this kind of thing does help a bit, but only a bit. What I went on to do is to implement a scheme whereby the time spent turning and reversing for each sensor modality is made proportional to the amount of sensor signals of that type received over some particular length of time. I do this by having a sensor signal integrator with a constant decay on it for each of the sensor input lines.

According to the performance criteria described previously, this control scheme gives the best results for the "don't get stuck" behaviour. It represents an interestingly different type of solution to my previous attempts. In the new system, although the topology of the mapping from the sensor spaces to motor actions is fixed, the geometry isn't. It varies all the time as the sensor signal accumulator values go up and down. Now, it is possible to show (with some quite careful work) that the actual sensor-to-motor action configuration operating in the vehicle is not very often the same, and in particular, it is not typically the same when the vehicle is in the same situations—this is because recent history now counts. In other words, this new scheme does not implement a fixed sensor to motor mapping that is designed to detect all the significantly different situations and to map them onto appropriate motor actions. It is therefore hard to explain what is going on in this version of the control program, to produce the observed behaviour, in terms of information processing. This is because it is now the

out. In other words, it's not just a matter of resolution, it's also a matter of accuracy and calibration, and that, as anybody who has built and used measuring devices knows, is typically a hard problem. The same argument applies to motor actions too, of course. See [6], for example, in which he talks about sensors delivering very uncertain values even in a stable world, and motor commands having very uncertain effects. My own experience with Lego vehicles fully confirms these observations.

dynamics of the control program that matters, not its logical structure.

It's not hard to see how a lot more dynamic variation can be introduced into this kind of scheme: topological as well as geometric, dynamic combinations of atomic motor actions, and dynamically changing signal processing—at the moment the IR lines are read five times and then if they are on three or more times in this five, the sensors are set to true, otherwise to false. We could have numbers of these kinds of processes running in parallel, which are fed from the same sensor device but each having different sample sizes and thresholds, and various kinds of novelty filter on them (see [27, p. 109] for a discussion of novelty filters, for example), and we could have all these dynamically changing too.

The complexity of such a system could easily be very high—even in a Lego vehicle, so high in fact that it would be impractical to try to enumerate all the possible configurations. But what if, for example, such a system resulted in the successful behaviour desired, as I now think it would. Then we may not have a situation in which a finite and fixed set of internal states (do or come to) detect all the distinct (relevant) states of the environment and then map them onto appropriate motor actions. Each kind of situation will not in general correspond to a particular internal agent state, yet the agent behaves successfully in its environment. If this is the case, then we can't associate particular states in the agent to particular states in the environment: We cannot say that the control program is designed to pick out a particular control state that corresponds to the state of the world and so identifies the actions to be taken. If we can't do this, then internal agent states can't be said to correspond to or to represent particular states of the environment. This means that the information processing stories we normally tell about how agents act appropriately in their environments do not work either: We can't assign a particular interpretation to the signals coming off the back of sensor devices because the way they are interpreted by the agent control processes into motor actions, or anything else, is not fixed, so they can't be said to be "carrying" information. It's as if the same messages are being read in a different way each time they arrive, but this does not prevent the vehicle from working well. It is hard to see that these messages channelled by the sensors are used to reduce the uncertainty of the vehicle about the state of its environment if it doesn't have particular states representing it as particular states of its environment.

What we have is not structural complexity in the control program, required to establish the necessary logic of information processing, but dynamic complexity, which produces the necessary dynamics in the sensorimotor interactions of the vehicle with its environment.

4.3.2 Sketch 2: Map-Building and Self-Organisation

In this series of experiments we have been investigating the use of self-organizing networks based on the techniques of Willshaw and von der Mals-

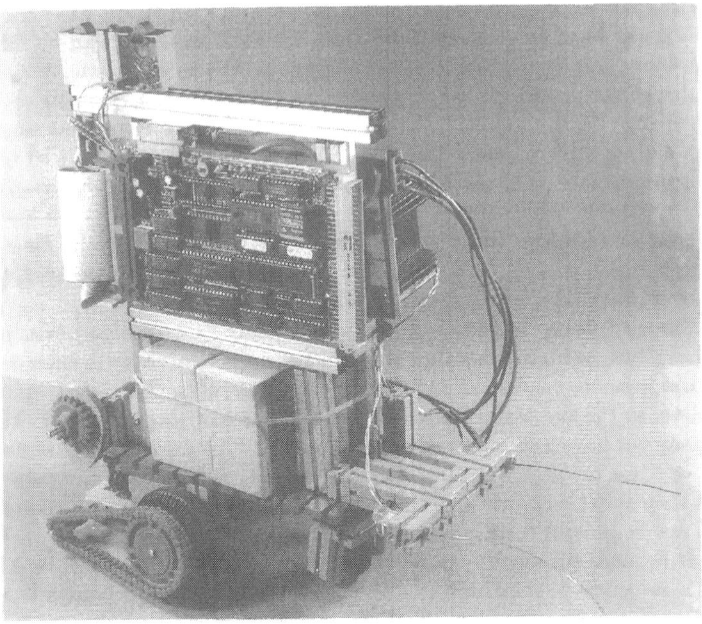

Fig. 4.6: The Really Useful Robot "Alder." This robot is built on a Fischertechnik^{TM} chassis and uses an ARC52 programmable controller—an 8-bit microprocessor with 16K of memory and an onboard BASIC interpreter. The interface board provides independent motor control (forward and reverse) for two motors and up to eight binary input lines. As shown, two whisker sensors are fitted, front-right, and front-left.

burgh [74] and Kohonen [27] to support the learning of simple navigation competencies.

For these experiments the robot was built to follow walls and placed in an enclosure built of straight walls and right-angle corners. Several different schemes for supporting map building have been investigated. First we used a feature detector (which used signals from the whisker sensors) to enable the robot to detect the convex and concave corners in its environment as it moved around the walls of the enclosure. As each corner was detected, its type (concave or convex) and the distance from the previous corner (estimated using a revolution counter mounted on one of the drive wheels) and its type, was used to construct an input vector for a one-dimensional self-organizing network. After several times round the enclosure the robot was able to use this network to recognize when it had returned to a nominated location (see Fig. 4.7). By extending the input vector to include the type of the previous two and three corners we were able to successively improve the accuracy of the location recognition until it was perfect (in the experimental enclosure used) [41].

In an attempt to move away from this rather inflexible feature detector-based scheme, we implemented a second scheme that used motor commands as the basis for the input vectors to the self-organizing network. In this version an input vector was constructed each time the motor state changed as a result of a new motor command produced as the robot wall followed its way around the enclosure. This meant that the number of input vectors generated increased significantly over the previous scheme. It also meant that it was harder to achieve reliable location recognition. In its most successful form this scheme used seven, two-dimensional, self-organizing networks, all working in parallel. Essentially this scheme performed a kind of frequency component analysis on the psuedo-periodic input vector sequence generated as the robot wall follows its way around its enclosure [43].

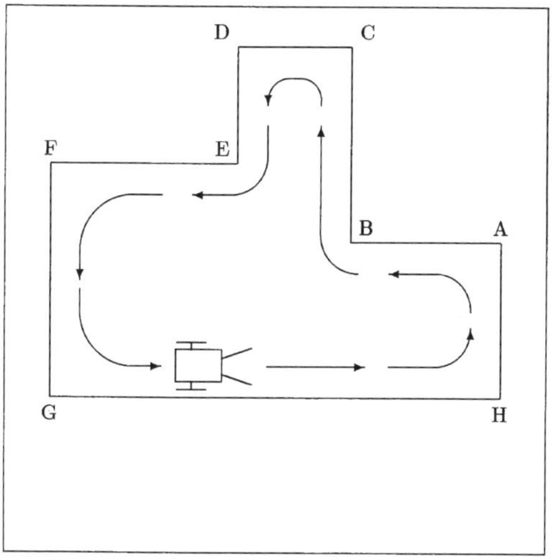

Fig. 4.7: A typical enclosure used for the map-building experiments using self-organising networks.

Although this scheme did remove the need for an explicitly programmed feature detector, we were dissatisfied with its large computational cost relative to the first scheme. We also disliked the need to have to set seven different threshold values (magic numbers) by hand in order to get the scheme to work well. This led us to devise a third map-building scheme, which again used no hardwired feature detectors but which was computationally much cheaper than the second scheme. In this third scheme, thc robot calculated a moving average based on the duration of the turn actions it executes to make contact with the wall as part of its wall following behaviour. Then, if a turn action occurs that is significantly different from this average, before contact with the wall is detected (significant turn action) an input vector is generated based on the type of turn (left or right) and the time since the last significant turn action [42]. This scheme proved to be as reliable as our first scheme and only a little more expensive in terms of computation. The use of the moving average calculation also proved to be an effective way of implementing the required novelty filter because it was robust with respect to the change in the average time taken by the robot to make turns of the same magnitude as the batteries drained.

There are three points to note about these map-building experiments with respect to information processing.

4.3.2.1 Not a Map of the World

First, the maps constructed by this robot, and used by it to recognise particular locations, are not maps in the conventional sense. In other words, they do not come to represent the geometry of the perimeter of the robot's enclosure. Rather, they come to represent what it is like for the robot to arrive at particular locations. If, after having constructed a map the robot were to be made to travel around the enclosure in the opposite direction, its map would be of no use to it in recognising the same nominated locations. This is because the experience of arriving at the same places would be different.

The self-organised structures in these experiments do not come to represent some objective aspect of the robot's environment, as classical information processing stories about what is going on during map-building would suggest. What is represented is certain properties that arise from the specific interaction between the robot and its enclosure as it wall-follows its way around the perimeter. If this interaction is changed, by making the robot move the opposite way around the enclosure, the structure captured in the self-organising network will not necessarily correspond to any structure in the new interaction.

4.3.2.2 Motor Signals Not Sensor Signals

The second point is that, for the last two map-building schemes developed, it is motor action signals that are used in forming the input vectors, not signals from sensors. What is going on is thus not to be understood as the robot's perception of its environment being used to build a model (a map) of its world, at least not straightforwardly so. We might talk about it using information about its motor actions instead, but this would not seem to offer much of an explanation for how it gets to know anything about its environment by this means. Another way of looking at it might be to say that the whole robot, or at least that part of it that controls the wall-following behaviour, is acting as a kind of sensor, with the motor action signals being its output. This might be a better description, but to go on to say that it is by this means that the robot picks up the required information from its world for it to form a map seems to be verging on the fanciful. It's certainly unnecessarily convoluted as an explanation of how the robot does what it does.

4.3.2.3 Redundancy Not Information

The third point concerns a property of self-organising networks and what is called redundancy in information theory. Let M_i be the maximum rate at which usable information can be supplied to our self-organising network, measured in bits/sec, and let A_i bits/sec be the rate at which it actually receives information (in the uncertainty reducing information theoretic sense described in section 2) as the robot makes its way around its enclosure. Then the *redundancy* is given by $M_i - A_i$ bits/sec. Let R_i bits/sec be the redundancy in the signals used by the robot to drive the self-organisation of its network. Now, redundancy here becomes a strange term because if R_i were zero there would be no self-organisation in the network, and hence no map building. This so-called redundancy is in fact a measure of the statistical structure in the signal, and it is this structure (if any) that drives the self-organisation in these networks. See [7] for a discussion of this kind of redundancy in unsupervised learning and its relationship to minimum entry encoding.

We can see the paradox here if we try to describe what is going on here in terms of the type of communication system presented in section 2 (see Fig. 4.1). The message source is the environment that produces the signals in the robot sensors that are used to construct the input vectors to the self-organising network. The encoding is then the construction of the input vectors and the communication channel for the application of the stream of input vectors to the network. The decoding is then the self-organising algorithm that takes input vectors and adjusts the weight vectors at the nodes of the network, so engendering its reorganisation. Now, if the stream of input vectors (messages) is understood to contain information about the structure of world the network uses to reduce its uncertainty about this structure—to come to model this structure—then we would have to call the redundancy required in the stream of input vectors information, which, as we have seen, it is not, at least not in the information theoretic sense.

These self-organising networks, at least as we have used them in this map-building work, are to be understood as implementing statistical structure extracting processes. The fact that we have implemented them as discrete systems (using computational techniques) does not make them information processing systems (though for some it seems that this is all it takes to qualify as one). We could implement such systems, albeit with considerably more difficulty, as continuous processes, both in time and value, as analogue systems. As such they would still best (most economically) be understood as statistical structure extraction processes, and probably be nearer the self-organising processes that are thought to occur in the brain (see [74, 75, 38] , for example). They are not well understood as processes that extract information from their environment and use this to build some kind of model of (or aspects of) that environment. As I noted in the first point, the structure in the stream of input vectors submitted to our networks does not represent or correspond to features of the robot's environment, but to properties of the particular form of the interaction between the robot and its environment. Statistical structure in these interactions is being modeled by our self-organising networks by a process which, as we have seen, can't easily be described coherently in information processing terms unless we are prepared to be very flexible and vague about what we mean by information.

4.3.3 Sketch 3: Computation and Real Control

If you build real robots, like the ones described earlier, for example, you quickly discover that there are things that critically affect the behaviour of the robot that cannot be brought under control just by writing the right code in the control program. This may seem an obvious point to make, but, although it might be easily admitted, it is often not appreciated by those who either have not built a robot or who only work with so-called simulation systems.

I have already pointed out that the shape and physical setup of the sensors makes a big difference to the performance of a Lego vehicle, as it does for any robot or animal [8]. If a particular robot is not well fitted morphologically to its tasks and environment, no amount of clever programming will ever overcome its deficiencies. In other words, reliable and robust task-achieving autonomous behaviour—intelligent behaviour—is not simply a matter of what goes on inside the robot's computer; it's not just a matter of the right control. An information processing story can say little or nothing about these other types of requirements. It can only attempt to identify the kinds of control and computations that are required.

There is, however, another aspect to getting real robots to work well that makes writing their control programs unusually difficult—unusual in the sense that it is not something that arises when writing conventional programs, or control programs for simulated robots, unless the simulator

[8] One of the reasons I developed the Lego vehicle technology was so that I could easily build autonomous mobile robots whose shape and sensor configurations I could change easily. It is often the case that small adjustments to the angle of IR-sensors or modifications to the shape of a bumper sensor can produce significant improvements in the performance of a vehicle operating in a particular environment. The facility for being able to 'hack' the code of the control program and 'hack' the shape of the robot at the same time is what also makes Lego vehicles a good educational device.

models real-time behaviour right down to code execution, which they seldom do. It is that the dynamics of the execution counts, not just which computations are executed. In other words, two programs that specify the same computations but in a different way—by a difference in the order of some code segments, for example—can produce quite different behaviour in the same robot.

For example, Fig. 4.8a presents the code for an early version of a function (called an `Action` in the Lego vehicle programming language) from the program that is used to control the Lego vehicle described in section 3.1. This function is concerned with the IR sensors: For each of the three IR sensors (left, front, and right) it first reads the IR-sensor device five times and counts how many times it is on; if it is on three or more times in the sample of five, it sets a signal variable (`lIRsig`, in the case of the left IR sensor) to true, and also increments the signal accumulator value (`irlSum`, for the left sensor) by a preset value (`delta`); if the sensor was on less than three times in the sample, the accumulator value is decreased by a preset value (`sink`); the code then checks for the accumulator value being less than zero, and sets it to zero if it is, and for it being above a preset maximum (`max`), in which case it is again reset to zero [9].

```
Action IRsensors Produces nothing
  Action Inner Space
    Fact delta : integer is  15; {signal accumulation increment}
    Fact sink  : integer is   1; {signal accumulation decrement}
    Fact max   : integer is 300; {max value of accumulation}
    Fact count : integer is   5; {number of readings in sensor sampling}
    Fact s1    : integer is   3; {threshold in sample below which sensor
                                   is off, must be less than counter!}

  i  Becomes 0
  sl Becomes 0
  Keep Doing i Becomes i+1
    If [Sensor(lIR) is on] Do sl Becomes sl+1 End If
  Until i=count
  If sl >= s1
    Do lIRsig Becomes true
       irlSum Becomes irlSum+delta
    Otherwise Do
      irlSum Becomes irlSum-sink
      If irlSum < 0 Do irlSum Becomes 0 End If
```

[9] In an earlier version of this function, the accumulator value saturated at the maximum value. In other words, when it was incremented above `max` it was reset to `max`, and remained there until it was decremented as a result of the IR sensor no longer being on enough. This seemed at first to be the appropriate dynamics, but after experimenting with various values for the incrementing, decrementing, and maximum values it was found that better vehicle performance was achieved by reseting the accumulator to zero on reaching its the maximum value. This latter scheme can be understood as implementing a simple kind of habituation, albeit for a short period of time. Not surprisingly, habituation is an important characteristic at this level of control and more sophisticated mechanisms are currently being developed for the Lego vehicle.

```
    If irlSum > max Do irlSum Becomes 0 End If
End If
i  Becomes 0
sf Becomes 0
Keep Doing i Becomes i+1
  If [Sensor(fIR) is on] Do sf Becomes sf+1 End If
Until i=count
If sf >= s1
  Do fIRsig Becomes true
     irfSum Becomes irfSum+delta
  Otherwise Do
    irfSum Becomes irfSum-sink
    If irfSum < 0 Do irfSum Becomes 0 End If
    If irfSum > max Do irfSum Becomes 0 End If
End If
i  Becomes 0
sr Becomes 0
Keep Doing i Becomes i+1
  If [Sensor(rIR) is on] Do sr Becomes sr+1 End If
Until i=count
If sr >= s1
  Do rIRsig Becomes true
     irrSum Becomes irrSum+delta
  Otherwise Do
    irrSum Becomes irrSum-sink
    If irrSum < 0 Do irrSum Becomes 0 End If
    If irrSum > max Do irrSum Becomes 0 End If
End If
End Action {IRsensors}
```

Fig. 4.8a: Version (a) of program code for reading IR sensor input and setting IR signal values.

Fig. 4.8b presents the code for a later version of this function. As can be seen, in this version all the sensor reading is collected together in one loop, instead of being distributed across three separate loops. This change makes very little difference to the execution time for this function, and it makes *no* difference to the logic of the computations carried out; it defines the same computation as the first version. It does, however, make a significant difference to the behaviour of the vehicle. Mostly it produces an improvement in its performance, but not always. There are certain situations in which it appears to produce less good behaviour. I say *appears* because it is very hard to quantify this kind of variation in the vehicle's performace.

```
Action IRsensors Produces nothing
  Action Inner Space
    Fact delta : integer is  15; {signal accumulation increment}
    Fact sink  : integer is   1; {signal accumulation decrement}
    Fact max   : integer is 300; {max value of accumulation}
```

```
    Fact count : integer is   5; {number of readings in sensor sampling}
    Fact s1    : integer is   3; {threshold in sample below which sensor
                                   is off, must be less than counter!}

  i  Becomes 0
  sl Becomes 0
  sf Becomes 0
  sr Becomes 0
  Keep Doing i Becomes i+1
    If [Sensor(lIR) is on] Do sl Becomes sl+1 End If
    If [Sensor(fIR) is on] Do sf Becomes sf+1 End If
    If [Sensor(rIR) is on] Do sr Becomes sr+1 End If
  Until i=count
  If sl >= s1
    Do lIRsig Becomes true
       irlSum Becomes irlSum+delta
    Otherwise Do
      irlSum Becomes irlSum-sink
      If irlSum < 0 Do irlSum Becomes 0 End If
      If irlSum > max Do irlSum Becomes 0 End If
  End If
  If sf >= s1
    Do fIRsig Becomes true
       irfSum Becomes irfSum+delta
    Otherwise Do
      irfSum Becomes irfSum-sink
      If irfSum < 0 Do irfSum Becomes 0 End If
      If irfSum > max Do irfSum Becomes 0 End If
  End If
  If sr >= s1
    Do rIRsig Becomes true
       irrSum Becomes irrSum+delta
    Otherwise Do
      irrSum Becomes irrSum-sink
      If irrSum < 0 Do irrSum Becomes 0 End If
      If irrSum > max Do irrSum Becomes 0 End If
  End If
End Action {IRsensors}
```

Fig. 4.8b: Version (b) of program code for reading IR sensor input and setting IR signal values.

The effect of modifying the code in this way can be explained in terms of the effect it has on the way the IR sensor devices are read by the executed control program, and on the way the vehicle's behaviour depends on this sensor reading in particular ways in particular situations. What makes this kind of thing quite difficult to deal with is that this dependence is not constant across different kinds of situations—moving down a corridor and moving about amongst chair and table legs, for example. The other thing to note is that these effects are much less pronounced when the robot moves relatively slowly (less than about 300 millimeters per second) in an otherwise static environment. If the robot is moving faster than this and/or there are other things in its environment that move relative to it, such as other robots (Lego vehicles) and people, then the nonuniformity of sensing produced as a result of the dependencies described here become significant. So much so that for my Lego vehicle it is not possible to describe the IR sensors as obstacle detectors because not only do they detect certain things much more easily than others (large white rough surfaces, like walls, best, and small shiny black surfaces, like chair legs, worst), their detection of the same obstacle depends on things like the speed and direction of approach of the vehicle.

Of course, some of what I have described here is caused by the details of the way everything is implemented, right down to the real-time execution of the program code. It is also true that improvements in performace could be obtained by using better designs of sensor devices. However, not all of what I describe could be made to go away by changing the details of the technology used and the details of its implementation. There are important aspects of the dynamics of the interaction between the Lego vehicle and its environment that count, and that cannot be made to go away by modifying its implementation. Information processing stories about how obstacles are to be avoided say nothing about these kinds of dynamics, and more importantly, computation and current programming languages offer the wrong abstractions for dealing with them.

4.4 Discussion

The foregoing remarks and observations drawn from my experience of building and experimenting with real robots is not meant to offer decisive proof against the appropriateness of information processing concepts in understanding autonomous system; they can't do that. They are, however, intended to illustrate that it is not such a straightforward business as we commonly suppose. In this section I will first make some more general comments arising from the difficulties identified and then make some specific comments on the nature of computers as machines and symbolic computations in the context of autonomous systems.

4.4.1 Some General Comments

There are three basic points I have tried to identify in the three sketches I presented in the previous section. These are:

- That the complexity required in successful controllers for robots that are to move around without becoming trapped lies in their dynamics, not in the complexity of their logical structure.

- That it is hard to offer coherent information processing descriptions of what is going on in the self-organising-based map-building and map-using systems we have built if you try to talk about the complete agent plus environment systems. It is, however, possible to talk just about the self-organisation process in information processing terms as long as it is abstracted from the agent, or larger system, it is embedded in—which is what much connectionist and neuroscience research does.

- That the morphology, sensor configuration, and dynamics of execution counts in real robot behaviour, and that information processing kinds of analyses or specifications of such systems fail to identify and to specify constraints and bounds on these aspects.

These problems are not, I believe, minor irritations on the edges of what is otherwise a basically sound approach to understanding autonomous systems; they are inevitable consequences of its underlying concepts and assumptions.

The concept of information and the closely associated concept of computation (by which I mean Turing Machine computation, not analogue computation), are both temporally neutral concepts. They do not embody any notion of time. We can, of course, talk about the rate of information processing and the rate of computation, and these can be critical to achieving the required performance in some particular system, but whatever the rate is, it is still the same information processing being done and the same computation being carried out. Complete specifications of information processing processes and computations do not identify any kind of temporal constraints. If there are any, these constraints have to come from other aspects of the system doing the information processing or carrying out the computations. They are therefore extra to the information processing and computational stories.

Descriptions of real autonomous systems, and real-time systems in general, and specifications of the computations they need to carry out cannot, therefore, constitute complete descriptions, or explanations, of such systems. The dynamics have to be added in somehow. For some types of system, such as certain kinds of operating systems and control systems, it is possible to abstract away from the dynamic aspects to a level at which information processing descriptions are useful; from a design point of view. In other words, it is possible to design such systems in a top-down fashion by first considering them as information processing systems and then as dynamic or real-time systems. Often this kind of situation only occurs once we understand well the nature of systems involved and the details of their interactions with their environments.

The question is can we make this kind of separation when it comes to understanding and designing autonomous agents? I believe not, but this is precisely what Newell's Knowledge Level theory of intelligent systems depends on (see next section). I believe that the dynamics of the interactions between an autonomous agent and its environment so completely pervade the functioning of such systems that there is no level of abstraction at which we can successfully escape its consequences. It is only the long established presumption of traditional AI and cognitive science approaches which presupposes that autonomous agents can be properly characterised as information processing systems, that leads us to construct such abstractions. It might work as a good first approximation, but I don't believe it can form the basis for a more complete understanding and explanation of autonomous systems.

4.4.2 Computers, Knowledge Systems, and the Dynamics of Interaction

In this section I want to make some specific remarks about computers and Newell's Knowledge Level [38, 45] which depends in a crucial way on their structure and operation.

According to Newell, the Knowledge Level is the level of abstraction at which we can both identify intelligent agents and explain their behaviour. At the Knowledge Level an agent is described as having *goals, actions,* and *knowledge* and as operating according to the *principle of rationality*: Knowledge is used to select actions that will contribute to achieving the goals. A particular autonomous system, natural or artificial, is then intelligent in its behaviour to the extent that it approximates its knowledge level description: If we behave in a way that does not make use of some knowledge we have, then our behaviour can be described as unintelligent.

This Knowledge Level is presented by Newell as being above a series of levels that can be identified in the description (and specification) of a computer, as in Fig. 4.9.

If Newell was right about his Knowledge Level being the proper level of abstraction for identifying and explaining intelligent behaviour in intelligent autonomous agents, then we should be able to use this level, and the series of levels below it, to design and build artificial autonomous systems. There are two related reasons for being suspicious of this possibility. First, the Symbol Level description of the symbol processing computations—the information processing—required to engender (at least to a sufficient approximation) the Knowledge Level specification for some particular agent does not identify the necessary dynamics of computation, nor the morphological requirements of our agents, nor do any of the levels below it. It is therefore a radically incomplete design description: One we could not use to actually build a robot without first adding a lot of other detail, which according to Newell, was supposed to be incidental to it behaving intelligently. The problem is not the incompleteness itself, but whether, having added everything else necessary to specify a realisable agent, the story will still be the same. In other words, will completion simply add to

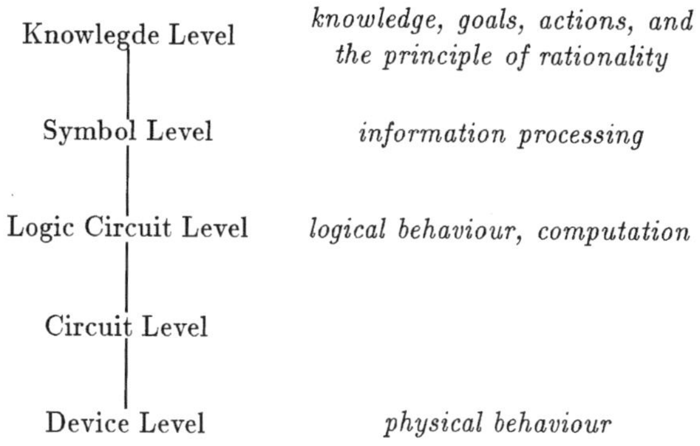

Fig. 4.9: Knowledge Level and the symbol processing and other computer levels it depends upon.

this Knowledge Level plus computers levels story, or will the completion result in a radical reconstruction of the story, which leaves little if any trace of this starting point?

The second point is a more subtle one and has to do with the kind of machine the computer is. If we look at the series of levels of a computer presented in Fig. 4.9 we see that at the bottom, like all physical machines (real machines), it depends on the physical behaviour of certain devices configured and arranged in particular ways—electronic circuits. Unlike other kinds of machines, however, such as steam engines, and analogue computers, for example, these physical devices are arranged so as to support a purely logical form of behaviour at the next level up (at the logic circuit level). In other words, the computer is a particular kind of machine in which the physics of the behaviour of the devices it is constructed from is effectively separated from the logic of the behaviour it can be configured (programmed) to produce. In other words, variations, due to noise and so on, in the behaviour of the implementing devices and the details of the physical behaviour of these devices are arranged (by careful design, choice of technology, and construction) not to affect the logic of its behaviour as a computing device. Of course, this is precisely what is required if we are to have a machine that can reliably carry out computations, as programmed—purely formal operations. More than anything else, early valve-based computers were more limited in their performance by the difficulty of keeping all their thermionic components operating long enough without failure.

The advent of the silicon-based transistor and very large scale integration (VLSI) circuits enabled the construction of the very remarkable machines we see everywhere today. I say very remarkable because no other kinds of machines are able to execute literally billions of sequential actions without fault and, most importantly, without any explicit error correcting or regulatory actions also being necessary. It is this effective separation of the physics of its implementing devices from the logical form of the behaviour they engender that makes computers a particular and distinctive kind of machine: The logical behaviour of the computer is dependent on, but not determined by the physical behaviour of its implementing devices. It is also this separation that enables the Symbol Level (information processing level) and thus Knowledge Level abstractions that Newell's theory depends on. If we could not build computing machines to the standards we can today, Newell's Knowledge Level hypothesis would have little or no basis.

This separation of the logical behaviour of computers from the physical behaviour of the implementing devices is what produces the formal medium that Newell sees as enabling the "Great Move" from what he calls *analogical* representational systems, which depend on the physical and dynamical properties of the representational media, to a *neutral* stable medium that is capable of being organised in the all the variety of ways required and of supporting further composition. As Newell said: "Far from representational constriction, this path opens up the whole world of infinitely rich representations" [38, p. 61]. In other words, the computer, by enabling the move from the physically determined representational behaviour to the formal medium of computation, unconstrained by the details of the physical behaviour of its implementing devices, liberates the representation builder in a big way. There is, however, an enormous cost involved, a cost whose true price classical AI has been busy trying to establish since its start. It is that we now have to specify explicitly all the necessary constraints on a representational system for it to meet the needs. This includes the general problem of controlling the formal inferences that our representational system can support so that only those beneficial to the agent's ongoing goal-achieving activities are actually made.

In making this move, Newell swapped the problem of finding the right kinds of material systems having the right kind of dynamics to meet all the representational demands of an autonomous agent with the problem of selecting from the indefinitely rich representations that can be composed in our neutral and stable computational medium. Composing the right representational system is, in general, a big unsolved problem in symbol processing AI, and one Newell said very little about in his enthusiasm for the computational medium offered by computers. He also threw out all the dynamics in order to have his neutral stable medium. Again, he said nothing about how and where it is to be reintroduced, as it surely must be, if we are to have a real autonomous agent able to support its complex interactions with the dynamic real world, as he described it.

The question all this raises is what kinds of machines are biological nervous systems, and brains in particular? AI, and the symbol processing kind, in particular, take it to be a kind of computer. This is the so called computational metaphor, but see [69] for an effective analysis of this rather unwarranted title. If this were true, then supposing it to also host, via a similar physical/logical behaviour separation, symbolic computations at some level of abstraction would seem reasonable, but brains and nervous systems don't seem to be like computers, McCulloch and Pitts [32] notwithstanding. The electrochemical processes that make up the nervous systems of mammals are not properly understood as being built from elementary devices whose dynamical behaviour is sufficiently simple that in combination they can host the logical behaviour of a formal medium: Brain processes are dynamical processes, not formal processes. (See [70], for some alternative metaphors that have more claim to biological reality.)

My suggestion is, therefore, that although we might be able to, as indeed we can, build certain types of intelligently behaving systems according to Newell's Knowledge Level and Symbol Level theory, it will not serve to adequately explain autonomous agents because it is fundamentally based on the wrong type of machine and as a consequence fails to identify the necessary dynamics of autonomous behaviour.

4.5 Autonomous Agents as Dynamical Systems

I want to end by pointing toward what I believe will be a more fruitful characterisation of autonomous systems, and thus of intelligent behaviour. This new characterisation has two parts to it. First, I want to redefine the relationship between an agent and its environment. The second part involves clearly identifying the fundamentally dynamical nature of this relationship. See [40] for a related discussion for the need of new characterisations of autonomous agents.

4.5.1 Agents, Environments, and Interaction Spaces

The conventional characterisation of an autonomous agent presents it as extracting information about the world it operates in via its various sensors, and of it using this information to construct internal models of its world that can support some kind of decision-making process that identifies further actions to take, in pursuit of some goal, for example. Agents are thus thought of as somehow "internalising" their "external" world. They are seen as being something extra to that external, objective world, and their internalised, subjective world being models from it. Hence the numerous abstracted agents that we see so often described in the AI literature (see Fig. 4.2). It is also this characterisation that leads people to talk about (and investigate) the problem of how an agent's sensory systems come to categorise their world—thus creating the ontology from which its models of the world are to be built, and of how they come to "ground" at least some of the symbols in their models or representations of their world—thus establishing "meaning" in the otherwise syntactic goings on. See [21] and [22], for example.

This characterisation fails to identify the fact that an agent's reality is created as a direct consequence of its interaction in its environment; it is not simply its external environment. What an autonomous agents experiences is what I call the *interaction space* that results from its ongoing interaction in its environment. It does not experience directly the objective, agent-free, reality of some external world. This interaction space is neither completely objective, nor completely subjective, as Lakoff pointed out (see [28]); it depends on both the environment and the way the agent interacts in it. Any categorisations, formed using novelty filters or self-organising processes, for example, are thus not categorisations of the external, objective world of the agent, but are categorisations of the interaction space created by the combination of the agent and its environment in an ongoing interactive process.

From this characterisation we can see that it is not simply a matter of an agent being situated in its environment, that is, having its sensors and actuators properly connected up to its environment. Being an agent is a result of an ongoing interaction that has the right dynamics. Being there is not enough (to borrow a slogan from Clark [11]): You have to interact in the right way, and interact not syntactically, as in the information processing characterisation, but dynamically and continuously. Put another way, and borrowing again, this time from hermeneutical philosophy, being an agent is a matter of continuously becoming that agent via the dynamics of an ongoing interaction between agent and environment. At this point we can see that this notion of the interaction space being the reality experienced by an agent and created between it and the environment it interacts in fits well with the hermeneutical philosophy of Heidegger [23], in which he argued that the separation of subject and object denies the more fundamental unity of *being-in-the-world (Dasein)*. (See [76, chap. 6] for a compact analysis of the rationalistic tradition that underlies the traditional agent–environment characterisation and the response to this of the hermeneutical philosophers.)

4.5.2 Dynamical Processes and Behaviour

In the second part of this newcharacterisation I want to emphasise the fundamentally dynamical process nature of the agent–environment interaction. I start by setting out the characterisations I want to use of agents and their environments.

An agent is abstractly characterised as a coherent system of dynamical interacting processes organised in a competence differentiating architecture. Some of these processes interact only with other agent processes, whereas others also interact with the agent's environment. These latter ones we will call *interaction processes*. An environment is also abstractly characterised as a system of processes, not necessarily coherent, and not organised by an architecture. Such a set of *environment processes* is typically a subset of the processes that constitute what we call the real world. Thus, the environment of one agent may not intersect with the environment of another agent: Each agent has its own reality and its own interaction space created by its particular interactions in its environment.

Given these characterisations of an agent and its environment we can characterise the behaviour of the agent, produced as an observable consequence of its interaction with it environment, as the dynamics of the interaction space. From this we can see that the behaviour of an autonomous agent is a dynamical property of the interaction space created between it and the environment it interacts in. It is not a property of the agent alone, to be explained in terms of the goals it has and the actions it can perform. This interaction space thus defines a phase space of a two component dynamical system: the agent component and the environment component. The behaviour of an agent can therefore be described in terms of the properties of this dynamical system. This is both convenient and attractive. It is convenient because the mathematical modeling and analysis of dynamical systems, and complex dynamical systems in particular, including dynamic chaos, can be drawn on to develop formal descriptions and specifications of behaviour. It is attractive because the science of complex dynamical systems, and the far from equilibrium phenomena and self-organising properties of dissipative structures in particular [52] offer us a uniform way of both talking about and describing both the observed behaviour of autonomous agents and the processes that constitute our agent. For some examples of how the behaviour of the kinds of robots discussed in section 3 can be described in terms of point attractors and limit cycles in interaction spaces see [65].

This dynamical systems characterisation of both an agent's behaviour and its constituting components also provides a uniform way of talking about the relationship between the dynamics of agent processes and those of its environment. It is a relationship in which the history of the ongoing interactions plays a fundamental role in forming the dynamical structures that arise within an agent, via its interaction processes. The best way I have for describing this relationship is in terms of Maturana and Varela's concept of *structural coupling*, "a history of recurrent interactions leading to the structural congruence between two or more systems" [37, p. 75].

This notion of structural coupling has been developed by Maturana and Varela in the context of cellular biological systems, which they describe as autopoietic unities that, once established, are subject to ongoing interactions with their environment that may result in internal structural changes:

> This ongoing structural change occurs in the unity from moment to moment, either as a change triggered by interactions coming from the environment in which it exists or as a result of its internal dynamics. As regards its continuous interactions with the environment, the cell unity classifies them and sees them in accordance with its structure at every instance. That structure, in turn, continuously changes because of its internal dynamics. [37, p. 74]

Although talking about cellular unities, this quote very nicely described what is going on in my Lego vehicle as its internal sensorimotor structure dynamically changes as a consequence of its interaction with its environment, and in so doing, continuously modifies its response to those interactions. The closeness of these ideas can be seen from Varela's development of these ideas, and in particular when he said [37, p. 75]:

> Let us begin with the notion of perceptually guided action. For the dominant computationalists tradition the point of departure for understanding perception is typically abstract: the information-processing problem of recovering pre-given properties of the world. In contrast, the point of departure for the enactive approach is the study of how the perceiver can guide its actions in its local situation. Since these local situations constantly change as a result of the perceivers activity, the reference point for understanding perception is no longer a pre-given, perceiver-independent world, but rather the sensorimotor structure of the cognitive agent, the way in which the nervous system links sensory and motor surfaces. It is this structure—the manner in which the perceiver is embodied—rather than some pre-given world, that determines how the perceiver can act and be modulated by environmental events.

The emphasis on a process-based characterisation presented here also fits well with the process-oriented views advocated by Whitehead [71, 72] in which he argued that the world, at physical, biological, and psychological levels of organisation is essentially a process, active and generative. To hold this process still, a look deeply into isolated parts can, he suggested, only produce a limited view. This move toward a process-oriented metaphysics is echoed in the work of Prigogine and Stengers [52] on the order that arises out of dynamically chaotic systems and the far from equilibrium effects seen in dissipative structures. For them, "physics and metaphysics are indeed coming together today in a conception of the world in which process, becoming, is taken as a primary constituent of physical existence and where existing entities can interact and therefore also be born and die".

4.5.3 Connecting Things Up

In this final section I relate these ideas to other work that is going on, in AI and the biological and neurosciences, which I think is either compatible or has a contribution to make to further development and investigation. This is not intended to be complete survey of related work, but to highlight what for me are some particularly exciting and significant ideas and results.

First, the application of complex dynamical ideas and, in particular, dynamical chaos, to an understanding of brain function (see [59], for example) serves as a strong pointer to the fact that the dynamics of material systems does perhaps form the basis of the representational structures built and used by biological systems, not the formal medium advocated by Newell. The identification of selectionist developmental processes (see [10, 11, 54]) offers further evidence that biological system's possess the powerful self-organising mechanisms required to develop and maintain the dynamic structural coupling that must exist between them and the environments they interact in. A different, but related kind of work concerns the details of the sensorimotor mechanisms found in biological systems, which implement the interaction processes that couple them to their environments in just the right way that enables them to continue as viable autonomous systems (see [29, 30, 50, 66, 68], for example).

The other area in which we can find related and supporting work concerns the use of analogical representations and complex dynamical ideas in AI. Here I would point in particular to the work of Steels (see [60, 61, 62]). More recently this has resulted in an initial experimental programming language, intended for use with robots like Lego vehicles, which attempts to offer the kinds of computational constructs that we need for specifying the computational components of the dynamical processes constituting our autonomous agents [64].

4.6 Conclusions

I have argued that the widely held dogma that that intelligent systems are information processing systems cannot be so straightforwardly used as we typically presume. I support this argument with examples of problems that arise from my work on real autonomous mobile robots. I further argue that the modern fashion for situatedness also fails to address the real problem of autonomous agents, and that the so-called symbol grounding problem is an inappropriate response to those who have pointed out that the world of an autonomous agent does not come ready categorized and neatly labeled. I end with some speculations on what might be a more satisfactory characterisation, which has much in common with some ideas of Humberto Maturana and Francisco Varela, and emphasises the dynamical process nature of the relationship between autonomous agents and the environments they interact in.

A polemic author ought not merely to destroy his victim. He ought to try a bit to make him feel his error—perhaps not enough to convert him, but enough to give him a bad conscience and to weaken the energy of his defence.

— William James [25, p. 304]

Acknowledgments

The development of the Lego vehicle technology described here was supported both financially and technically by the Department of Artificial Intelligence, Edinburgh University. The work of the "Really Useful Robot" was supported by a grant from the U.K. Science and Engineering Research Council (grant number GR/F/5852.3) and also involved John Hallam, Pete Forster, and Ulrich Nehmzow. The ideas expressed here have benefited from discussions with a large number of people. Important among these have been: Amaia Bernaras, Rod Brooks, Jo Decuyper, John Hallam, Stevan Harnad, Leslie Kaelbling, Brendan McGonigle, Ulrich Nehmzow, Rolf Pfeifer, Peter Ross, Luc Steels, Francisco Varela, Paul Verschure, and Barbara Webb. I also acknowledge the contribution of enthusiasm and ingenuity of the the two classes of students who built Lego vehicles for the practical exercises of the Intelligent Sensing and Control course I taught in Edinburgh in 1989 and 1990.

References

[1] Albus, J. S. (1981). *Brains, behavior, and robotics.* Peterborough, NH: BYTE Books.

[2] Andersson, R. L. (1988). *A robot ping-pong player: experiment in real-time intelligent control.* Cambridge, MA: MIT Press.

[3] Anderson, T. L., & Donath, M. (1991). Animal behaviour as a paradigm for developing robot autonomy. In P. Maes (Ed.), *Designing autonomous agents: Theory and practice from biology*

to engineering and back (pp. 145–168). Cambridge, MA: MIT Press, Bradford Books.

[4] Arkin, R. C. (1991). Integrating behaviour, perception, and world knowledge in reactive navigation. In P. Maes (Ed.), *Designing autonomous agents: Theory and practice from biology to engineering and back* (pp. 105–122). Cambridge, MA: MIT Press, Bradford Books.

[5] Ash, R. B. (1965). *Information Theory.* New York: Dover Publications.

[6] Ashby, R. B. (1956). *An introduction to cybernetics.* London: Chapman & Hall.

[7] Barlow, H. B. (1989). Unsupervised learning. *Neural Computation, 1*(3), 295–311.

[8] Brooks, R. A., Connell, J. H., & Ning, P. (1988). *Herbert: A second generation mobile robot* (Memorandum No. 1016). Cambridge, MA: MIT, AI Lab.

[9] Brooks, R. A. (in press). Artificial life and real robots. In Proceedings of the First European Confence on Artificial Life, Cambridge, MA: MIT Press.

[10] Changeux, J. P. (1985). *Neuronal man: The biology of mind.* (L. Garey, Trans.). Oxford: Oxford University Press.

[11] Clark, A. (1987). Being there: Why implementation matters to cognitive science. *Artificial Intelligence Review, 1*, 231–244.

[12] Connell, J. H. (1987). Creature design with the subsumption architecture. *Proceedings of IJCAI-87,* (pp. 1124–1126).

[13] Covrigaru, A. A., & Lindsay, R. K. (1991). Deterministic autonomous systems. *AI Magazine, 12*(3), 110–117.

[14] Cummins, R. (1984). *The nature of psychological explanation.* Cambridge, MA: MIT Press, Bradford Books.

[15] Cummins, R. (1989). *Meaning and mental representation.* Cambridge, MA: MIT Press, Bradford Books.

[16] Cutting, J. E. (1986). *Perception with an eye for motion.* Cambridge, MA: MIT Press, Bradford Books.

[17] Donnett, J., & Smithers, T. (1991). Lego vehicles: A technology for studying intelligent systems. In J. A. Meyer & S. W. Wilson (Eds.), *From animals to animates* (pp. 540–549) Cambridge, MA: MIT Press, Bradford Books.

[18] Dretske, F. I. (1981). *Knowledge and the flow of information.* Oxford: Basil Blackwell.

[19] Edelman, G. M. (1989). *Neural Darwinism: The theory of neuronal group selection.* Oxford: Oxford University Press.

[20] Gibson, J. J. (1979). *The ecological approach to visual perception.* Boston: Houghton Mifflin.

[21] Harnad, S. (1990). The symbol grounding problem. *Physica D, 42*, 335–346.

[22] Harnad, S. (1992). Connecting object to symbol in modeling cognition. In A. Clark & R. Lutz (Eds.), *Connectionism in context* (pp. 421–425). Berlin: Springer-Verlag.

[23] Heidegger, M. (1962). *Being and time* (J. Macquarrie & E. Robinson, Trans.) New York: Harper & Row.

[24] Holenstein, A. A., & Badreddin, E. (1991). Collision avoidance in a behavior-based mobile robot design. *Proceedings of IEEE Robotics and Automation* (pp. 898–903).

[25] James, W. (1975). *Pragmatism and the meaning of truth.* Cambridge, MA: Harvard University Press.

[26] Koch, C. (1990). The biophysics of computation: Towards the mechanisms underlying information processing in single neurons. In E. L. Schwartz (Ed.), *Computational neuroscience* (pp.910–940). Cambridge, MA: MIT Press, Bradford Books.

[27] Kohonen, T. (1987). *Self-organization and associative memory* (2nd ed.). Berlin: Springer-Verlag.

[28] Lakoff, G. (1986). *Women, fire, and dangerous things: What categories tell us about the nature of thought.* Chicago: University of Chicago Press.

[29] Lohmann, K. J. (1992). How sea turtles navigate, *Scientific American, 264*(1), 82–88.

[30] Long, M. E. (1991). Secrets of animal navigation. *National Geographic* June 1991.

[31] MacKay, D. M. (1991). *Behind the eye.* Oxford: Basil Blackwell.

[32] McCulloch, W. S., & Pitts, W. H. (1965). A logical calculus of the ideas immanent nervous activity. In W. S. McCulloch (Ed.) *embodiments of mind* (pp. 19–39). Cambridge, MA: MIT Press.

[33] McFarland, D., & Houston, A. (1981). *Quantitative ethology: The state space approach.* London: Pitman.

[34] McFarland, D. (1991). Defining motivation and cognition in animals. *International Studies in the Philosophy of Science, 5*(2), 1–18.

[35] Malcolm, C. M., Smithers, T., & Hallam, J. (1989). An emerging paradigm in robot architecture. In T. Kanade, F. C. A. Groen, & L. O. Hertzberger (Eds.), *Intelligent Autonomous Systems. Proceedings of the Second Intelligent Autonomous Systems Conference* (pp. 284–293).

[36] Mataric, M. J. (1991). Navigating with a rat brain: A neurobiologically-inspired model of robot spatial representation. In J. A. Meyer & S. W. Wilson (Eds.), *From animals to animates* (pp. 169–175). Cambridge, MA: MIT Press, Bradford Books.

[37] Maturana, H. R., & Varela, F. J. (1987). *The tree of knowledge: The biological roots of human understanding.* (R. Paolucci Trans.). Boston: New Science Library.

[38] Merzenich, M. M., Recanzone, G. H., Jenkins, W. M., & Nudo, R. J. (1990). How the brain functionally rewires itself. In M. A. Arbib & J. A. Robinson (Eds.), *Natural and artificial parallel computation* (pp. 177–210). Cambridge, MA: MIT Press.

[39] Millikan, R. G. (1984). *Language, thought, and other biological categories: New foundations for realism.* Cambridge, MA: MIT Press, Bradford Books.

[40] Nehmzow, U., Hallam, J., & Smithers, T. (1989). Really useful robots. In T. Kanade, F. C. A. Groen, & L.O. Hertzberger (Eds.), *Intelligent autonomous systems* (pp. 284–292). Amsterdam: North-Holland.

[41] Nehmzow, U., & Smithers, T. (1991a). Mapbuilding using self-organising networks in "really useful robots." In J. A. Meyer & S. W. Wilson (Eds.), *From animals to animats* (pp. 152–159). Cambridge, MA: MIT Press, Bradford Books.

[42] Nehmzow, U., & Smithers, T. (1991b). Using motor actions for location recognition. In Brougine, J. and F. Varela (eds.), *Proceedings of the First European Conference on Artificial Life.* Cambridge, MA: MIT Press. pp. 232–249.

[43] Nehmzow, U., Smithers, T., & Hallam, J. (1991). Location recognition in a mobile robot using self-organising features maps. In G. Schmit (Ed.), *Information processing in autonomous mobile robots.* Berlin: Springer Verlag.

[44] Neisser, U. (1967). *Cognitive psychology.* San Francisco: W. H. Freeman.

[45] Newell, A. (1982). The knowledge level. *Artificial Intelligence, 18*, 87–127.

[46] Newell, A. (1990). *Unified theories of cognition.* Cambridge, MA: Harvard University Press.

[47] Newell, A., & Simon, H. A. (1976). Computer science as empirical inquiry: Symbols and search. *Communications of the ACM, 19*, 113–126.

[48] Palmer, S. E., & Kimichi, R. (1986). The information approach to cognition, In T. Knaand & L. C. Robertson (Eds.), *Approaches to cognition: Contrasts and controversies.* Hillsdale, NJ: Lawrence Erlbaum Associates.

[49] Pfeifer, R., & Verschure, P. (1992). The challenge of autonomous agents: Pitfalls and how to avoid them (this volume, chap. 9).

[50] Pichon, J. M., Blanes, C., & Franceschini, N. (1989). Visual guidance of a mobile robot equipped with a network of self-motion sensors, *SPIE, 1195*, 44–53.

[51] Powers, W. T. (1973). *Behavior: The control of perception.* Chicago: Aldine.

[52] Prigogine, I., & Stengers, I. (1984). *Order out of chaos: Man's new dialogue with nature.* Glasgow: Fontana.

[53] Pylyshyn, Z. W. (1984). *Computation and cognition: towards a foundation for cognitive science.* Cambridge MA: MIT Press, Bradford Books.

[54] Reeke, G. N. & Edelman, G. M. (1988). Real brains and artificial intelligence. In S. R. Graubard (Ed.), *The artificial intelligence debate: False starts and real foundations* (pp. 143–174). Cambridge, MA: MIT Press.

[55] Rosen, R. (1986). On information and complexity, In J. L. Casti & A. Karlqvist (Eds.), *Complexity, language, and life: Mathematical approaches* (pp. 174–196). New York: Springer-Verlag.

[56] Rumelhart, D. E., McClelland, J. L., & the PDP Research Group. (1986a). *Parallel distributed processing: Explorations in the microstructure of cognition, Vol. 1: Foundations.* Cambridge, MA: MIT Press, Bradford Books.

[57] Rumelhart, D. E., McClelland, J. L., & the PDP Research Group. (1986b). *Parallel distributed processing: Explorations in the microstructure of cognition, Vol. 2: Psychological and biological models.* Cambridge, MA: MIT Press, Bradford Books.

[58] Shannon, C. E. (1948). A mathematical theory of communication. *Bell System Technical Journal, 27*, 379–423, 623–656.

[59] Skarda, C., & Freeman, W. J. (1987). How brains make chaos in order to make sense of the world. *Behavioral and Brain Sciences, 10*, 161–195.

[60] Steels, L. (1987). *Self-organisation through selection.* (Memorandum No. 87–5). Brussels: VUB, AI Lab.

[61] Steels, L. (1987). *Artificial intelligence and complex dynamics.* Paper presented at the IFIP workshop on concepts and tools for knowledge-based systems, Mount Fuji, Japan.

[62] Steels, L. (1990). Exploiting analogical representations. *Robotics and Autonomous Systems, 6*, 71–88.

[63] Steels, L. (1991). *The robot ecology manifesto.* Unpublished manuscript, Brussels: VUB, AI Lab.

[64] Steels, L. (1992). *The PDL reference manual.* (Memorandum No. 92–5). Brussels: VUB, AI Lab.

[65] Smithers, T. (1991). Taking eliminative materialsim seriously: A methodology for autonomous systems research. *Proceedings of the First European Confence on Artificial Life.* Cambridge, MA: MIT Press.

[66] Suga, N. (1990). Biosonar and neural computation in bats. *Scientific American, 262*(6), 34–41.

[67] Sutton, R. S. (1991). Reinforcement learning architectures for animats. In J. A. Meyer & S. W. Wilson (Eds.), *From animals to animates* (pp. 288–296). Cambridge, MA: MIT Press, Bradford Books.

[68] Wehner, R. (1987). "Matched filters"—Neural models of the external world. *Journal of Comparative Physiology A, 161*, 511–531.

[69] West, D. M., & Travis, L. E. (1991). The computational metaphor and artificial intelligence: A reflective examination of a theoretical falsehood. *AI Magazine, 12*(1), 64–79.

[70] West, D. M. & Travis, L. E. (1991). From society to landscape: Alternative methaphors for artificial intelligence. *AI Magazine, 12*(2), 69–83.

[71] Whitehead, A. N. (1975). *Process and reality: An essay on cosmology.* New York: The Free Press.

[72] Whitehead, A. N. (1985). *Science and the modern world.* London: Free Association Books.

[73] Wiener, N. (1948). *Cybernetics or control and communication in the animal and the machine.* New York: Wiley.

[74] Willshaw, D. J., & von der Marlsburgh, C. (1976a). How patterned neural connections can be set up by self-organisation. *Proceedings of the Royal Society, London, B., 314*, 1–340.

[75] Willshaw, D. J., & von der Marlsburgh, C. (1976b). A marker induction mechanism for establishment of ordered neural mappings: Its application to the retinotectal problem. *Philosophical Transactions of the Royal Society of London (Biological Sciences), 287*, No. B-1021, 203–243.

[76] Winograd, T., & Flores, F. (1986). *Understanding computers and cognition: A new foundation for design.* Norwood, NJ: Ablex.

[77] Young, Y. (1988). *Philosophy and the brain.* NewYork: Oxford University Press.

Part II

Technical Contributions

5. Integration of Representation Into Goal-Driven Behavior-Based Robots

MAJA J. MATARIĆ[1]
Massachusetts Institute of Technology

5.1 Introduction

Inaccurate sensors, world unpredictability, and imperfect control often cause the failure of traditional planning and navigation methods for real-time mobile robots. More reactive approaches to navigation have been explored by [1, 4, 33]. In particular, Brooks [4] proposed the *subsumption architecture* as an incremental method for building layers of robot competencies, consisting of simple rules that tightly couple sensing and action.

The subsumption architecture has been used successfully in fully reactive systems such as [6, 5, 10, 15]. So far, these systems have been limited to applications requiring no explicit internal representation, which imposed a fundamental limitation on the domain of applications for the architecture. The classical problem of path planning, for example, requires some representation of space. Any solution superior to random walk necessitates an internal model of the robot's current location, the desired goal location, and the relationship between the two.

Path planning is discussed extensively in the literature [21, 23, 34]. Most solutions rely on centralized world models, whose compatibility with completely reactive systems is debatable [7]. *Hybrid* systems offer a compromise by employing a reactive system for low-level control and a planner for higher level decision making. They separate the control system into two or more communicating but basically independent parts.

In contrast, we address the problem of integrating representation into a fully reactive, nonhybrid system, with the goal of maintaining a map of the environment and using it for path planning. We introduce a distributed map representation that merges directly into a homogeneous subsumption-based system, thus eliminating the need to separate the planning and execution parts of the system. Our approach extends the repertoire of integrated, fully reactive systems to domains requiring internal spatial representation.

Our system's task is to explore an office environment and to construct and maintain a map based on landmarks it discovers. The user can select a particular landmark (e.g., a specific corridor), or landmark type (e.g., the nearest corridor) as the goal. The robot then employs the map to plan and execute the shortest known path to that landmark. After reaching the destination, the robot is either given another goal or it continues to explore and update its map. If the robot fails to reach the goal, it detects its failure and changes the map appropriately.

All algorithms we describe were implemented on a mobile robot. The data were gathered by running the robot in unaltered office environments with static and dynamic obstacles, including furniture, other robots, and people.

5.2 The Robot, Toto

Toto, the testbed robot we constructed, consists of a circular omnidirectional three-wheeled base capable of following an arbitrary continuous path. On the base is mounted a ring of 12 ultrasonic ranging sensors, ranging from 0.9 to 32 feet, and a flux-gate compass, providing four bits of bearing (Fig. 5.1). The robot is programmed in the Behavior Language, a rule-based parallel programming language that compiles into the subsumption architecture [4].

The robot was tested over a period of 2 months, in over 40 trials, in a cluttered office environment. The data were gathered by attaching a marker to the base of the robot and recording its path on the floor covered with 1-square-foot tiles.

5.3 Sensor Characterization

Real sensors are noisy and inaccurate. Maximizing their reliability often involves data interpretation using complicated physical models. In contrast to explicit error modeling, we minimized overhead computation by using

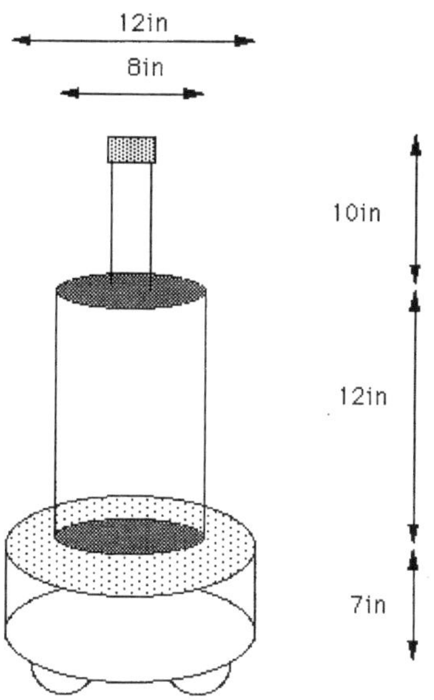

Fig. 5.1: The robot testbed: an omnidirectional three-wheeled base equipped with a ring of 12 ultrasonic ranging sensors and a flux-gate compass.

qualitative, functional descriptions of the sensors describing merely the properties relevant to the robot's task.

Much work has been done on formalizing the limitations of ultrasonic ranging sensors, and suggesting various analytical approaches to their application [19, 20]. Our method relies on a single sufficient characteristic of the sensor: its high accuracy (near 95%) for incident angles less than 15 degrees from the surface normal [32]. Long returns may result from specular reflection and are thus less reliable. We utilize the returns in the short range, as well as the qualitative properties of the data, such as relative differences between readings rather than their exact values.

The error characteristics of the compass are quite different. Its absolute heading reading is grossly inaccurate in the presence of interfering magnetic fields and metal structures in the environment (up to two of the available four bits of resolution, or 50%), although it is locally consistent to up to 90% accuracy. To maximize its utility, we structured our algorithms to rely on the repeatability rather than on the absolute accuracy of the sensed compass direction.

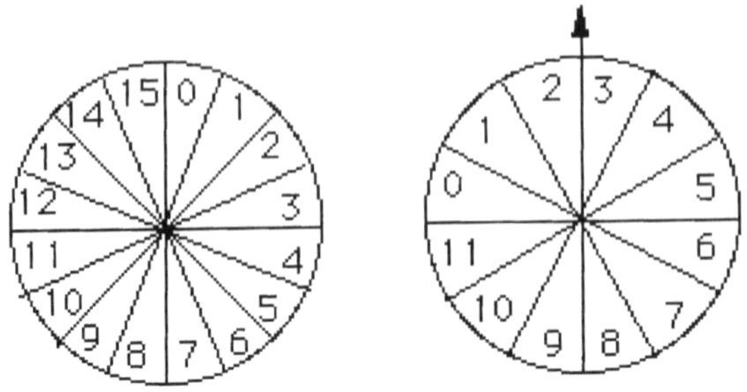

Fig. 5.2: This figure illustrates the organization of the compass and sonar regions. The sonar cones remain constant relative to the shown forward-pointing vector. The compass reflects the local magnetic field. The two sensors are used independently.

5.4 The Basic Navigation Algorithm

The robot's control system consists of three competencies, integrated into a homogeneous, behavior-based representation: (a) basic navigation: obstacle avoidance and boundary tracing,(b) landmark detection, and (c) map-related computation: map construction, map update, and path planning. The competencies were designed and added incrementally, each relying on those that follow.

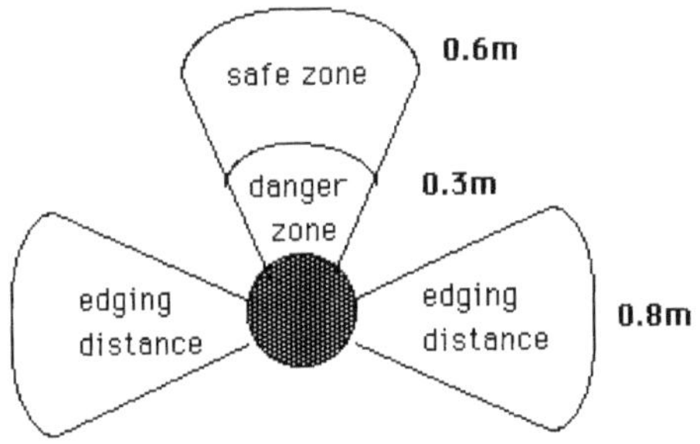

Fig. 5.3: The perceptual zones around the robot corresponding to the relevant obstacle and boundary conditions in the environment. The regions are used to implement basic collision-free navigation rules that combine into a robust boundary-tracing behavior.

Lower level competencies do not depend on the higher level ones, but we designed them by keeping in mind the entire, integrated system. The basic navigation algorithm was designed to facilitate landmark recognition as well as map construction [24]. Its primary task was to keep the robot moving safely through an unaltered office environment, avoiding collisions with objects and people. The rules for reactive wandering were augmented with a rule that made the robot maintain a small distance from objects, (i.e., avoid open areas). This behavior is useful as the accuracy of the sonars is maximized in the proximity of detectable objects, which is where the robot can obtain the most information about the environment.

The robot's velocity was limited by the sonar refresh rate: 200msec per pair of sensors, a new data set for the entire sonar ring was obtained at 0.83 Hz. This limited the robot's velocity from the maximum of 2 m/sec to 0.2 m/sec. Based on the circular arrangement of the sonars, obstacle avoidance and boundary tracing were implemented by segmenting the space around the robot into relevant sensory regions (Fig. 5.3). The area in front of the robot was divided into two regions: the danger zone and the safe zone. The threshold between the zones (0.3 m) was derived from the robot's velocity and the minimum range of the sonar sensors (0.25 m). It guarantees that at least two sets of sonar data are available before reaching an obstacle, thus decreasing the probability of collision.

An object in the danger zone is an obstacle. An object in the safe zone causes the robot to turn appropriately to avoid it. The edging distance is a threshold dividing the area on each side of the robot. The robot stays within the edging distance of the boundary it is following. The following basic behaviors utilize the zones to produce boundary tracing:

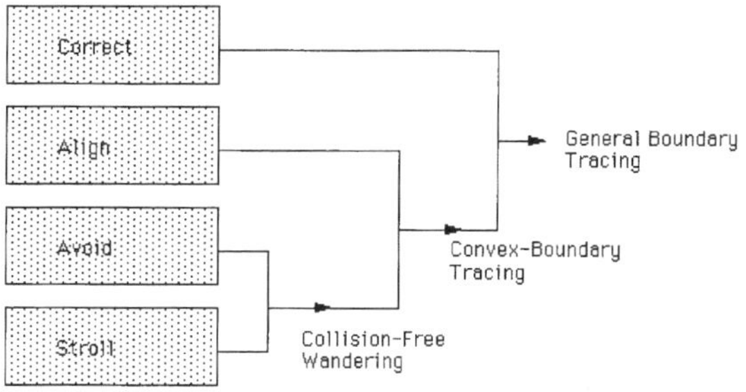

Fig. 5.4: A schematic showing the incremental interaction of the low-level navigation behaviors resulting in boundary tracing. The addition of each new behavior adds to the overall competence of the robot.

```
(defbehavior stroll
  (cond
      ((and (<= (min (sonars 1 2 3 4) danger-zone))
            (not stopped))
         (stop))
      ((and (<= (min (sonars 1 2 3 4) danger-zone))
            (stopped))
         (move backward))
```

```
    (t
       (move forward))))
```

Stroll: If an obstacle is detected within the danger zone, the robot stops. If stopped within a danger zone, it backs up. This allows the robot to escape tight situations, and minimizes unnecessary motion in avoiding transient obstacles. If no obstacles are detected, the robot is repeatedly given a target distance, resulting in smooth, continuous motion. *Stroll* alone provides safe forward motion.

```
(defbehavior avoid
   (cond
     ((and (<= (sonar 1 or 2) safe-zone)
           (<= (sonar 3 or 4) safe-zone))
        (turn left))
     ((<= (sonar 3 or 4) safe-zone)
        (turn right))))
```

Avoid: The robot turns (by a small, fixed angle $\alpha = 30$ degrees = width of sonar cone) in the opposite direction from an obstacle within the safe distance of its front sonars. If obstacles are detected on both sides, oscillation is prevented by consistently choosing the same default direction (left). In conjunction with *stroll*, this rule generates collision-free wandering behavior.

```
(defbehavior align
   (cond
     ((and (< (sonar 7 or 8) edging-distance)
           (> (sonar 5 or 6) edging-distance))
       (turn right))
     ((and (< (sonar 9 or 10) edging-distance)
           (> (sonar 11 or 0) edging-distance))
       (turn left))))
```

Align: If an object is detected within the edging distance range of one of the rear-lateral sonars (10 and 9 or 8 and 7), and not by the lateral sonars (0 and 11 or 5 and 6) on the same side, the robot makes an α-degree turn in that direction. The combination of *avoid*, *stroll*, and *align* allows the robot to follow straight and convex curved boundaries.

```
(defbehavior correct
   (cond
     ((and (< (sonar 11) edging-distance)
           (> (sonar 0) edging-distance))
       (turn left))
     ((and (< (sonar 6) edging-distance)
           (> (sonar 5) edging-distance))
```

Correct: This behavior prevents the robot from losing track of a lateral boundary containing a sharp turn by monitoring the pair of sonars on each side of the robot (0 and 11 or 5 and 6). If the rear of the two sonars (11 or 6) detects an object within the edging distance, and the front (0 or 5) does not, the robot makes an α-degree turn in the same direction. By turning, it gets the boundary in the range of both of the sensors in the pair, effectively returning to a position aligned with the boundary. In conjunction with the rest of the wandering behaviors, *correct* allows the robot to track arbitrarily sharp turns. Figure 5.4 illustrates the incremental addition of navigational competencies resulting in boundary tracing behavior.

The boundary-following behavior does not distinguish between, or differentially treat, various kinds of boundaries in the environment. The behavior is general, independent of what types of objects and structures form the boundaries, as long as they are detectable by the sonars.

Figure 5.5 shows a cumulative plot of four real-time runs in a large, unaltered office area. The room is cluttered with chairs, tables, doors, a water fountain, moving people, and other robots. The data show reliable boundary following in all trials, independent of the robot's starting position. The robot also remains in the middle of empty corridors if the corridor width is less than the sum of the edging distance on both sides of the robot. In a wider corridor, the robot follows the wall it initially approaches. Even without the use of position control to direct the robot to specific Cartesian positions, the navigation rules result in stable paths that show repeatable convergence around the detected object boundaries.

5.5 Landmark Detection

The robust, repeatable navigation behavior enabled the robot to safely wander about and explore its environment. Next we added the ability to detect landmarks used in spatial mapping. Sonar-based systems usually perform landmark detection by matching sensory patterns to stored landmark models or signatures (e.g., [12]). These approaches are "static" in their use of a discrete snapshot of the world based on a single set of sensor data. However, the expected accuracy of any one data point is low, and different sonar signatures are generated in different trials due to sensor error and noise. Static matchers compensate by maintaining error estimates and utilizing positional precision that is often difficult to maintain due to wheel slipping and other factors producing further cumulative errors.

We explored an alternative, "dynamic" approach to landmark detection, based on continuously monitoring the robot's sensors and taking advantage of the robot's underlying boundary-tracing behavior. The landmark detector looks for features in the world that have physical extensions detectable over time (i.e., it monitors for consistencies in the sensory data as the robot is moving next to objects in the environment). Spurious sensor errors are filtered out through dynamic averaging. Three specific sensory conditions are monitored: the compass bearing, to determine whether the robot is moving straight, and the sonar data on both sides of the robot, to check for a persisting boundary on either or both sides. Whenever the robot repeatedly detects short readings on its right side, and its averaged compass bearing is stable, the confidence counter for a right wall is incremented. An analogous rule applies to left walls. Simultaneous sufficient confidence in both walls indicates a corridor. When the appropriate combination of confidences reaches a preset threshold τ, the corresponding landmark is detected, and the confidence counter is reset. τ is the minimum length of a continuous landmark boundary, represented in counter units. To adapt the algorithm to other types of environments, τ is set to the shortest landmark we want the robot to detect. In our case, based on the constant velocity assumption, τ is equivalent to the maximum length of nonlandmark obstacles in the office environment (chairs, table legs, trash cans, filing cabinets).

We chose three large, stable, and reliably detectable landmark types: left walls (LW), right walls (RW), and corridors (C). A default landmark type was added, corresponding to long irregular boundaries (I). It enables the system to represent the environment as a collection of contiguous strings of features describing the path the robot traversed. Wherever in the environment the robot happens to be, it finds and follows a boundary enabling it to classify the area into one of its four landmark types.

The landmarks used by the system are designed to be reliably detectable, but due to their size produce a rather sparse representation of space. By introducing additional sensors or position control, the granularity of landmarks can be refined. Although additional behaviors would be required for detecting different landmark types, the connectivity and path planning properties of the representation would remain linear.

The qualitative, procedural nature of the landmark detection algorithm adds robustness to the system by not relying on sensor precision or position control. Figure 5.6 illustrates the locations of landmark detection over three trials in a room cluttered with furniture and people. Even without position control, the data show some clustering. The same landmarks, with slight deviations in the compass bearing due to the averaging process, are detected repeatably independent of the robot's starting position or the exact path followed.

Besides following object boundaries, the robot must also be able to find landmarks located in the middle of open areas, separated from the continuous boundary it begins to explore. This ability is provided by a behavior that occasionally moves the robot out into an open area. When stimulated to go into an open area, the robot continues to move straight until it encounters an object whose boundary is either new, or recognized as one it has followed before. The following sections describe how the mapping algorithm distinguishes between the two possibilities, and how the open-space behavior is triggered.

5.6 The Mapping Algorithm

The robot's top-level task is to map the structure of the environment based on the spatial relationships of the landmarks, and to use this map to find paths to any previously visited landmark the user chooses as the goal. This differs fundamentally from building a detailed map of the world that includes features of smaller size and higher probability of impermanence. The aim is to produce and maintain a coarse-scale map that allows the robot to get within the sensing range of the goal. Reaching an exact location can be accomplished by augmenting the system with special-purpose motion planning based on the specific task and sensors used. The system is suitable for various applications that require the use of a map, such as sentry and surveillance tasks, as well as prioritized tasks such as hazardous area maintenance, plant watering, or supply delivery in a large office complex.

Reaching places that cannot be sensed from the robot's current position necessitates some form of path planning, which, in turn, requires a world model. The traditional approach to path planning involves some type of a reasoning engine that generates a plan by manipulating a Cartesian map usually stored in a centralized data structure (e.g., [8, 14, 16, 21], etc.). The success of the plan depends on the accuracy of the geometric information in the map. In contrast to Cartesian metric representations, graphs are convenient for encoding topological, qualitative information (e.g., [8, 9, 17, 18], etc.). Similarly, our approach directly constructs and utilizes a graph in which each node represents a unique landmark, and neighbor links indicate physical adjacency, thus producing a structure isomorphic to the topology of the environment.

5.6.1 The Distributed Nature of the Representation

Whenever a node is activated, it spreads *expectation* to its neighbor in the direction of robot's travel along the path, priming it for upcoming activation. Matching an expecting node to a found landmark verifies the correctness of the graph. The notion of expectation provides a contextual clue by expanding the matching window to two nodes instead of one. This information helps disambiguate between nodes with identical type and similar compass bearing.

When the robot initially returns to a previously visited landmark, the node corresponding to the location will not be expecting activation, because the topological link between it and the beginning of the path has not yet been established. The match is recognized by comparing the location of the landmark to the stored position estimate. Although the estimate is very inaccurate, the matching tolerance is bounded by the size of the landmark, and it suffices for disambiguating two otherwise identical landmarks. The use of the position estimate does not constitute position control, however, because it is used exclusively for landmark disambiguation and not for controlling the robot's motion. The combination of expectation and position estimation allows for uniquely disambiguating the landmarks.

Consequently, matching always produces a unique match or no match. If no match is found, the landmark is assumed to be new and is assigned to a free node. The newly added landmark is connected to the currently active landmark by a topological wire. Figure 5.7 shows the graph representation the robot constructed for the office environment shown in Fig. 5.6. Figure 5.8 illustrates an environment containing multiple cycles, and its corresponding graph.

The unique representation of landmarks eliminated false positive matches in all trials. Due to sensor noise, false negatives occurred in approximately one third of the trials when the robot, while following a boundary, failed to recognize it as a landmark. If this happened during the discovery phase, it resulted in a sparser map that would later get augmented if the robot was allowed repeated runs through the same environment. In the converse case, failing to detect a previously detected landmark was ignored if the subsequent landmark matched in type and position. Otherwise it was recognized as a new location and added to the network as an alternative direction to pursue. This case accounted for situations in which the environment could change, such as a doorway that could be open or closed. Finally, failing to detect a landmark while on the way to a goal did not affect the goal-finding behavior, unless the skipped landmark was the goal itself, or a junction of two or more paths in the network.

5.6.2 Path Planning and Optimization

The map provides the structure for relating the robot's current position and the goal. Its distributed nature allows for the path to be computed by the individual map components using local operations only. We use a variation of *activation spreading* from the goal in all directions throughout the graph. Activation is propagated through the nearest-neighbor links. The goal node repeatedly sends out a *call* that eventually reaches the currently active node. Equivalent to parallel search, this process is guaranteed to terminate in worst case linear time $O(n)$ in the size of the graph [27].

Path optimization by topological distance is a natural consequence of this process. Whenever the robot follows the landmarks in the direction of the spreading call, it is guaranteed to proceed on a shortest topological path to the goal. The call originating from the node closest to the robot's current position will reach it first, given uniform activation dissipation. Weighting each landmark by its physical length allows for computing the physically shortest path within the graph. As a call propagates from the goal to the current node, it adds the lengths of all the landmarks it passes. On reaching the active landmark, the value of the call approximates the physical length of the traversed path. The shortest incoming call is chosen at each landmark. Making a local greedy choice at each node results in the global, physically shortest-known path within the graph, in $O(n)$ [28].

Graph cycles do not cause problems because of the greedy nature of the algorithm. Because the length of a cycling call increases monotonically, it is never selected as the optimal path. Additionally, the maximum length of any path is bounded by the size of the graph so indefinite activation propagation cannot happen.

The activation from the goal node is received by all of the nodes in the graph. As the robot traverses a path, it chooses the optimal direction to pursue from any landmark. Consequently, if the robot veers away from the optimal path, or is intentionally placed elsewhere in the environment by the user, once localized it will pursue the optimal path from the current location [26].

The goal is reached when the currently recognized landmark matches the goal landmark. This condition terminates the activation spreading, and the robot can pursue another goal or continue exploring the environment and augmenting and verifying the map. If the path to the goal is blocked, the robot will persistently fail to make a transition from the current landmark to its neighbor. After a fixed time period, it gives up pursuing the blocked path, terminates activation spreading, and removes the topological link between its current position and the one it failed to reach. When the change in the graph is complete, activation spreading from the goal is started up again, in order to find another path, if one exists. The ability to detect failure and update the network structure allows the system to adapt the map representation to a dynamically changing environment.

In evaluating the performance of the system, the robot was presented with various obstacles including furniture and people walking in its way. If the desired path was temporarily blocked, the low-level navigation behavior ensured that no collision occurred by turning the robot away from the obstacle. Simultaneously, activation from the goal forced the robot to turn in the direction of the desired path. The conflict of the two motivations resulted in taking the first free turn toward the direction of the goal. Only if the path to the goal was completely blocked was it eventually abandoned.

The user can interact with the system in a number of ways depending on the type of the specified goal. The goal types vary from very specific (e.g., a particular corridor, the first discovered landmark in the graph, etc.), to less general (e.g., nearest north-going corridor), to very general (e.g., nearest corridor). All landmarks that match the goal descriptor become goals and spread activation. Based on the greedy algorithm, the robot always pursues the path to the nearest one.

Figure 5.9 shows an environment used for testing path finding and optimization. After exploring the environment and learning its structure, the robot is given the corridor as the goal. Given a choice of paths from its current position (LW8), the system takes into account that the shortest topological path does not correspond to the shortest physical one (Fig. 5.10). In seven consecutive trials, the system correctly chose the topologically longer but physically shorter path to the goal.

5.7 Hardware Implications

The system we present is best suited for coarse-grained parallel hardware. In general, graph structures with arbitrary, dynamically assignable connections between nodes can escalate to full connectivity and do not scale well. In contrast, our approach employs only a few global broadcast connections, in addition to nearest-neighbor connections between adjacent graph nodes.

To further limit the graph connectivity, we utilize some domain knowledge about the robot's environment. Based on the boundary-following behavior, the robot has no more than a small, fixed number f of directions to pursue from any given location in an office environment. Consequently, we can bound the outdegree of the graph to f. In our implementation, $f = 8$, bounded by the resolution of the compass in the half-plane (from any convex boundary the robot can pursue at most as many directions as it can distinguish with the compass). This results in the total connectivity linear $O(n)$ in the size of the graph.

The choice of a parsimonious representation that encodes only the necessary information simplified the control system and resulted in notably small object code. For example, a network of 10 landmarks takes up 51K. The division between code and data is blurred because the graph representation, which comprises most of the code, is actually data. This means that scaling to larger maps requires only a linear increase in hardware. This contrasts with approaches relying on a reasoner that may suffer from a combinatorial explosion with an increase in the problem size.

The approach we present has been shown to be biologically feasible and to resemble some properties of the spatial mapping mechanism of a rat [27]. In particular, the distributed nature of the representation, and its direct integration with action, has biological analogs [29].

5.8 Related Work

Path planning systems initially relied on purely deliberative, nonreactive solutions (e.g., [3, 8, 14, 16, 21, 30], etc.). More recently, most path-planning systems implemented on physical robots have introduced a reactive layer and have been implemented in the hybrid style (e.g., [2, 21, 31], etc). Exceptions include Connell [9], who suggested a completely reactive subsumption-based scheme for navigation by path remembering, but this scheme was never fully developed or implemented. Lumelski and Stepanov [22] described an entirely local navigation strategy independent of a map. Using Cartesian coordinates of the goal, the system relied on position control to either reach the goal or recognize failure. Although general, the system does not build or maintain a representation of the environment in order to optimize its paths to the goal. Kuipers and Byun [18] described a qualitative spatial learning method based on a landmark strategy similar to ours. The key differences lay in the nature of its landmarks (they are signature based), the lack of metric information (no metric path optimization is done), the static world assumption (no moving obstacles are allowed), and the fact that the system was tested in simulation. [11] and [13] are examples of relevant graph discovery and exploration work. However, these are theoretical results that, in order to be applied to robots, require a perfect ability to determine the local graph structure. Such ability has not yet been demonstrated in physical, nonsimulated robots.

5.9 Limitations and Extensions

In order to implement a nonhybrid architecture, we attempted to minimize the translation overhead between the robot's sensor space and the map representation. We those a topological scheme, and instead of place-and-path graphs, used extended landmarks and their adjacency relationships. These primitives were chosen because they are directly available from the robot's sensors and its low-level, reactive control system.

Consequently, the method we describe is based almost entirely on topological information. This simplifies computation but also limits it to optimizing paths only within the previously traversed path set. In an extension of the existing approach, the rough position information already available in the system could be used for making geometric inferences. For instance, the information could be used to generate shortcuts by producing novel, previously unexplored paths [25]. A related extension to the system would enable the robot to explore by following directions into as yet undiscovered areas.

The current system allows the user to select a specific landmark or a landmark type as a goal, by pressing buttons on the top of the robot. Although the landmark primitives are well suited to the robot's sensors and its task, they are not intuitive for the user. A mechanism for translating between the robot's and the user's map representation would make the interaction with the robot easier. Additionally, such a mechanism would allow for translating the robot's internal representation into a form that could be used by other robots equipped with different types of sensors. Using the combination of the topological structure (the graph) and the metric data (the landmark lengths, the rough position estimates, the robot's velocity, and the landmark threshold), it is possible to transform the map into other forms more accessible to people or other robots. Currently, the robot's representation is well suited for its sensors and its task. However, if a different representation is needed in the future, the described transformation tool would be an interesting extension of this work.

5.10 Conclusion

We have described a strategy for integrating a distributed spatial representation into a fully reactive, subsumption-based mobile robot. The robot performs navigation, spatial mapping, and path planning, in real time based on real sensory data. Additionally, the robot can interact with a human operator and receive a variety of goal directives. The strategy is implemented as a collection of concurrently executing behaviors performing both representation and action tasks.

The approach we presented derives its strengths from three main properties of the representation: It is qualitative, procedural, and distributed. The qualitative nature keeps the granularity of the representation low, but minimizes the computational overhead. Qualitative sensor characteristics are used to construct a fault-tolerant navigation behavior that facilitates a simple procedural landmark detection algorithm. The distributed representation utilizes the benefits of parallel computation in allowing for constant-time localization and linear-time path planning. The decentralized nature of the map permits the planning computation to be performed by the map itself, rather than by a separate planner. The system detects failures and dynamically adapts the map.

The presented architecture is an alternative to the hybrid approach of separating the reactive and the planning parts of the control system. By removing the distinction between the control program and the map, the described distributed representation introduces added power to fully reactive, subsumption-based architectures by extending their domain to applications requiring internal spatial models and interaction with the user.

5.11 Acknowledgments

This report describes research done at the Artificial Intelligence Laboratory of the Massachusetts Institute of Technology. Support for the research was provided in part by the Artificial Intelligence Center of Hughes Research Labs, and in part by the University Research Initiative under Office of Naval Research contract N0014-86-K-0685. Rodney Brooks originally proposed the idea of a distributed representation. Jose Robles provided many helpful comments on earlier drafts of this chapter, as did Rodney Brooks, Nancy Pollard, and Sundar Narasimhan.

References

[1] Agre, P., & Chapman, D. (1987). Pengi: An implementation of a theory of activity. *Proceedings of Sixth National Conference on Artificial Intelligence, AAAI-87,* 268–272.

[2] Arkin, R. (1989). Towards the unification of navigational planning and reactive control. *AAAI Spring Symposium on Robot Navigation: Working Notes,* 1–5.

[3] Brooks, R. (1983). Solving the find-path problem by good representation of free space. *IEEE Transactions on Systems, Man and Cybernetics, Vol. SMC-13*(3), 190–197.

[4] Brooks, R. (1986). A robust layered control system for a mobile robot. *IEEE Journal of Robotics and Automation, RA-2,* 14–23.

[5] Brooks, R., & Connell, J. (1986). Asynchronous distributed control system for a mobile robot. *SPIE's Cambridge Symposium on Optical and Opto-Electronic Engineering Proceedings, 727,* 77–84.

[6] Brooks, R. (1989). A robot that walks: Emergent behavior from a carefully evolved network. *Neural Computation, 1*(2), 253–262.

[7] Brooks, R. (1991). Intelligence without representation. *AI Journal, 47,* 139–159.

[8] Chatila, R., & Laumond, J. (1985). Position referencing and consistent world modeling for mobile robots. *IEEE International Conference on Robotics and Automation,* 138–145.

[9] Connell, J. (1988). Navigation by path remembering. *SPIE Mobile Robots III, 1007,* 383–390.

[10] Connell, J. (1989). A colony architecture for an artificial creature. (Tech. Rep. No. 1151). Cambridge, MA: MIT AI Lab.

[11] Deng, X., & Papadimitrou, H. (1990). Exploring an unknown graph. *Proceedings of the 31st Annual Symposium on Foundations of Computer Science, 1,* 355–361.

[12] Drumheller, M. (1986). Mobile robot localization using sonar. (Memorandum No. 826). Cambridge, MA: MIT AI Lab.

[13] Dudek, G., Jenkin, M., Milios, E., & Wilkes, D. (1988). *Robotics exploration as graph construction.* (Tech. Rep. Stanford University No. 23).

[14] Elfes, A. (1986). A sonar-based mapping and navigation system. *Proceedings of the IEEE International Conference on Robotics and Automation,* pp. 490–510. 1986.

[15] Flynn, A., Brooks, R., Wells, S., & Barrett, D. (1989). *Squirt: The prototypical mobile robot for autonomous graduate students.* (Memorandum No. 1120). Cambridge, MA: MIT AI Lab.

[16] Giralt, G., Chatila, R., & Vaisset, M. (1984). An integrated navigation and motion control system for autonomous multisensory mobile robots. In M. Brady & R. Paul (Eds.),*First international symposium on robotics research,* (pp. 191–214). Cambridge, MA: MIT Press.

[17] Kuipers, B. (1987). A qualitative approach to robot exploration and map learning. *AAAI Workshop on spatial reasoning and multi-sensor fusion.*

[18] Kuipers, B., & Byun, Y. (1988). A robust, qualitative approach to a spatial learning mobile robot. *SPIE sensor fusion: Spatial reasoning and scene interpretation*, pp. 366–375.

[19] Kuc, R., & Di, Y. (1986). Intelligent sensor approach to differentiating sonar reflections from corners and planes. *Proceedings of the International Congress on Intelligent Autonomous Systems.* pp. 124–135.

[20] Kuc, R., & Siegel, R. (1987). Physically based simulation model for acoustic sensor robot navigation. *IEEE Transactions PAMI, 9* (6), 766–778.

[21] Lozano-Perez, T. (1987). A simple motion-planning algorithm for general robot manipulation. *IEEE Journal of Robotics and Automation, RA-3*(3), 224–238.

[22] Lumelski, V., & Stepanov, A. (1986). Dynamic path planning for a mobile automation with limited information on the environment. *IEEE Transactions on Automatic Control, CA-31*(11).

[23] Khatib, O. (1986). Real-time obstacle avoidance for manipulators and mobile robots.*International Journal of Robotics Research, 5*(1), 90–98.

[24] Mataric, M. (1989). Qualitative sonar based environment learning for mobile robots. *PIE Proceedings of conference on Mobile Robots, IV.*

[25] Mataric, M. (1990a). *A distributed model for mobile robot environment-learning and navigation.* (Tech. Rep. No. 1228). Cambridge, MA: MIT Press.

[26] Mataric, M. (1990b). Environment learning using a distributed representation. *Proceedings of the IEEE International Conference on Robotics and Automation*, 402–406.

[27] Mataric, M. (1990c). Navigating with a rat brain. In Meyer & Wilson (Eds.), *Proceedings of the 1990 International Conference on Simulation of Adaptive Behavior* (pp. 169–175). Cambridge, MA: MIT Press, Bradford Books.

[28] Mataric, M., & Brooks, R. (1990). Learning a distributed map representation based on navigation behaviors. *Proceedings of USA–Japan Symposium on Flexible Automation*, 499–506.

[29] McNaughton, B. (1989). Neuronal mechanisms for spatial computation and information storage. In L. Nadel, A. Cooper, P. Culicover, & R. M. Harnish (Eds.), *Neural connections, mental computation*, (pp. 285–350). Cambridge, MA: MIT Press.

[30] Moravec, H., & Cho, D. (1989). A Bayesian method for certainty grids. *Proceedings of the AAAI Spring Symposium on Robot Navigation*, 57–60.

[31] Payton, D. (1991). Internalized plans: A representation for action resources. In P. Maes (Ed.), *Designing autonomous agents* (pp. 89–103). Cambridge, MA: MIT Press.

[32] Polaroid Corporation. (1987). *Polaroid ultrasonic ranging system handbook.* Cambridge Ma.

[33] Rosenschein, S., & Kaelbling, L. (1986). The synthesis of digital machines with provable epistemic properties. In J. Halpern (Ed.), *Proceedings of the Conference on Theoretical Aspects of Reasoning About Knowledge* (pp. 83–98). Los Altos, CA: Morgan Kaufmann.

[34] Yap, C. K. (1987). Algorithmic motion planning. In J. T. Schwartz & C. K. Yap (Eds.), *Algorithmic and geometric aspects of robotics* (pp. 95–143). Hillsdale, NJ: Lawrence Erlbaum Associates.

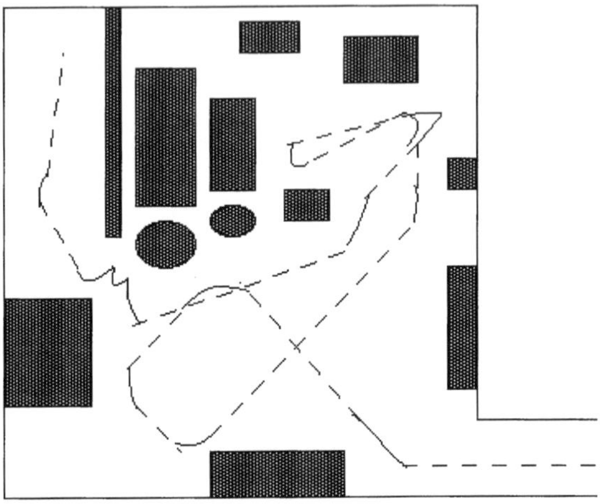

Fig. 5.5: A plot of four independent real robot runs manifesting consistent boundary following in an unaltered room. The data consist of inflection points in the robot's actual traversed paths, connected by straight line segments.

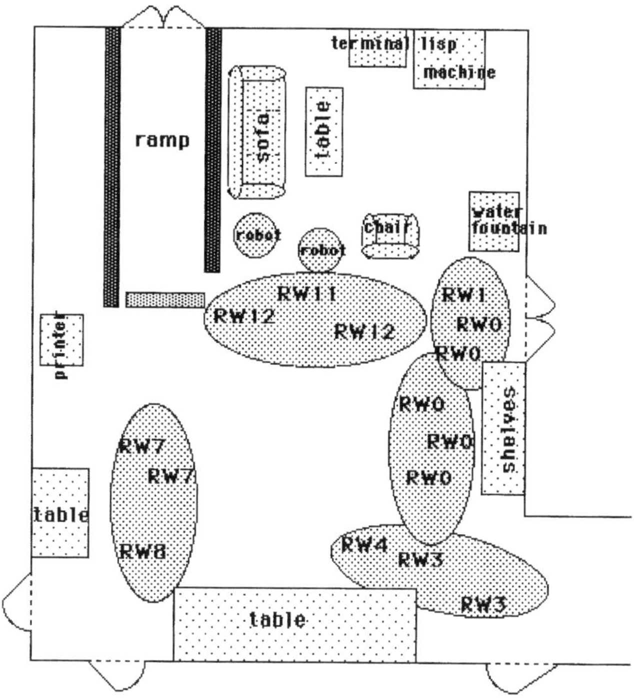

Fig. 5.6: The robot's landmark detection performance over three trials in the same room. Transient obstacles and people are not shown. Each landmark consists of the type and the associated compass bearing (e.g., RW0 = right wall north). The shown landmark locations correspond to the exact position of detection. The subscript indicates the trial. The locations corresponding to the same landmark are indicated by a common shaded area.

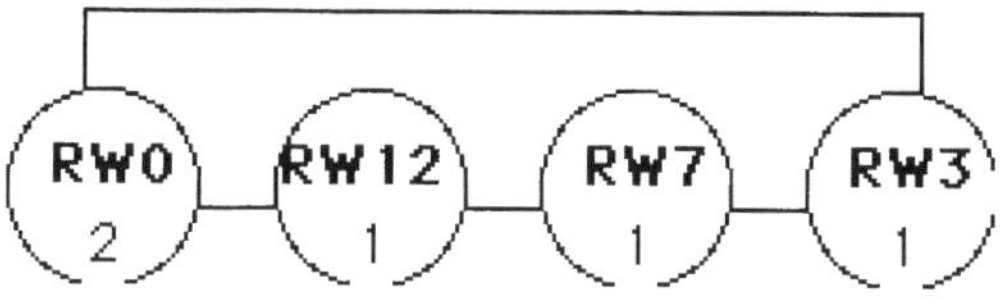

Fig. 5.7: The graph the robot produced in the environment shown in Fig. 7, in the second trial. The first trial produced (RW0, RW11, RW7, RW4), whereas the third trial produced (RW0, RW12, RW8, RW3); the three networks have correct, identical topology, and the difference in compass values falls within c's error margin. The nodes are ordered left to right by discovery time. Besides the landmark type and compass bearing, the figure also shows the relative landmark length.

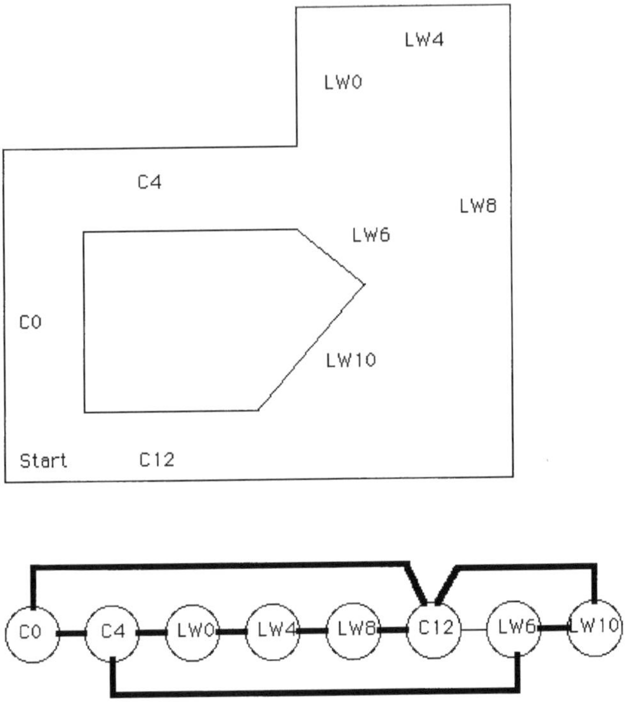

Fig. 5.8: An example of an environment containing multiple cycles on the robot's traversal path, and the graph the robot produced.

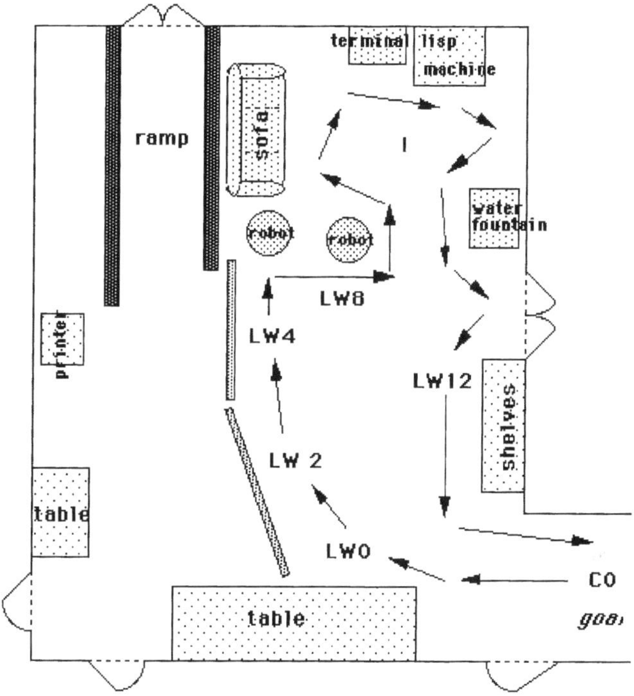

Fig. 5.9: In the shown environment, the robot records a cluttered area as a long irregular boundary (indicated by landmark type I).

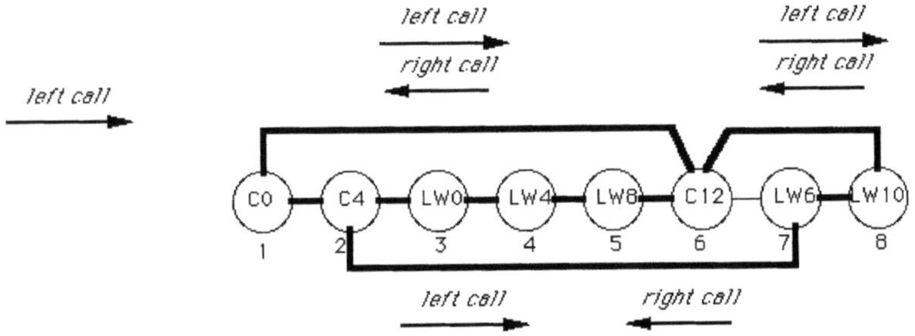

Fig. 5.10: The graph the robot constructed of the shown environment. Shaded nodes indicate the robot's current location and the goal, which the arrows indicate in the direction of activation propagation. To test the robot's ability to use the correct measure of optimality, the corridor was chosen as the goal when the robot was located at LW8. The topologically shortest path involves going through a cluttered area with a long irregular boundary. Consequently, the robot consistently chose the topologically longer but physically shortest path around the room.

6. Autonomy and Self-Sufficiency in Robots

DAVID McFARLAND
Balliol College

6.1 Introduction

The purposes of this chapter are to distinguish between autonomous and nonautonomous agents, and to seperate the concepts of autonomy and self-sufficiency. Looking at nature, we can easily see that some organisms are self-sufficient but not autonomous, such as plants and some primitive animals. Equally, we can see that some animals are autonomous but not self-sufficient. An example is the kind of overdomesticated lap dog that could not survive without the free meals provided by its owner.

In robotics it is entirely conceivable that there can be agents that are self-sufficient without being autonomous. Solar powered automatic weather stations are an example. Equally, we can conceive of robots that are autonomous (i.e., self-governing) without being self-sufficient, because they depend on an outside source of power. My purpose here is to define autonomous agents and then to examine some implications of self-sufficiency in robots.

6.2 Defining Autonomous Agents

In everyday usage, autonomy implies freedom from outside control or self-government. Agents capable of behaviour may be controlled entirely by outside agents. Such agents are not autonomous in the usual sense of the word. Once an agent has some degree of self-control, or self-government, then it has some freedom from outside control, and it has some autonomy.

An agent whose behaviour is entirely controlled by an outside agent has no will of its own, or self-government. In everyday usage, such agents are called *automata*, their actions being involuntary. Most present-day robots are automata.

6.2.1 The Agent as Automaton

Let us first consider the agent as an automaton. The freely mobile robot is in a similar situation to an animal, in that its state is influenced both by environmental conditions and by the robot's own behaviour. The robot does not have a physiology as such, but it has some equivalent state variables, such as fuel supply and operating temperature. For example, the robot will be designed to operate within certain upper and lower temperature limits, analogous to the tolerance limits of animals. At any particular time the robot will be operating at a particular temperature, the operating temperature, and it is probable that this will have little effect on performance over a wide range, the operating temperature range. The situation for animals is similar in principle.

The robot may or may not be equipped with devices for taking corrective action if the operating temperature comes close to the edge of the operating range. A robot designed to operate within a building might not require any such devices, but we can imagine that some robots are equipped with a fan that cuts in at a certain temperature threshold, or with a heater that comes on if the temperature drops too low. Such robots would be able to operate in a wider range of environments than those without any thermoregulatory devices. Similarly, we can imagine robots that take certain action when their fuel level becomes low, and even those that automatically refuel themselves. Thus we can begin to construct a robot state space similar to that proposed for animals [17].

In defining the state of a robot we are simply following standard practice in control systems theory [4] and automata theory [1, 2]. The state variables describe the state of the system and provide information that (together with a knowledge of the equations describing the system) enables us to calculate the future behaviour from a knowledge of the inputs or environmental stimuli. The n state variables provide the axes for an n-dimensional state space, within which the changing state of the system describes a trajectory—hence the term *state-space approach.*

When an automaton, whether animal or robot, is in a particular state it obeys a particular behavioural rule. Let us look, first, at an animal example. In his study of the digger wasp, *Ammophila compestris*, Baerends [3] found that the female, when about to lay an egg, digs a hole, kills or paralyses a moth caterpillar, carries it to the hole, deposits an egg on the caterpillar and stows it away in the hole. The female wasp then repeats this procedure with the second and subsequent eggs. Meanwhile, the first egg has hatched, and the larva has begun to consume the caterpillar. The wasp now returns to the first hole and provisions it with more caterpillars. She then may start another hole, or she may provision the second hole, depending on the circumstances. In this way the female wasp may maintain up to five nests simultaneously (see Fig. 6.1).

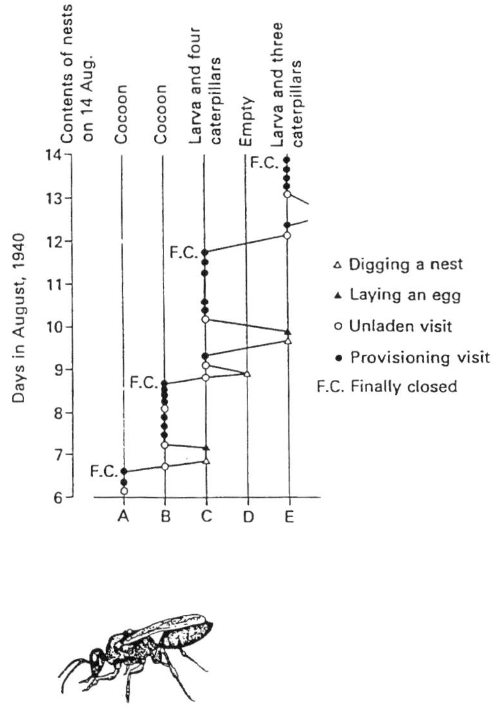

Fig. 6.1: Diagram of the nesting activities of an individual male *Ammophila* wasp.

Baerends found that the wasps inspect all the holes each morning before leaving for the hunting grounds. By robbing a hole he could make the wasp bring more food than usual, and by adding caterpillars he could induce her to bring less food than usual. However, he could manipulate the wasp in this way only if he made changes to the nest before the wasp's first visit of the day. Changes made later in the day had no effect. The female wasp seems to operate by simple rules. There is a standard routine for laying an egg, which involves digging a hole and providing a caterpillar. There is a standard early morning inspection routine that usually determines which nest will be provisioned during the day. There is a standard stopping routine by which the wasp closes up the nest when sufficient caterpillars have been supplied. Although the wasp is capable of assessing the extent of provisions when she visits a nest, she does not always use this ability. Moreover, each routine, once started, is followed to its conclusion. Thus, a wasp will go on and on provisioning a nest if the caterpillars are removed systematically each time they are supplied. This example shows that complex behaviour can be programmed on the basis of a set of rigid rules. The wasp behaves in an automatonlike way. The consequences of its behaviour that affect its state are consequences that are presumed by nature to be immutable.

Ethologists recognise that an animal in a particular state is likely to behave in a particular manner, and they have gone some way to define precisely what is meant by the state of an animal, and to represent the essential state variables in quantitative terms [17]. Some of these state variables may have to do with hormonal levels, others with perception of environmental cues, and others with memory of recently performed behaviour. The state variables in combination can be represented as a hyperspace of n dimensions. This will be divided up into regions (cells in a three-dimensional space, and patches in a two-dimensional space) according to the activity that is to be performed when the state of the animal falls within each region. In other words, although the animal may appear to have various options open at any given time, the activity that is performed is controlled entirely by the state of the animal. In this respect, the animal is like a physical system. It is an automaton.

The alternative is that the animal is not an automaton, but is some kind of autonomous agent. I would now like to spend some time discussing what this might mean.

6.2.2 Autonomous Agents

Autonomy implies freedom from control. In ordinary terms, "A controls B if and only if the relation between A and B is such that A can drive B into whichever of B's normal range of states A wants B to be in for something to be a controller its states must include desires—or something 'like' desires—-about the states of something (else)" ([7], p. 52).

Certain types of machines are controllable and others are not controllable. A controllable machine is one that can be made to behave as the controller wishes, provided the controller knows enough about the state of the machine. To completely control a machine, the controller would have to know the state of the machine, the environmental forces acting upon it, and the rules for translating state into behaviour. For example, a boy can control a toy car by radio if he knows enough about the state of the vehicle (that is, the essential state variables), the forces acting on the vehicle, such as gravity, friction, and so on, and the rules for translating this information into car behaviour. These rules must include not only how the controls work in general, but the detailed effects of manipulation of the controls on the behaviour of the car.

In addition, as Dennett [7] pointed out, to control a machine, the controller must want to make the machine behave in a particular way. In other words the controller must have some relevant motivation.

Autonomous agents are self-controlling as opposed to being under the control of an outside agent. To be self-controlling, the agent must have relevant self-knowledge and motivation, because these are the prerequisites of a controller. In other words, an autonomous agent must know what to do to exercise control and must want to exercise control in one way and not in another way.

The main differences between automata and autonomous systems are outlined in Fig. 6.2 (from [14]).

AUTOMATON	AUTONOMOUS AGENTS
follows rules	evaluates alternatives
to control must know the state and the rules	to control must know the state, the history and the evaluation criteria

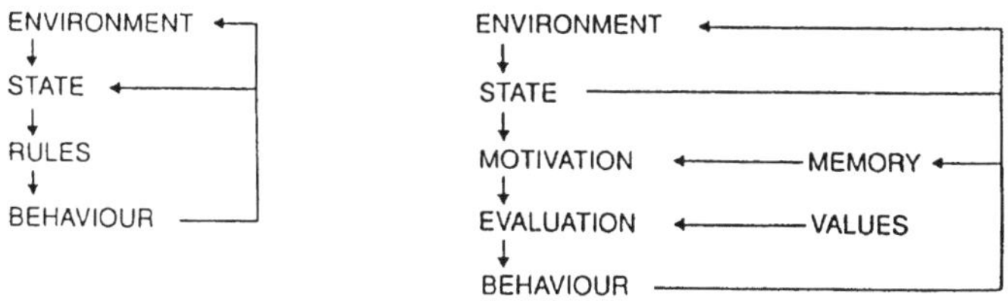

Fig. 6.2: Essential features of an automaton and an autonomous agent.

An important implication of autonomy is that the autonomous agent cannot be completely controlled by an outside agent. For example, we normally think of a dog as being autonomous in the sense that its behaviour is not readily controllable. Humans can control the behaviour of dogs to some extent, but the extent of this control depends partly on the animal's internal state and partly on its internal organisation or architecture. Thus, a man is usually more successful in influencing the behaviour of a dog than a cat, because the one is more amenable than the other. Dogs like to be cooperative, whereas cats do not. Autonomous robots, like dogs and cats, would be self-controlling and uncontrollable by outside agents.

The reason that an autonomous agent cannot be controlled by an outside agent is that the state of the autonomous agent is not completely observable. It is well known in systems theory that to be completely controllable an agent must be completely observable. Moreover, if an autonomous robot is not to be completely controllable and observable (and this is what we usually mean by autonomy) then an investigator's model of such a robot would not be minimal or unique. A model that contains no redundant elements is said to be minimal. A model that is the only one that can account for the data is said to be unique. Kalman [10] showed that a model is minimal if and only if it is completely controllable and completely observable. Moreover a minimal model is unique. Kalman's results apply only to linear systems, but they can be extended to nonlinear systems by making use of the close correspondence between dynamical systems theory, which Kalman used, and the theory of finite automata. Kalman [10] compared his theorems with Moore's results on automata [19], and Arbib [1, 2] investigated this relationship in considerable detail. The advantage of finite automata theory is that the question of linearity does not arise unless extra structure is added (i.e., unless the system switches between modes what have different structures; see also [17]).

In short, an investigator cannot expect to be able to produce a complete (minimal and unique) model of a robot whose internal workings are not completely observable, and for this reason he should not expect to be able to completely control the behaviour of such a robot.

The crucial question is - what is it about an autonomous system that makes it incompletely observable? Both automata and autonomous agents take decisions, in the objective sense of the term. That is, they switch from one type of behaviour to another, depending on the circumstances and on the decision criteria. It is these decision criteria that are the key to the argument.

6.2.3 Decision Criteria

Suppose we consider a committee set up to make an appointment to a university post. In stage 1 of this process the committee has to search for candidates. They have a breadth of search problem in that they cannot possibly hope to screen all the people in the world who might possibly be suitable. Often this problem is circumvented by advertising for applicants. But this is an essentially arbitrary procedure, because those likely to see the advertisement are a subsection of the potential pool of applicants. Sometimes a search committee is set up, using the grapevine or professional headhunters. Even here some arbitrary criterion for stopping the search is required. In AI it is widely recognised that the process of limiting the breadth of search is a matter of heuristics.

Stage 2 of the process is to reduce the list of candidates to a short list. Here again fairly arbitrary criteria are used. Those with no PhD, few publications, or those above a certain age may be rejected without further scrutiny.

Stage 3 of the process involves choice of one of the candidates on the short list. The choice must be based on certain criteria, such as teaching suitability and research potential, in the case of a university post. Suppose the committee arrives at an agreed short list of six candidates, which we refer to as a,b,c,d,e,f. Their task is to decide which is the best applicant taking both teaching and research into account. We assume that these abilities are independent and have to be assessed separately. A possible approach would be for the committee to arrive at an agreed rating of teaching ability for each candidate, scored on a 10-point scale. A separate 10-point rating would be agreed for research potential. Possible results of this dual exercise are shown in Fig. 6.3 (from [14]).

The question is which is the best applicant? This question cannot be answered without specifying some optimality criteria for combining teaching rating T and research rating R to give a single strength of canditature C. For example, if teaching and research were thought to be of equal importance, the (optimality) criterion might be additive, so that $C = R+T$. In this case candidate b would score $6+5 = 11$;$c = 3+8 = 11$; $f = 8+2 = 10$. So candidates b and c would be equal. In Fig. 6.3(a), lines joining points of equal candidature (called isoclines) appear as straight lines, which are characteristic of an additive optimality criterion. If research was thought to be more important than teaching, the optimality criterion might be $C = R + T/2$, in which case $b = 6 + 5/2 = 8.5$; $c = 3 + 8/2 = 7$; $f = 8 + 2/2 = 9$; and f emerges as the best candidate. Alteration of the weighting given to teaching and research changes the slope of the isoclines, as shown in Fig. 6.3(b). Alternatively, a multiplicative optimality criterion might be more suitable, so that $b = 6x5 = 30$; $c = 3x8 = 24$; and $f = 8x2 = 16$. Multiplicative criteria produce hyperbolic isoclines, as illustrated in Fig. 6.3(c).

All optimal decision making (in which the aim is to choose the best option) involves decision criteria of the type outlined here (see [6, 16]). We now have to ask what factors influence the optimality criteria. In the university context, factors such as government attitude and financial pressures are likely to determine policy concerning the balance between teaching and research. As far as the selection committee is concerned, these are ecological factors.

In the case of animal decision making, it is clear that natural selection will have had a hand in shaping the decision criteria. The mechanism of decision making is not the issue here. It may be that some animals make decisions by simply switching from one activity to another when certain criteria are met, as in an automaton; whereas other animals employ some process of evaluating alternatives. In both kinds of decision making the criteria are important. There is now quite a large literature on the

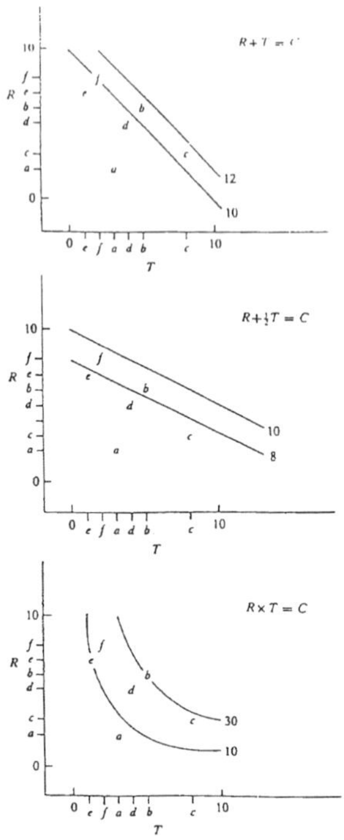

Fig. 6.3: Applicants for a university post are scored separately for estimated teaching (T) and research (R) ability. The scores obtained by applicants a, b, c, d, e, and f are shown as labeled points on the graph. Lines joining points of equal canditature (isoclines) are labeled according to the candidature value calculated on the basis of optimality criteria indicated in the inset formulae.

optimality criteria for animal behaviour (e.g., [17, 27]). In a nutshell, an animal maximises fitness if it deploys its behavioural options in a manner that optimises with respect to the cost function that is characteristic of its environment. In general, the cost function "specifies the instantaneous level of risk incurred by (and reproductive benefit available to) an animal in a particular internal state, engaged in a particular activity in a particular environment" [13].

6.2.4 Cost Functions

It is important to realise that the notion of optimising with respect to a cost function applies to an automaton as well as to an autonomous agent. It may be helpful at this point to spell out a particular example.

Let us now look at an example of a simple cost function that has received considerable attention from animal behaviourists.

Consider the two-dimensional quadratic cost function:

$$C(x) = Kx_1^2 + Lx_2^2 + Mu_1^2 + Nu_2^2 \tag{6.1}$$

where $C(x)$ is the instantaneous cost, x_1 and x_2 are state variables, u_1 and u_2 represent the rates of performing two activities, and K, L, M, and N are scaling parameters, which we will assume to have value one, for our present purposes. The behaviour of an automaton would conform to this cost function if it obeyed the following simple rule:

if $x_1 u_1 > x_2 u_2$ perform activity u_1 else perform activity u_2.

We will call this Rule B.

The effect of applying this rule can be seen in Fig. 6.4. In this figure, Rule B is contrasted with an even more simple rule (Rule A), which is to perform that activity for whichever x is larger. Fig. 6.4 shows that the two rules give different behaviour (shown here in terms of the reduction in x), and different cumulative costs, as calculated on the basis of the cost function. Rule B is less costly and comes close to the optimal solution for this problem [26].

Notice that it is possible for the rules governing behaviour to conform to some extremal or optimality principle, without there being any obvious sign of this in the formulation of the control system. Of course, the cost function could be explicitly represented, as would be necessary in a planning system. In fact, it is worth considering this approach.

6.2.5 Planning

Planning is the generation of a sequence of activities, designed to achieve a particular end, without performing the activities. Basically, a planned sequence of activities is generated by (a) reviewing alternatives, and (b) drawing up a short list of feasible possibilities. These possibilities are then assessed in terms of the particular end that the planning system is designed to achieve.

Let us analyse this possibility a little further. The first stage of planning is to review the alternatives, but how many? In AI terminology, this is the breadth of search problem. For example, there are 792 somatic muscles in the human body. In theory, because these are supposed to be voluntary muscles, one could decide to contract any one of them, or any combination of them. Does this mean that, in planning what movement to make next, one must review 792 alternatives? This is obviously computationally impossible. The breadth of search must somehow be limited.

One possibility is that it is limited by motivational state. The agent simply does not consider those alternatives that have no current motivational relevance. In other words, the planning system comes up with a short list of behaviour candidates, not as a result of exhaustive search, but as a result of motivational filtering [15].

The second stage of planning is to evaluate the consequences of performing each of the candidate activities. This review of the consequences must be based upon knowledge of the probable outcomes, and the results of the review must be stored. This aspect of planning requires some form of cognitive evaluation. It is cognitive because some of the knowledge manipulated in the review is declarative knowledge. For example, I know that the likely consequence of pushing this switch is that the picture on my word-processor screen will change.

The third stage of planning is to decide among the evaluated alternatives on the basis of some criterion. There are many ways in which such a decision may be made (see [20] for a discussion). For an intelligent agent to be well adapted, the decision-making mechanisms must be related to some optimality criterion such as fitness or utility. This means that the decision-making mechanism must be able to refer to some representation of the cost function.

In summary, we can identify the tasks that have to be accomplished by an autonomous robot using a planning approach: (a) review the options and reduce them to a manageable number of candidates, (b) estimate the consequences of the alternative activities, (c) assign utility to the consequences, and (d) choose the candidate whose consequences yield the highest expected utility. We tend to view these operations as a sequence, but this does not necessarily mean that they are performed in sequence. It may be that they occur in parallel.

We can apply the planning approach to the situation outlined in Fig. 6.4 (from [14]). Instead of using a rule of thumb, we use a planning approach, as outlined in Fig. 6.5. If we plan one step ahead (PLAN1), then we simply ask what next activity will result in the lower cost as calculated from the cost function. In planning two steps ahead (PLAN2) we ask which subsequent activity yields the lower cost. We simply follow through this procedure, using the numbers in our original example, and calculate the cumulative cost, step by step. What we find is that the simple planning approach to the problem gives a very similar cost profile to Rule B, as illustrated in Fig. 6.4.

Note that both the rule-following automaton and the planning system have identical associated cost functions. In the case of the automaton it is embedded in the structure. In the case of a planning system it is explicitly represented and referred to in the course of the planning process.

6.2.6 Conclusions

The inner workings of an automaton are observable in principle and could be investigated by various types of black box analysis. The cost function is not observable, because there is a uniqueness problem (see [17], p. 160). We

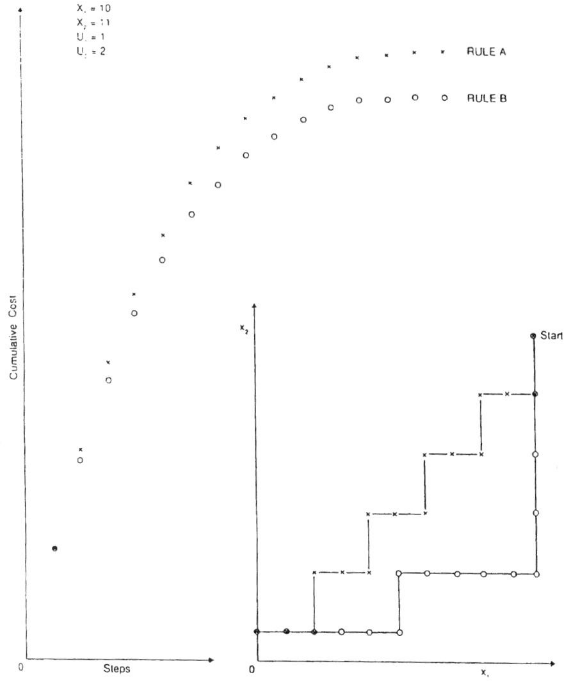

Fig. 6.4: The cumulative effect of following rules (large graph) and the changes of state that result (small graph).

cannot infer cost functions from behaviour, because there will be more than one cost function that could give rise to the same behaviour. Nevertheless, as we can discover the mechanisms responsible for the behaviour of an automaton, we can use this knowledge to control its behaviour.

The inner workings of an autonomous system are not observable in principle, because they make reference to a cost function representation that is just as inaccessible to us as it is in the case of an automaton. Moreover, even if we built an autonomous system so that it was initially observable, we could not keep track of its inner workings once it had become autonomous. Many of its decisions would depend, not only on the cost function, but also on the personal history of the agent.

An autonomous system is self-controlling. It has the knowledge and the motivation to control its own behaviour. Its behaviour cannot be controlled by an outside agent, because the outside agent cannot obtain the necessary knowledge. This knowledge cannot be obtained, because the inner workings of the autonomous agent are in principle unobservable. They are unobservable because they depend on a representation of a cost func-

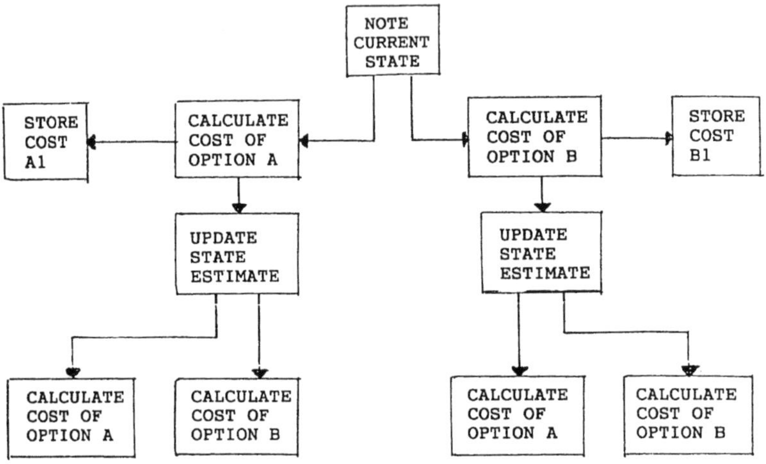

Fig. 6.5: Simple planning procedure based upon cost criteria.

tion that cannot be uniquely specified from behaviour. They may also be unobservable because they change as a result of the personal history of the agent.

The problem in designing autonomous robots is to deploy a compromise between decision making by rules and decision making by cognition. Because there will be many dimensions involved, it may be possible to rely on rules in some situations and planning in others. Therefore we need to think about autonomy in a multidimensional context.

6.3 Self-Sufficiency in Robots

For a robot to be self-sufficient it must maintain itself in a viable state for long periods of time. To do this it must be able to replenish its energy source in a way that is not directly dependent on human intervention.

Indirect dependence on humans is another matter. It will often be the case that a robot is designed for a particular environment or niche in which indirect dependence on manmade energy sources is inevitable. In this respect, robots are not in principle different from animals. Many animals are dependent on special sources of energy that are characteristic of their ecological niche.

To replenish its energy source independently of human intervention the agent must have some appropriate behaviour. The form of the behaviour will depend on the type of energy source. Thus a robot may be able to go to a nest to recharge batteries, or it may seek sources of light or heat to activate specialised energy-gathering apparatus, such as solar cells.

The behaviour by which a robot obtains its energy itself expends energy and uses time that the robot might otherwise use for other purposes. Obviously, if refueling took all the robot's time and energy, the robot would have no time or energy for other purposes, and we have to ask how much this would matter. Thus the issues involved in self-sufficiency affect the whole design concept and viability of the robot. Essentially, this is an issue about the consequences of robot behaviour.

6.3.1 The Consequences of Robot Behaviour

The consequences of behaviour are of three main types: (a) those that alter the state of the robot itself, (b) those that alter the robots environment, and (c) those that are irrelevant. For example, it may or may not be irrelevant that the robot casts a shadow. We are here primarily concerned with the first condition, although the second condition may be important in considering the design purposes of the robot.

The consequences of behaviour, insofar as they affect the robot's state, can be represented in a state space, in which the state of the robot is portrayed as a point. As a consequence of the robot's behaviour, the state changes, and so the point describes a trajectory in the space. On a two-dimensional page it is possible to portray the trajectory in only a single plane of the space, but we can imagine that the changing state describes an equivalent trajectory in a multidimensional space. The state changes continually, both as a result of the robot's own behaviour and as a result of outside influences. The advantage of this type of representation is that it enables us to portray very complex changes in state in a relatively simple manner.

The freely mobile robot is in a similar situation to an animal, in that its state is influenced both by environmental conditions and by the robot's own behaviour. The robot does not have a physiology as such, but it has some equivalent state variables, such as fuel supply and operating temperature. For example, the robot will be designed to operate within certain upper and lower temperature limits, analogous to the tolerance limits of animals. At any particular time the robot will be operating at a particular temperature, the operating temperature, and it is probable that this will have little effect on performance over a wide range, the operating temperature range. The situation for animals is similar in principle, as illustrated in Fig. 6.6.

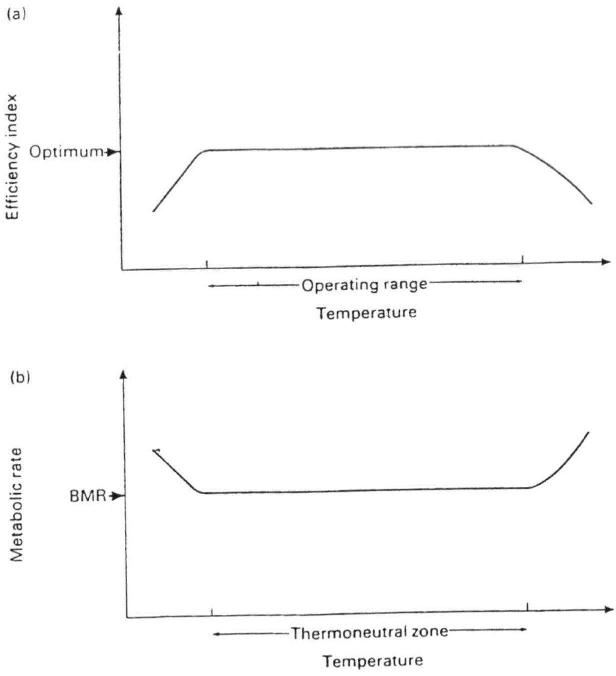

Fig. 6.6: Comparison of robot (a) and mammal (b) body temperature, and its behaviourial consequences.

The robot may or not be equipped with devices for taking corrective action if the operating temperature comes close to the edge of the operating range. A robot designed to operate within a building might not require any such devices, but we can imagine that some robots are equipped with a fan that cuts in at a certain temperature threshold, or with a heater that comes on if the temperature drops too low. Such robots would be able to operate in a wider range of environments than those without any thermoregulatory devices. Similarly, we can imagine robots that take certain action when their fuel level becomes low, and even those that automatically refuel themselves. Thus we can begin to construct a robot state space.

Robots designed to carry out a particular task, such as laying bricks, would probably be designed to monitor other state variables pertaining to the task. Thus a brick laying robot should keep track of the amounts of bricks and mortar available, and of the number of bricks laid, as shown in Fig. 6.7. It is worth noting that one axis in this figure is based upon the robot's perception (i.e., a cue-state variable), whereas the other is based upon memory.

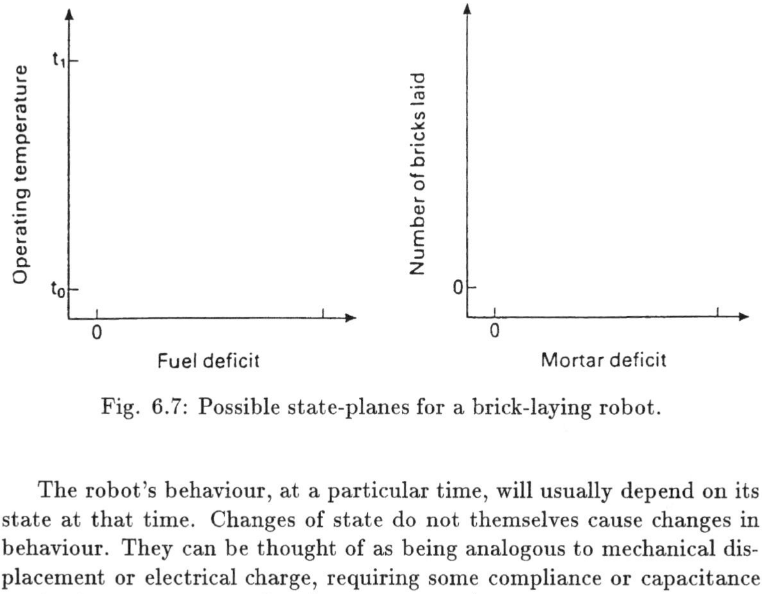

Fig. 6.7: Possible state-planes for a brick-laying robot.

The robot's behaviour, at a particular time, will usually depend on its state at that time. Changes of state do not themselves cause changes in behaviour. They can be thought of as being analogous to mechanical displacement or electrical charge, requiring some compliance or capacitance mechanisms to exert an effort (force or voltage) on the mechanisms responsible for behaviour [12]. In the case of animal behaviour, the displacements in physiological state have to be monitored by sensors that relay nervous messages to the brain. For example, the osmosity of the blood is monitored by osmoreceptors in the hypothalamus. In the case of robots, there will presumably be equivalent sensory devices for the fuel deficit, operating temperature, and so on. It is important to recognise that there are two stages in this monitoring process, as illustrated in Fig. 6.8. The first involves monitoring the state-variables with appropriate sensors, and the second involves some sort of calibration of the monitored message. Obviously, the same monitored displacement in state will have different significance for different robots. Morover, decisions have to be made among various different displacements in state, all monitored by different kinds of sensors. Clearly, these parallel messages must all be calibrated in terms of their significance, or importance, to the robot making the decisions.

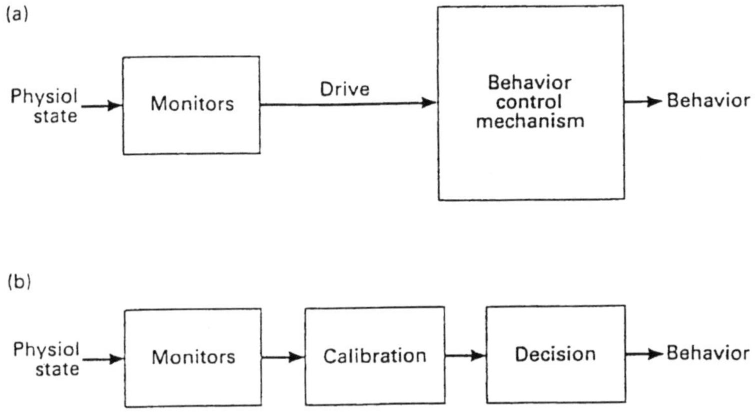

Fig. 6.8: How monitored physiological state affects behaviour: (a) the traditional view, (b) the decision-theory view.

One way to achieve such calibration is to overlay the state space with a cost (or fitness) landscape. This is derived from the cost function (see earlier) that is characteristic of the robot niche. Isoclines (or contour lines) in the cost landscape join points of equal cost. An everyday example may help to illustrate this.

Let us consider a motorist on a long journey, keeping an eye on the fuel gauge. At what point (on the fuel gauge) should the motorist stop for fuel? To answer this question we need to know the risk of running out of fuel as a function of the position of the fuel gauge. In other words, we need to know cost as a function of state. This largely depends on the ecology of the situation, the distribution of petrol stations in particular. If there were a petrol station every 10 km, then the motorist could allow the fuel to deplete until there were just 10 km worth of fuel left (a simple threshold policy). If, on the other hand the stations were normally distributed, then the risk (of running out of fuel) would increase as the square of the depletion (for the reasons given in [16]), and if the distribution conformed to some other function, then the risk function would also be different. The evaluation of the risk function by the motorist would depend on various factors, such as the seriousness of running out of petrol in terms of lost time, extra expense, and so on. In other words, much would depend on whether the motorist was risk averse or risk prone. Thus the function employed by the motorist in decision making would depend partly on the ecology of the situation (as appreciated by the motorist) and partly on various aspects of the motorist's makeup and internal state.

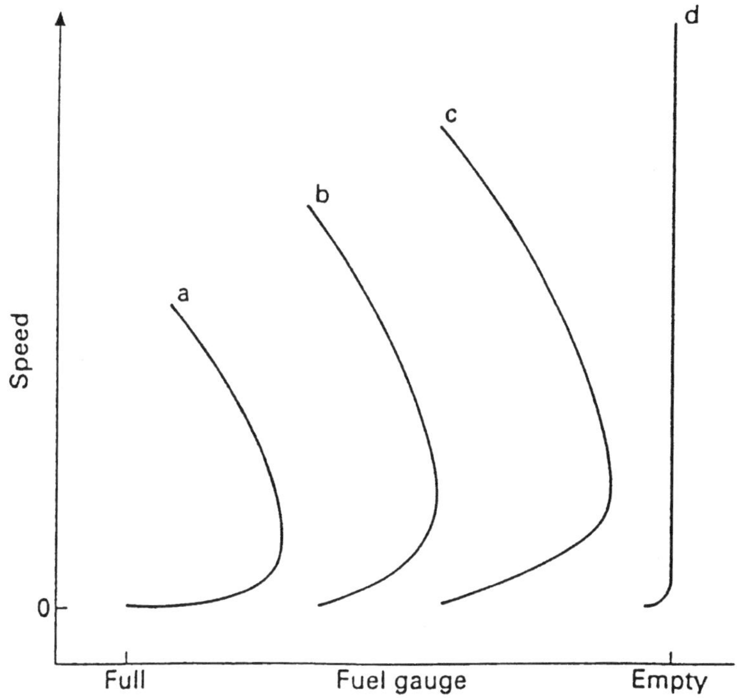

Fig. 6.9: Trade-off between speed and fuel supply for a motorist. The isoclines a, b, c, and d are for increasing distance.

Another important factor is the fact that petrol consumption varies with speed. Fig. 6.9 shows the distances that can be covered as a function of speed and fuel supply. The exact shape of the functions will vary with the make of car, but usually there is a particular (cruising) speed at which the rate of fuel consumption per distance covered is minimal. If there is an urgency factor (desired journey time), then the motorist will want to drive as fast as possible (ignoring safety considerations for the moment), provided there is sufficient fuel. When fuel supply is low, the motorist has to sacrifice speed in the interests of economy, as shown in Fig. 6.10. In other words, in deciding at what speed to drive, there is a continual trade-off amongst various variables. Fig. 6.10. is, in effect, a cost landscape because a point on the surface represents the cost of each behaviour (driving speed), in terms of fuel availability and time deadline.

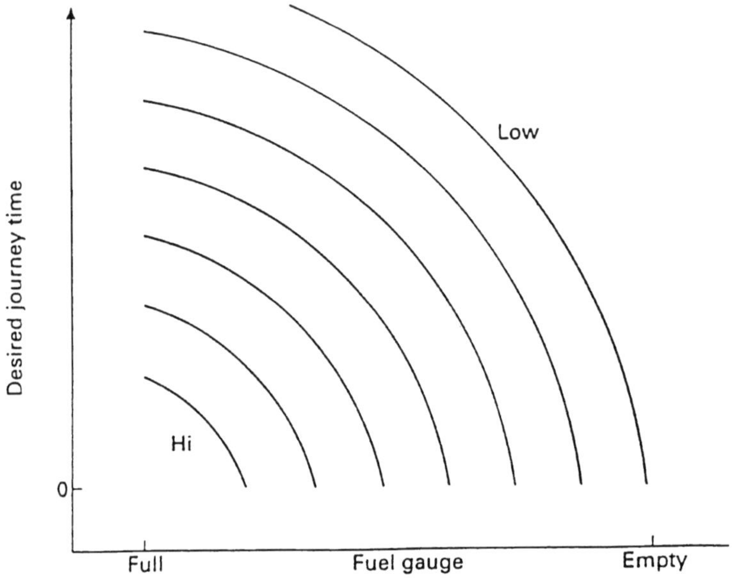

Fig. 6.10: Trade-off between journey time and fuel supply for a motorist. The isoclines are for speed of travel.

6.3.2 Stability

A fundamental notion of any system that has physical embodiment is that of stability. In general a system is stable if, for a bounded input, the output is bounded. In terms of the state-space representation, a system is stable if, for a bounded input, the state vector of the system is bounded. Systems with state vector $bf\ x$, which may be reduced to the form

$$dbfx/dt = f(bfx) \tag{6.2}$$

are suitable for the application of Liapunov's direct method of stability analysis. Because the systems in which we are interested can be reduced to this general form, the Liaponov method is the most appropriate general approach to stability.

The Russian mathematician Liaponov developed two methods of stability analysis. The first of these methods involved an approximation and considered stability only in the vicinity of the origin of the state space. The second, or direct method, which appeared in Liapunov's doctoral thesis in 1892 and was published much later [11], did not have these restrictions. It provided the necessary and sufficient conditions for the asymptotic stability of linear systems and sufficient conditions for the asymptotic stability of nonlinear systems. Until recently, the main difficulty encountered in applying Liapunov's direct method has been that no means were available for generating the correct Liapunov function for solving a given stability problem. Many of these difficulties have now been overcome, and there is now an extensive literature that allows the designer to apply Liapunov's direct method in a systematic way (see [4, 5, 21, 22, 23], for a general introduction).

When a system is displaced from an equilibrium state it may return to that state, or to some other equilibrium state, following a transient period. In such cases the system is said to be asymptotically stable. An alternative is that the disturbed system may enter a limit cycle, continually oscillating around a closed trajectory. Such a system is globally stable provided it periodically returns to a particular state.

These stability ideas can be applied to the design of robots. Let us assume that it is unacceptable for the robot to run out of fuel. To violate this obligatory criterion is the equivalent of death. This means that there is a lethal limit on one of the major state variables, as illustrated in Fig. 6.11.

Let us also assume that, the robot is designed to do certain jobs and that it is unacceptable for the robot to fall behind schedule. The customer will not expect the robot to keep entirely up to schedule, but the customer will expect the progress with tasks to stabilise at some level. In other words, the customer expects some kind of asymptotic stability, in which the trajectory tends toward the origin, as shown in Fig. 6.11. On this basis we can say that, in terms of the rate of change of state, there is a hard and fast obligatory criterion. Of course, the extent to which a given robot in a given situation can cope with this stability criterion will depend to some extent on the demands of the environment. There may be some environments in which the situation deteriorates so quickly that the robot can never keep up. An equivalent situation exists in animal behaviour, because the animal must be able to adapt to the physiological exigencies imposed by the environment [25].

In general terms, the state of a system stays within a particular region as a result of various interacting processes, the consequences of which can be represented as vectors in an adaptation space, such as that shown in Fig. 6.12 after [25]. In this space vectors representing processes that tend to change the state of the system can often be combined into a single resultant

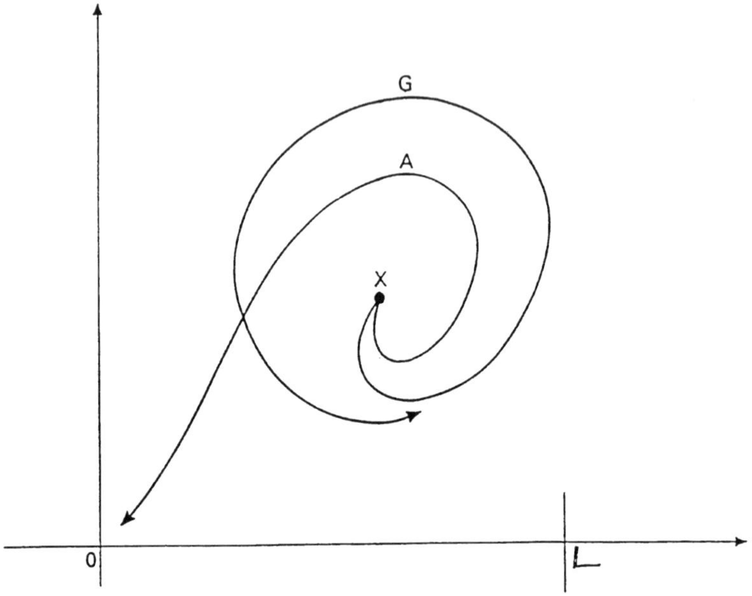

Fig. 6.11: Globally stable (G) and asymptotically stable (A) trajectories. L marks a lethal boundary.

vector, called the drift vector, representing the rate of change of state due to these processes. The drift vector $\dot{z}\_d$ is opposed by an adaptation vector $\dot{z}\_A$, which represents the combined effect of the various processes designed to counteract the drift. If the drift becomes so strong that the adaptation processes are unable to restrain it, then the system becomes unstable (see the Adaptation Theorem of [25]).

It is important to realise the rates of drift and adaptation that are important. Fig. 6.13 (from a simulation by McFarland & Bosser [16]) shows how a robot could reduce an initial debt in a three-dimensional system (i.e., a system with three state variables, W, B and F). This figure shows asymptotic stability, the trajectory homing in toward the origin. However, the situation may not be so stable if the rates of increase of these state variables are much higher (technically called the rate of drift, i.e., the rate at which the state moves away from the origin as a result of energy expenditure and environmental forces). Suppose, for example, that an environmental variable changed much more quickly than implied in Fig. 6.13. At some point the robot will be unable to keep up with the situation. (See Fig. 6.14

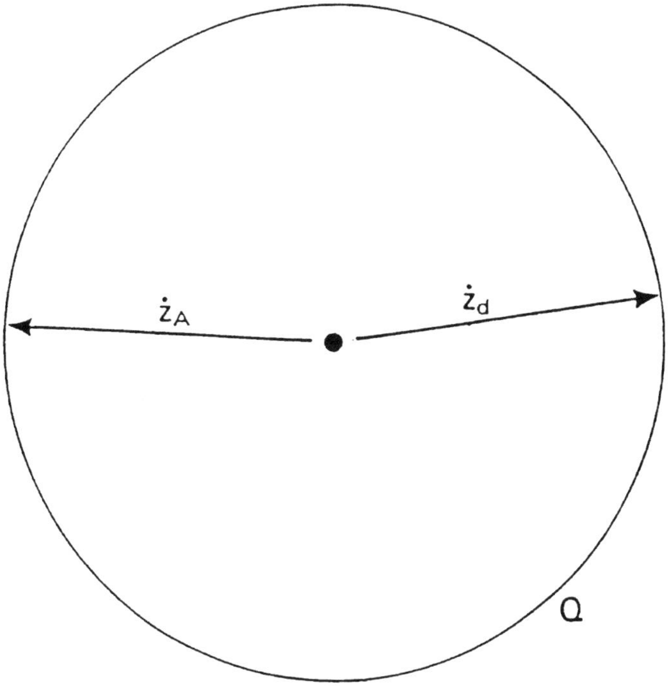

Fig. 6.12: Adaptation space Q, defined in terms of limiting velocity vectors. A rate of drift is opposed by a rate of adaptation. When the drift is greater than the limit set by Q, the adaptation is no longer adequate and the animal will die in the near future.

from a simulation in [16]). For example, we can see the trajectory that would result if variable W changed at double the rate implied in Fig. 6.8 (based on values from a simulation by [16]). Here the trajectory is not asymptotically stable, because it comes back almost to its starting point. It may be globally stable (as in Fig. 6.12, repeating the same cycle over and over), but it is probably on the verge of being unstable.

Suppose we have determined that the robot will become unstable if B 100 and dW/dt 2.0. What about the other consequences of behaviour? Obviously we can apply similar thinking to the rates of change of other variables. There must also be values of these variables at which the robot becomes unstable because it is unable to keep up with the accumulating workload.

Ultimately the workload depends on the requirements of the customer. Suppose we are designing a robot to be marketed by one or more robot retailing companies. These companies are our customers. The customers de-

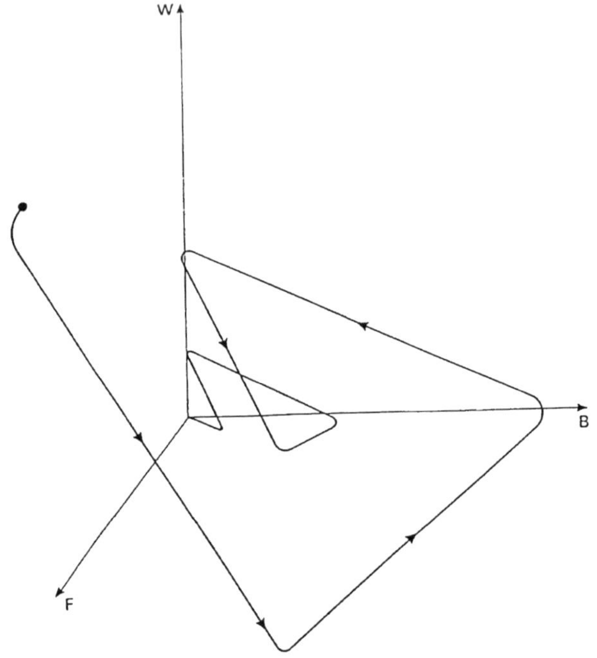

Fig. 6.13: Asymptotically stable trajectory resulting from reduction of a high initial debt.

cide whether or not a particular product is likely to sell well in a particular marketplace. The equivalent situation in nature is the selective pressures that are characteristic of a particular ecological niche. Effectively, these "decide" what design criteria are relevant in the prevailing environment. Similarly, customers will buy our robot only if it satisfies certain design criteria.

In other words, in designing a robot for the marketplace we must first determine the minimal relevant acceptance criteria. We assume that the robot has to find a niche in the marketplace, and that it can do this only if certain basic criteria are met. What are these criteria? So far, we have assumed only the most parsimonious obligatory criteria—that is, those criteria we can be sure every customer will accept. Basically, we have assumed that every customer will want the robot to be, at least, asymptotically stable (see earlier). At this later stage of the design process we can take account of customers' whims, by imposing facultative criteria.

Thus a particular variable may have little direct relevance to stability, but may have high priority for other reasons. The situation here is

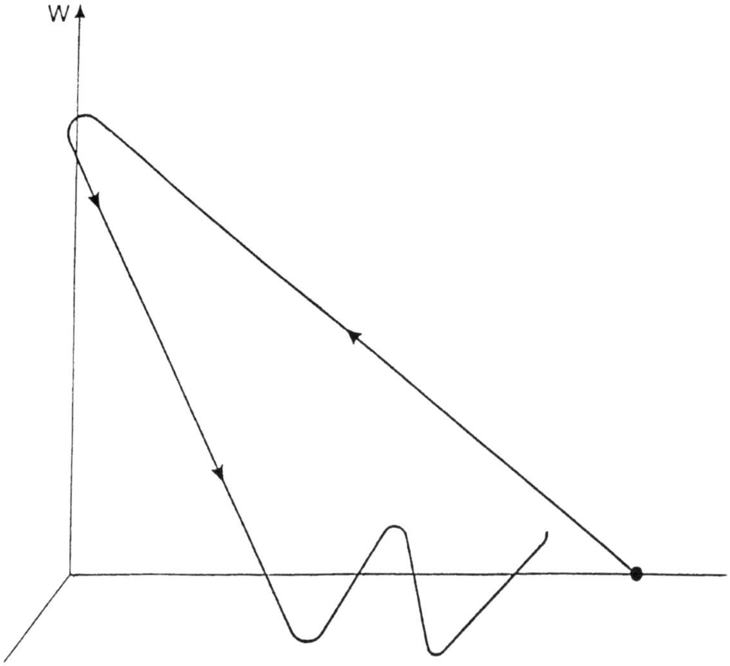

Fig. 6.14: Globally stable trajectory resulting from low initial debt but high drift.

similar to that of animals. Factors directly relevant to survival, such as physiological regulation and predator avoidance, have high priority. These are effectively the stability criteria. But there is another factor, which has little relevance to survival, but nevertheless has high priority, and that is reproduction. To maximise lifetime reproductive success, animals should adopt a life history strategy that maximises a joint function of individual survival and reproductive potential [8, 18, 24]. The animal must survive to reproduce, but there is little point in struggling to survive when reproductive potential is zero. Similarly, the robot must be stable to carry out those tasks that the customer requires, but there is little point in attempting to maintain stability at the expense of those tasks.

6.3.3 Behavioural Resilience

To be stable and self-sufficient the robot should neglect no important behaviour. The question that arises is whether the robot has sufficient time to do all those activities that are important. In some animals we can expect behavior that has the prime function of promoting the survival of the individual over behavior that promotes other aspects of fitness, such as territorial mating and parental behavior. However, species vary in this respect. Some aspects of behavior are essential, but others like thermoregulatory behavior may be important only when physiological mechanisms cannot cope. Thus, drinking is a daily necessity for some species, but other species can manage without drinking at all. Each activity has value in terms of fitness, and animals must be designed to allocate priorities to activities in a general way, as well as from minute to minute.

We can approach the problem by considering a measure of the cost to the animal, or robot, of abstaining from each activity in its natural repertoire [9]. If an animal did no feeding, for instance, the cost would be high, but if it abstained from grooming the cost might be relatively low. An animal that had a high tendency to both feed and groom but did not have time to do both would sacrifice less, in terms of fitness, if it devoted its available time to feeding.

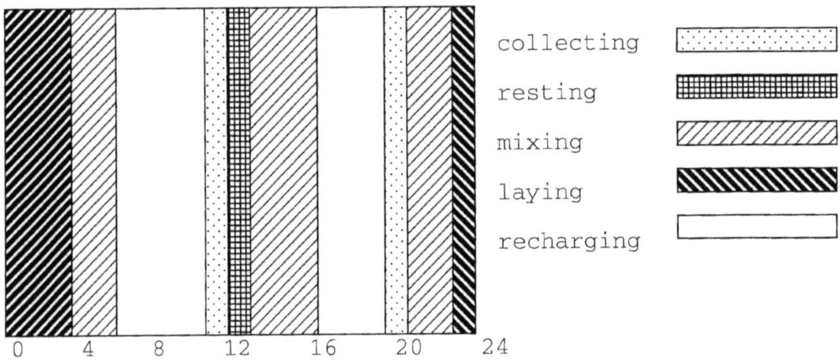

Fig. 6.15: Diagram showing how a self-sufficient robot might spend its time throughout the day.

Suppose a self-sufficient robot fills its typical day with useful activities, as illustrated in Fig. 6.15. In an environment that was much the same from day to day, the robot would adjust its activities to the time available. Suppose, however, there is a change in the environment such that it now takes very much longer to recharge the batteries. The robot can respond to the changed circumstances by spending the same amount of time recharging as before and settling for less charge. Alternatively, it could insist on the same charge as usual, or it could compromise between the two extremes. If the animal spent a longer time obtaining the usual charge, then there would be less time available for all the other activities in its repertoire. These would have to be squashed into the remaining time. The extent to which an activity resists squashing can be represented by a single parameter called *resilience.*

In the case where the robot recharges for the normal amount of time and ends up with a reduced charge (see Fig. 6.15), the resilience of recharging is relatively low because it has not compressed the other activities even though the robot's need for energy is increased. In the case where the robot insists on the normal charge (see Fig. 6.16), the resilience of recharging is relatively high because it ousts the other activities from the time available without itself being curtailed in any way.

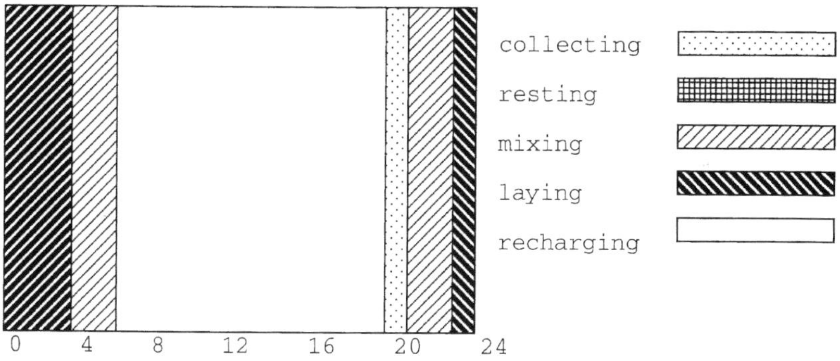

Fig. 6.16: Diagram showing how the robot in the previous figure might adjust its daily routing when required to spend much more time recharging.

Behavioral resilience is a measure of the extent to which each activity can be squashed in terms of time by other activities in the agent's repertoire. It also reflects the importance of an activity in a long-term sense. During periods when time is a budget constraint, activities with low resilience will tend to be ignored. Indeed, if an activity completely disappears from an agent's repertoire when time is rationed, we might call it a luxury or leisure activity.

Mathematically, resilience is closely related to the weighting factors of the cost function and to the economic notion of elasticity of demand (see [17]).

References

[1] Arbib, M. A. (1966). Automata theory and control theory—A rapprochement. *Automatica, 3*, 161–189.

[2] Arbib, M. A. (1969). Automata theory. In R. E. Kalman, P. L. Falb, & M. A. Arbib (Eds.). *Topics in mathematical system theory* (pp. 163–233). New York: McGraw-Hill.

[3] Baerends, G. P. (1941). Fortpflanzungsverhalten und Orientierung der Grabwespe Ammophilia campestris. *Jur. Tijdschr Ent., 84*, 68–275.

[4] Barnett, S., & Cameron, R. G. (1985). *Introduction to mathematical control theory.* (2nd ed.) Oxford: Clarendon Press.

[5] Bell, D. (1969). Liapunov's direct method in nonlinear control systems analysis. In D. Bell & A. Griffin (Eds.). Modern control theory. London: McGraw-Hill.

[6] Bunn, D. (1982). Analysis for optimal decisions. New York: Wiley.

[7] Dennett, D. C. (1984). *Elbow room.* Oxford: Oxford University Press.

[8] Freeman, S., & McFarland, D. (1982). The Darwinian objective function and adaptive behaviour. In D. McFarland (Ed.), Functional ontogeny. London: Pitman.

[9] Houston, A., & McFarland, D. (1980). Behavioural resilience and its relation to demand functions. In J. Staddon (Ed.), *Limits to action: The allocation of individual behaviour* (pp. 177–203). New York: Academic Press.

[10] Kalman, R. E. (1963). Mathematical description of linear dynamical systems. *J.S.I.A.M. Control, series A, 1*, 152–192.

[11] Liapunov, A. M. (1907). Probleme general de la stabilité du movement. *Ann.ac. Sci. Toulouse, 9*, 203–474.

[12] McFarland, D. J. (1971). *Feedback mechanisms in animal behaviour.* London: Academic Press.

[13] McFarland, D. (1977). Decision-making in animals. *Nature, 269*, 15–21.

[14] McFarland, D. (1991). Defining motivation and cognition in animals. *International Studies in the Philosophy of Science, 5*,

[15] McFarland, D. (1992). Animals as cost-based robots. *International Studies in the Philosophy of Science, 6*, 133–153.

[16] McFarland, D. & Bösser (1993). *Intelligent behaviour in animal and robots.* Cambridge, MA: MIT Press.

[17] McFarland, D., & Houston, A. (1981). *Quantitative ethology: The state-space approach.* London: Pitman.

[18] McNamara, J. M., & Houston, A. I. (1986). The common currency of behavioural decisions. *American Naturalist, 127*, 358–378.

[19] Moore, E. F. (1956). Gedanken-experiments on sequential machines. In C. E. Shannon & J. McCarthy (Eds.). *Automata studies* (pp. 129-153). Princeton, NJ: Princeton University Press.

[20] Rachlin, H. (1989). *Judgment, decision and choice.* New York: Freeman.

[21] Riggs, D. S. (1970). *Control theory and physiological feedback mechanisms.* Baltimore: Williams & Wilkins.

[22] Rouche, N., Habets, P., & Laloy, M. (1977). *Stability theory by Liapunov's direct method.* New York: Springer-Verlag.

[23] Schultz, D. G. (1965). *Advances in control systems (Vol. 2).* London: Academic Press.

[24] Sibly, R. M. (1989). What evolution maximises. *Functional Ecology, 3*, 129–135.

[25] Sibly, R. M., & McFarland, D. J. (1974). A state-space approach to motivation. In D. J. McFarland (Ed.), *Motivational control systems analysis* (pp. 213–250). London: Academic Press.

[26] Sibly, R. M., & McFarland, D. J. (1976). On the fitness of behaviour sequences. *American Naturalist, 110*, 601–617.

[27] Stephens, D. W., & Krebs, J. R. (1986). *Foraging theory.* Princeton, NJ: Princeton University Press.

Part III

Position Papers

7. Autonomous Robots: A Question of Design?

JOHN HALLAM
University of Edinburgh

7.1 Introduction

"Robotics is the intelligent connection of perception to action." This characterisation opens the Proceedings of the First International Symposium on Robotics Research, edited by Brady and Paul [1]. It is interesting in that it characterises the field of robotics without attempting to define the term *robot* itself; it covers all the mainstream work with both mobile and assembly robots as well as a number of unusual limiting cases. It also suggests, as was the almost universal view at the time but is now controversial, that intelligence, perception, and action are in some way separable into distinct functional components of the system.

Robotics is a young field of study in which dreams abound; perhaps, though, the most universal of these, both inside the field and out, is that of the autonomous general-purpose robot, able to perform competently in a variety of situations without the need for reprogramming or extensive supervision. This dream is of both commercial and scientific import: Successful, versatile, inexpensive robotic systems would have a tremendous economic and social impact, making it possible to relieve people of dangerous, physically demanding, or monotonous jobs (and, of course, creating the problem of what those people would then do); equally, the construction of such a robot would give and require considerable insight into how the many different kinds of natural creatures are uniquely suited to their own environmental niches, by teaching us about the relationships between environment, agents, behaviour, and tasks.

The aim of this chapter is to consider the possibility of achieving autonomy in a robotic system, the ability to function competently over an extended period without (or, perhaps, *despite*) human intervention. We focus on the scientific and engineering prerequisites and consequences of this aim, leaving aside, for the most part, the important social, economic, and philosophical consequences. We choose to begin with Brady and Paul's neat characterisation because it encapsulates both the dream of autonomous robots and the essential ingredients for its practical realisation.

7.2 Robots as Artifacts

One of the interesting features of modern robotics, particularly in relation to autonomy, is a tendency to view the problem of constructing a competent autonomous robotic system as one of performance. A robot is autonomous when it is able to, and does, take responsibility for the consequences of its own action when there is no interventionist rescuer available to fix the problems it manages to create for itself. The robot is thus faced with a multiplicity of possible situations it may encounter and a collection of possible responses to those situations. The problem of autonomy is has to do, then, with choosing appropriate sensory and action patterns—effectively a question of the performance of the robot in response to the challenges offered by its environment.

If this were the whole story, autonomous robotic systems might in fact be constructed in the near future. However, the reasonableness of the performance viewpoint disguises the essential difficulty with autonomous robotics: The robots are artifacts, and artifacts must be *designed.* The central questions of designing a system capable of interacting with its environment without recourse to rescue remain to be answered. Without the basic design rules—and design rules imply a well-understood technology and methodology—it is impossible to answer in prospect rather than in retrospect the key question of whether a particular robot design will meet the requirements of a given task in a given environment for any situation of interesting complexity.

Of course, this does not mean that we cannot build robotic systems, only that we run the risk of being surprised by their performance when (if) they reach production. The current state of knowledge, vis à vis autonomous robotic systems, is rather like that obtained during the early years of cathedral construction: The empirical design rules for the towering Gothic buildings were inferred in the course of several centuries of success and failure, and their design was an intuitive insight on the part of the architects involved until a theoretical analysis of stone structures eventually became possible. Nevertheless, numbers of beautiful (and enduring) buildings were successfully built.

In the remainder of this contribution we explore one of the problems that besets designers of autonomous robotic systems using a research project currently in progress at Edinburgh as a pointer to what might eventually be possible.

7.3 Intelligence as Orchestrated Activity

At the time of their writing, Brady and Winston [1] declined to give a definition of intelligence to supplement their characterisation of robotics, saying, "Unfortunately, a definition of intelligence seems impossible at the moment because intelligence appears to be an amalgam of so many information-processing and information-representation abilities" (pp. 2).

This is still the case and for the same reason: Intelligence is an amalgam of conscious, semiconscious, and subconscious skills, which we are only beginning to see how to disentangle.

One of the key practical problems of intelligence, then, is the orchestration, on different levels, of thought and action. Our ordinary, everyday experience illustrates this well. Some of the jobs we do require sustained conscious concentration for success; some happen almost entirely subconsciously. There is also a gradual migration between these two ends of the spectrum toward the subconscious end. For example, consider driving. Most good drivers spend time thinking about what is going to happen a short time ahead rather than what is going on now; they do not need to spend attention on changing gear, manipulating the pedals, indicating their intentions or even, perhaps, on watching what is happening; they automatically attend to the relevant details on the road to support their thinking. Much of their skill is subconscious (but not, therefore, unintelligent). The speed and fluency of their response to conditions on the road is a consequence of this automation. Conversely a novice driver spends attention directly on controlling the vehicle—managing the pedals, changing gear, and watching in the mirror all require conscious supervision at the outset. This results in a slower, more laborious performance than that of the expert.

The same can be said of many activities, particularly (but not only) those involving a significant element of physical skill: dancing, playing a musical instrument, most sports, and so on. The expert no longer has to attend to the detail of physical performance, and can concentrate on the tactics and strategy of the activity—on a good day. On a bad day, everything becomes bogged down in the details again.

The conclusion we may draw from this discussion is that, in human skill, the orchestration of activity, in which parts of the system are responsible for each component of the skill, differs at different degrees of expertise, and the various possible patterns of responsibility for action have consequent advantages and disadvantages with respect to the competence as a whole.

Exactly the same situation arises in autonomous robotics, except that we see the problem *from the designer's viewpoint rather than the observer's.* The design problem is to choose the orchestration of activity within the robot in such a way that the desired competence is achieved robustly, efficiently, and economically by the complete system. A good orchestration depends both on the deployment of activity and on the agents (the "players") themselves. What makes the problem interesting is that we have a number of mutually interacting levels on which to address the design and no general understanding of the trade-offs involved in choosing any particular level or type of agent with which to proceed.

A well-understood example will clarify this point. Consider the peg insertion task in which a tightly fitting peg is to be inserted into a hole by a robot. The key difficulty to overcome is jamming: If the robot tries to force the peg into the hole out of alignment, the forces acting on the peg and hole around the point(s) of contact will tend to jam the peg tight.

There are four qualitatively different levels at which we can address this problem:

- Pegs and holes could be fitted with chamfers (and suitable compliance in the insertion process), so that they auto-locate as the peg is pushed home. In this case, the problem is eliminated by engineering the environment. Chamfers on holes and pegs, part feeders, and careful work-cell engineering are all examples of this approach.

- The robot could be fitted with a remote centre compliance device (that of Nevins and Whitney, [11]) that changes the configuration of forces on the peg to prevent jamming. This alleviates the problem by an alteration of the robot's morphology.

- The robot controller could be augmented to permit compliant motions of the end effector. This third option results in the addition of a new class of *controlled motions* of which the robot is capable, the space of possible actions has been altered.

- The robot could follow a carefully crafted "intelligent" strategy in searching for the hole and inserting the peg. This solution corresponds most closely to the human style of problem solving by means of deliberate, strategic, consciously directed activity.

This spectrum of possibility for addressing a problem illustrates a general point: The terms in which a problem is described need not be directly related to the manner in which its solution is implemented. In particular, we may describe a problem explicitly in symbolic or mathematical form, while solving it using a simple mechanical contrivance. The error of implementing the description,[1] although resulting in correct performance, is

[1] Using the formal mathematical description, or derivations of it, directly as an ingredient in the algorithm controlling the behaviour.

probably the single biggest cause of wasted effort (both human and machine) in robotics!

In research into the engineering of human competence, this is also important: It is unsafe to suppose that the plausible story advanced by an individual asked how (or even why) they do something bears a close relationship to the truth of how the task is actually accomplished; we are rarely at a loss for an intellectually satisfying rationalisation of our actions. For robotics, however, a rationalisation is insufficient. We need to be able to identify the different approaches to a given problem and quantify the trade-offs between them in terms of cost, performance, ease of engineering, generality, and so on.

In the peg-insertion problem, a few of the trade-offs are obvious. It may not be economically viable or it may be impractical for some reason to engineer the environment to suit the robot. Adding extra hardware may limit unreasonably the load-bearing capabilities or the physical dexterity of the robot. Making the controller more complex, to add qualitatively new motor capability to the robot, may either be impossible (the robot uses a proprietary controller that cannot easily be modified) or result in an unacceptable performance penalty (the controller now cycles too slowly). The deliberate strategic peg-insertion may be frustratingly or uneconomically slow, or may rely on repeatability, which cannot be engineered into the robot. On the other hand, any or all of the four approaches, or a suitable combination of them, may solve the problem in a repeatable, efficient, and economic way.

Carefully conducted research into skilled human performance can provide considerable insight on this kind of question. For example, consider the competent driver's ability to brake in such a way as to stop close behind another vehicle or at a traffic light. A psychophysical study by Lee [6] shows that human performance is well accounted for by the theory that brake timing and forces are controlled using the *time-to-contact* parameter—a visually-derived estimate of how long it will be until the observer strikes the object being looked at, computed on the assumption of constant relative velocity. This is surprising as one might assume that successful braking requires knowledge of the distance to the target and of the vehicle's speed and acceleration, together with some simple reasoning; in fact, the time-to-contact is independent of the size, relative speed, and relative distance of an object (the respective dependencies cancel out) and can be computed solely on the basis of image appearance and its rate of change. For a longer discussion of a greater variety of tasks thought to be dependent on time-to-contact and similar visually derived parameters, the interested reader is referred to the excellent book by Bruce and Green [2, chap. 12].

Although Lee's result is initially surprising, on reflection it is perhaps obvious. It makes good engineering sense to bring to bear a source of information that is easy to access, reliable, and robust, and of general applicability. A single general mechanism may perhaps support the variety of human and animal skills involving the visual cuing of timed action. The psychophysical experimentation, by revealing an interesting choice in the orchestration of these skills, both illuminates the design trade-offs to some extent, makes possible further theoretical analysis of the proposed model, and suggests useful experimental applications of the theory in robotics.

7.3.1 The SOMASS System

The peg-insertion example illustrates one aspect of the problem of orchestrating activity in a complex system—that of obtaining adequate performance at reasonable cost. There is a second aspect, however, which follows from our perspective on robots as artifacts: we must consider the design effort and the implementation difficulty of specifying and constructing a given system. Here, too, the trade-offs between different approaches are obscure. In general, we may say that it is easier to design and build a number of simple, relatively independent systems as opposed to a single monolithic complex one, so that a design that decomposes the problem into a set of independent parts is to be favoured. However, independence can be a tricky thing to assess in advance and for most problems a number of different decompositions are both possible and plausible.

To illustrate this point within the context of activity orchestration, we consider an example of a successful system, SOMASS, that encapsulates a particular approach to system decomposition. Its domain of operation is assembly, and it is one of the few complete robotic assembly systems in the world—complete in the sense that its input consists of a description of the shapes of the pieces and final assembly and a set of approximate positions for the pieces in the robot's workspace, and its output is a finished object in the hand of the spectator (well, on the robot's worktable...). The first implementation of the system used no sensors (apart from those used to control the robot's joint positions) and required only 6 man-months to design and build. The interested reader should consult [7, 10] for a full description of the system.

In order to permit the construction of a complete system—-of critical importance in robotic work [9]—the problem of shape representation was simplified by restricting the assembly domain to the SOMA world [3, 4, 5]. SOMA parts comprise collections of cubes glued together face-to-face so that each part has at least one concavity. The simplest set of parts, the SOMA4 set, consists of seven parts that can be assembled into a large cube of side three basic units (*cubits*) in 240 different ways (ignoring symmetries) as well as into a rich variety of other shapes. The SOMA domain was chosen as a research model because it retains the crucial assembly property of shape-dependent part mating (unlike the popular "blocks world", for example), while providing a rich world of things to build.

SOMASS is a hybrid system: It incorporates both conventional symbolic reasoning and tacit knowledge in the form of skills or behaviours providing a nontrivial agent for the planner to instruct. The planner reasons about the disposition of SOMA parts in the finished assembly, determines whether there exists a sequence of intermediate partial assemblies that are gravitationally stable (the robot has only one hand) and permit the necessary finger clearances for successful construction, and sorts out any regrasping needed. The executive agent (and not the planner) knows the physical size of a cubit and the approximate initial disposition of the parts. It comprises a collection of handcrafted behaviours that reliably acquire a part (given an approximate location for it), reorient it, and place it in a specified position and orientation. The planner plans *part* grasps and rotations; the executive agent fills in the necessary translations, and interprets part motions into *robot* motions at run time.

This separation of knowledge between planner and agent is not accidental. The planner is kept ignorant of all the detail of the uncertainty in the parts (being real parts made of wood and plastic in various sizes, they are not especially precise in side, shape or internal alignment) and even of the basic unit of size. This considerably simplifies its construction without depriving it of any of the information needed to play its part in the system. In particular, the planner never needs to reason about whether an assembly might fail because of part tolerance, physical characteristics such as friction or stiction, and the like: The handcrafted executive agent guarantees that failure will not occur for these reasons.

The interesting point about SOMASS, for our purposes, is that it takes a particular, and somewhat unusual, approach to the activity orchestration problem. The conventional view in assembly robotics has tended to be that the planning component of the system should anticipate and deal with the various possible reasons for assembly failure; this has, in practice, proved computationally and intellectually intractable. SOMASS, on the other hand, takes the position that the planner should concentrate on those aspects of the problem that can tractably be expressed in symbolic form, leaving the execution agent to cope with the specifically manipulative difficulties of the assembly problem. Because the agent is handcrafted, most of the consequences of the uncertainties in the parts and their manipulation are dealt with by the human programmer who has years of experience of object manipulation to call on when diagnosing and repairing failures in the tacit skills of the executive agent. The reliability of the complete system when faced with previously untested assemblies (about 2% failure in 45 hours of testing on some 4,000 lines of previously untried automatically generated robot program [8]) and the relatively small amount of effort required to design and build it (about 6 man-months) can be attributed to the separation between planner and agent and the choice of the virtual assembly machine at the interface between them.

7.3.2 Discussion and Summary

The peg-insertion example and the SOMASS system illustrate our contention that there are qualitatively different ways of addressing a given problem, corresponding to different decisions about the orchestration of activity, and the definition of the "players" in a robotic system, and that these decisions have significant consequences both in terms of the performance of the engineered system and in terms of the effort expended in its design and realisation. The interesting scientific question is then which orchestration strategy is appropriate for a given problem and, consequently, what the trade-offs between the different options are for various problem classes. With this kind of understanding, it will become possible reliably to answer questions of orchestration in prospect in situations of useful practical complexity.

At present, the trade-offs between deliberate and automatic action and between engineering of environment and agent are only partly understood in a number of specific problems, and the design rules for robotic behaviour exist as folklore and intuition rather than as a codified body of knowledge or a set of analytic design tools. The rules can only be elicited by building robots; and, as in cathedral construction, the issue cannot be dodged entirely; robotic projects and systems can fail as spectacularly, in their own way, as cathedrals!

Having said that, however, the issue *can* be dodged to some extent. Conservative engineering and careful application of the available insights can take us a long way. From a scientific point of view, though, the failures are rather more interesting than the successes; they lead to refinement of the principles underlying the design and perhaps ultimately to an understanding of the principles that are at work in the control of action in natural systems, where faulty orchestration is punished more finally than in robotics.

7.4 Conclusion

The task of designing intelligent autonomous robots is not as easy as it might, at first, appear. The key difficulty is one of design rather than of performance, and the limitations of the usefulness and competence of robots are a reflection of the problems faced by designers in choosing appropriate agents and orchestrating their contributions to composite solutions to robotic problems in a principled way.

In consequence of this, today is both an exciting and a dangerous time to be involved in robotics. It is dangerous because modern technological developments allow us to engineer a great range of different sensory and effector systems, but we lack the insight to design autonomous systems using them in a principled way. Our robots may fail, unforseeably.

On the other hand, lack of understanding has never been a complete barrier to producing things that work, and many robot applications will succeed by dint of conservative engineering or just plain luck.

It is an exciting time because the successes of robotics and, more significantly, its failures provide us with a chance to explore and formulate general laws of organisation for autonomous systems. The necessity of addressing problems like the orchestration of activity opens the way to a fruitful interdisciplinary dialogue between roboticists, psychophysicists, engineers, and biologists that can only enrich all the disciplines in the long run.

7.5 Acknowledgments

The author acknowledges with gratitude the helpful comments and constructive criticism offered by Bob Fisher, Bridget Hallam, Chris Malcolm, Mark Orr, and Tim Smithers in the preparation of this chapter; and the hours of enjoyable discussion with them and others spent in the preparation of the ideas it contains. The SOMASS project, directed by Chris Malcolm, is funded by the ACME Directorate of the SERC under grant no. GR/E/6807.5. Computing and other facilities were provided by the University of Edinburgh.

References

[1] Brady, M., & Paul, R. (Eds.).(1984). *Robotics research: The first international symposium.* Cambridge, MA: MIT Press.

[2] Bruce, V., & Green, P. R. (1990). *Visual perception: Physiology, psychology and ecology* (2nd ed.). London, UK: Lawrence Erlbaum Associates.

[3] Carson, G. S. (1973, November). Soma cubes. *Mathematics Teacher*, 583–592.

[4] Gardner, M. (1961). *More mathematical puzzles and diversions.* New York: Penguin.

[5] Gardner, M. (1972, September). Pleasurable problems with polycubes. *Scientific American.*

[6] Lee, D. (1976). A theory of visual control of braking based on information about time-to-collision. *Perception, 5*, 437–459.

[7] Malcolm, C. (1987). *Planning and performing the robotic assembly of soma cube constructions.* Unpublished master's thesis, University of Edinburgh, Edinburgh, Scotland.

[8] Malcolm, C., & Smithers, T. (1988). Programming assembly robots in terms of task achieving behavioural modules: First experimental results. *International advanced robotics programme: Second workshop on manipulators, sensors, and steps towards mobility* (pp. 15.1–15.16). Manchester, UK:

[9] Malcolm, C., Smithers, T.,& Hallam, J. (1989). An emerging paradigm in robot architecture. In T. Kanade, F. C. O. Groen, & L. O. Hertzberger (Eds.), *Intelligent Autonomous Systems, 2* (pp. 284–293). The Netherlands: Amsterdam.

[10] Malcolm, C., & Smithers, T. (1990). Symbol grounding via a hybrid architecture in an autonomous assembly system. *Robotics and Autonomous Systems, 6*, 123–144.

[11] Nevins, J. L., & Whitney, D. E. (1978, February). Computer controlled assembly. *Scientific American*, 62–74.

8. A Boy Scout, Toto, and a Bird

How Situated Cognition is Different from Situated Robotics

W.J. CLANCEY
Institute for Research on Learning

8.1 Introduction

We are at an exciting turning point in the development of intelligent machines. Situated robot designers [9] have given the AI community concrete examples of alternative architectures for coordinating sensation and action. These examples suggest that, for some navigation behaviors at least, predefined maps of the world and control structures are unnecessary. This work has developed in parallel with and lends credence to similar criticisms of models of human reasoning [22, 24]. However, it is crucial to understand that situated robotic designs are pragmatic, emphasizing engineering convenience and new ways of building machines. Brooks et al. [4] are not trying to model human beings, and to a significant degree their robotic designs violate situated cognition hypotheses about the nature of human knowledge and representation construction. I sketch out some of these distinctions here and suggest how they might be used to discover alternative architectures for robotics.

I believe that the fundamental question for robotic designers is how to construct an intelligent machine without bounding its behavior by the designer's preconceptions about the world [5]. By not building in maps and procedures that rigidly control behavior, situated robot designers seek more flexible, robust mechanisms, such that what the robot does develops in the course of historical interactions with the world. I have also argued that this research leads us to reconsider the relation of knowledge-level descriptions of behavior (an observer's descriptions of patterns in what the robot does over time in some environment) to the mechanisms that coordinate sensation and action (e.g., a subsumption architecture designed by an engineer). I claim that a mechanism that reconstructs and recoordinates processes, rather than stores and retrieves labeled descriptions or procedures, is more consistent with what we know about human memory and perception [6, 8]. Such a process possibly cannot be built today, because we don't know how to build the kind of self-organizing mechanism that is required [9]. But articulating how human cognition is different from a classical architecture helps delineate what aspects of situated robotic designs are still cast in the classical mold and remain to be freed of prevailing assumptions about the nature of memory and representations.

8.2 Situated Cognition Hypotheses

To begin, here are some of the hypotheses about cognition that essentially distinguish situated (human) cognition research from what Brooks et al. call *classical AI*:

- Knowledge is an explanatory concept like energy, a capacity for interactive behavior. Knowledge can be represented, but "knowledge is never in hand" [17] p.89. "The map is not the territory" [11] p.25.

  Knowledge-level descriptions (e.g., prototype hierarchies, scripts, strategies) constitute an observer's model, characterizing patterns in behavior—the product of internal mechanisms and some environment—not structures or mechanisms inside the agent. Just as there is no such thing as "all in the information" in some situation, there is no such thing as completely describing an agent's behavior. Descriptions are always with respect to the frame of reference of an observer interacting with an agent in its environment; descriptions embody the observer's point of view (including values and goals) and are themselves the product of interactions.

  Cognitive models (including expert systems) replicate the patterns of human behavior—how it appears in recurrent interactions—without replicating the mechanism that produce human behavior. Such descriptions are necessary and valuable; they help specify what a cognitive architecture must be capable of accomplishing. In human behavior, such models, in the form of natural language grammars, disease hierarchies, operating procedures, and so on, are extremely valuable for coordinating group behavior, or in general designing, controlling, diagnosing, and repairing complex systems [7].

- Meaningful structures are not fixed, given, or static in either the environment or in human memory: *Human memory* is not a place where things (e.g., schemas, categories, rules, procedures, scripts) are stored. Such representations—when they are not stored in the environment—are always constructed each time they are used. Representations are not manipulated by people in a hidden way, but must be perceived to be interpreted; that is, they must be in the environment (including silent speech and imagery). Interpretation is a process of commentary, constructing secondary representations that give meaning to experiences and perceptions by placing them in a context, thus relating them to activity [1, 5, 22].

Information is not given to the agent. Information is constructed by people in a process of perception; it is not selected, noticed, detected, chosen, or filtered from a set of given, static, pre-existing things [15, 18]. Each perception is a generalization, a new construction. No category is merely retrieved or reinstantiated. In people every utterance is a new representation.

- *Human learning* occurs all the time. Every perception and coordinated movement is a generalization [23], in the sense that it recomposes previous categorizations and sequences of behavior [6]. Perception and action are dialectic in people: What we perceive and what we say our perceptions mean arises together with what we are doing and our sense of what we are doing [3, 20]

  An important kind of learning occurs in cycles of behavior as we represent and comment on what we have done in the past (e.g., explanation-based learning). Knowledge-based approaches to machine learning model the learning that occurs in cycles of behavior, not the constant generalization that occurs with every action in people.

To summarize, human behavior is situated because all processes of behaving, including speech, problem-solving, and physical skills, are generated on the spot, not by mechanical application of scripts or rules previously stored in the brain. Knowledge can be represented, but it cannot be exhaustively inventoried by statements of belief or scripts for behaving. Knowledge is a capacity to behave adaptively within an environment; it cannot be reduced to (replaced by) representations of behavior or the environment.

Representations are created by an interaction of neural and external processes in what we call perception. As the product of interactions with the environment (sensory, gestural, and interpersonal), representations cannot correspond to an external, objective reality. Representations are themselves interpreted interactively, in cycles of perceiving and acting—they are always outside the main loop; they are the product of interactions, not the physical substrate from which behavior is generated. Today's computer programs create and interpret representations grammatically, by applying patterns and rules. People construct a new representation with every interpretation.

8.3 Toto's Maps

We don't know how to design a machine today that respects our current hypotheses about human cognition. Situated robotic designs are valiant attempts to break away from past ways of programming, but they, perhaps necessarily, still embody many of classical AI's assumptions. For example, consider Mataric's robot dog Toto [13, 14]. Toto has an innovative design that enables it to learn the relative location of landmarks in some environment. But I would like to distinguish Toto's advances as a novel engineering design from its relation to situated cognition theory. To be brief, here is how Toto's design violates the hypotheses stated previously:

- *Memory*: Toto's design is based on predefined categories for modeling the world, such as wall, bearing, obstacle. Descriptions of landmarks (e.g., "leftwall," compass bearing) are stored in a graph during Toto's operation.

- *Learning* : Toto uses the classical approach of comparing the current landmark to a stored description of type, bearing, and position. This matching process uses a predefined calculus for manipulating the representation, just as in rule-based systems. For example, the calculus represents the equivalence of a left wall heading south and a right wall heading north [13]. Toto doesn't learn with every interaction; for example, it doesn't update its graph if an obstacle isn't a known landmark.

In summary, Toto adheres to classical views about information as given, memory as description storage, and learning as controlled, grammatical manipulation of descriptions.

On the other hand, Toto's design is consistent with and indeed motivated by the view that knowledge-level descriptions of behavior (e.g., wall following) needn't be encoded in the mechanism as a map of the environment and fixed procedure for moving about. The fact that Toto constructs a map is not novel in itself. What is new and especially interesting is how Toto stores the map and how map building is coordinated with primitive behaviors. In particular, the map is not globally available. Stored information is only accessible in the context of moving through the environment, when the history of interactions activates the nodes in the landmark graph. Furthermore, the graph is dynamically created as "jumper links," so that landmark recognition activates the next landmark detection process. This effectively replicates the "next-next-next" nature of human memory, what Bamberger calls the "felt path" [3]. The separation of the map from the motion and sensing behaviors also appears to be a good idea, insofar as we view the map as an internally constructed representation that other processes apprehend and respond to (in the manner of Minsky's B and A brains [16]). My complaint, however, is that descriptions of current landmarks and a sense of similarity with past categorizations should be co-constructed with the robot's high-level coordination of its primitive behaviors (reflex movements). That is, how "what is out there" is categorized should arise with the process of categorizing "what the robot is doing now." As it stands, the design violates Brooks' own principle that perception is not an input to action; Mataric and Brooks have simply moved the serial, left-to-right precedence to a serial, bottom-to-top precedence.

The claim of situated cognition (in my formulation) is that perception and action arise together, dialectically forming each other. Perceiving landmarks is not retrieving past descriptions and matching against current categorizations [15, 20]. In the human, there is no structure stored in the past to compare the present to [10, 18]. Toto's "active representations" graph models the process of activation by which processes of past perceiving and moving are coordinated, but descriptions of past encounters are stored. In people the processes themselves are literally reconstructed by reactivating neural nets that actually do the coordination (the sensing and the moving), not nets that store descriptions. Simply put, the claim is that people navigate through familiar space without referring to representations; sensations are directly coupled to actions without intermediate acts of description. In comparing and disambiguating descriptions—"the landmark I am sensing now" and "the landmark description I stored in my graph"—Toto is simulating reasoning, which is more complex behavior than we expect to see in a model of a dog.

This brief analysis illustrates that we need conventions for describing alternative robotic mechanisms, so we can better describe what is new and what work remains to be done. What distinguishes situated robotics and classical AI is muddled because how classical programs work has been poorly articulated relative to our current needs. Useful concepts can be derived by first comparing classical programs to situated cognition hypotheses; this gives us comparative descriptions like "memory-as-structure storage versus memory as a capacity for recomposing past coordinations" and "learning via perceptual generalization (within a cycle; what people must do because they don't store representations) versus learning via grammatically manipulating representations (in cycles of perception and action, e.g., explanation-based learning in machines)." The most glaring problem is that how people create and use representations has been almost universally misconstrued in classical AI [8]. Situated robotics has yet to address how coordination of sensation and action in complex spaces or in sequences of behavior over time is reconstructed, without storing descriptions of either behavior or the world [19].

We must distinguish representations used by people (road maps, journal papers) from assumed structures in the head that aren't perceivable. The processes of constructing and interpreting representations that occur in cycles of human behavior is radically different from hidden manipulation of neural structures. To call both perceived structures like maps and unperceivable neural structures "representations" is to confuse what intelligence is. In this respect, Toto models how people use coordinate systems in cycles of behaving.

Situated cognition theories suggest that representations don't mediate human behavior within each cycle [24]; in particular, we can walk through a room without referring to an internal map of where things are located, by directly coordinating our behaviors through space and time in ways we have composed and sequenced them before (a process memory, cf. Rosenfield [19]. It is bizarre to postulate that dogs represent what people get by quite well without, and even more strange to assume that dogs have developed coordinate representational languages (e.g., "bearing," "left-wall orientation"). Indeed, how could a dog want to go somewhere (a particular place or kind of place) without having a descriptive language? The situated cognition claim is that the coordination is accomplished in dogs by reactivation of past neural compositions (sensory-effector maps and maps of maps producing sequences of behavior).

We must distinguish more carefully between what it means for a Boy Scout to use a compass bearing, what it means for Toto to store descriptions of landmarks, and how birds might migrate by interacting with a magnetic field [2]. I claim that the Boy Scout is more like the bird than Toto, because he doesn't literally store descriptions. It may be tempting to say that a process memory enables the same behavior as structure storage (e.g., the Boy Scout can say, "I remember that its bearing was 45 degrees"). But this again confuses how behavior appears with the flexibility and generative capabilities of different architectures.

8.4 Recommendations

To proceed effectively and systematically, robot designers and their critics might concentrate on the following:

1. Be clear what design alternatives you are using and why. Speak in terms of memory, perception, learning. What representations of the world are built in? What is stored? How are sensation and action coordinated? How are routines learned? Attempt to develop a language for classifying systems:

   1. Categorical perception versus only direct sensation.

   2. Maps, map primitives, or grammars for creating maps are hardwired.

3. Composite behaviors (e.g., sentence templates), primitive behaviors (e.g., reflexes), or constraints between behaviors are hardwired.

4. Opposing behaviors built in (e.g., left and right turn) sensors are fixed or mobile.

2. Experimentation:

1. State hypotheses and purpose of the experiment (not just its design).

2. Change the environment systematically, and justify your choice of a microworld. Experimentally explore and describe surprises, but work within a framework that defines a space of experiments.

3. Specify a robot's behavior using classical representations (e.g., scripts, grammars, situation-action rules) so we can compare the capacities or "knowledge" of different designs (including after learning). Similarly, specify environmental assumptions using classical representations (e.g., quantitative and qualitative models). Principled robot design requires systematically describing behaviors and environments.

4. Define the enterprise in terms of specific constraints:

1. Functional: Are you designing for a particular environment? For particular learned behaviors?

2. Biological: Are you replicating animal capacities?

3. Computational: Are you doing a bottom-up experiment to see what a given mechanism can do?

5. Don't view the design of a society of robots as a different research problem. Ignoring the effect of other agents is just a variation of ignoring how the environment can structure behavior (presumably the view we are arguing against). Look for ways that emergent multiagent patterns of interaction can be perceived by individuals and structure individual behavior [21].

6. Move toward construction of processes, not just activation of prewired constraints between behaviors. Move from the idea of predetermined, layered control (subsumption architecture) to creating new compositions (literally new networks) that can be reactivated (and potentially generalized rather than simply re-enacted). Programs like Toto, compared to people, are both too reactive (no learning of procedures, composite behaviors that effectively become new primitives) and too predetermined (no learning of categories, new ways of coordinating behaviors outside the subsumption layering). Correlating multimodal sensation might be a practical and not too complex starting point.

8.5 Conclusions

We shouldn't expect progress to be monotonic; we need to take a broad view of the difficulty of articulating what we are doing. For example, some might view Winograd's early work (SHRDLU) as a mistake, particularly in light of his subsequent rejection of that approach. But progress requires clearly and valiantly pushing a point of view, so the community can reflect on it and see where it falls short. In this respect, Mataric's design of Toto is a major contribution to AI, and especially valuable as a foil for explaining situated cognition hypotheses. With such artifacts in hand, we can say better what we have done, what we are trying to do, and what to try next. Given the tentativeness of our theories and the compromises inherent in our engineering designs, we would be well advised to retain some humility—looking back a few years (or even months) from now, we may realize that we've made the same mistakes as classical AI. Before we proclaim that the path through the desert is now found, we should remember that it is unlikely that any trend or school of thought, whether behaviorism, gestalt psychology, or classical AI, is entirely wrong.

8.6 Acknowledgment

I am grateful to Maja Mataric for providing useful explanations of Toto's design, as well as thoughtful suggestions for improving these comments.

References

[1] Agre, P. (1988). *The dynamic structure of everyday life.* Unpublished dissertation. Cambridge, MA: MIT, Department of Engeneering and Computer Science.

[2] Baker, R. (1981). *The mystery of migration.* New York: Viking Press.

[3] Bamberger, J. (in press). *The mind behind the musical ear.* Cambridge, MA: MIT Press.

[4] Brooks, R. (1991). Intelligence without reason. Chapter 1 in this volume.

[5] Clancey, W. J. (1991). The frame of reference problem in the design of intelligent machines. In K. VanLehn (Ed.), *Architectures for intelligence* (pp.343–380). Hillsdale, NJ: Lawrence Erlbaum Associates.

[6] Clancey, W. J. (in press-a). Review of *The invention of memory. Journal of Artificial Intelligence.*

[7] Clancey, W. J. (in press-b). Model construction operators. *Journal of Artificial Intelligence.*

[8] Clancey, W. J., & Roschelle, J. (in preparation). Situated cognition: How representations are created and given meaning. *Educational Psychologist.*

[9] Freeman, W. J. (1991, February). The physiology of perception. *Scientific American*, 78–85.

[10] Gibson, J. J. (1966). *The senses considered as perceptual systems.* Boston: Houghton Mifflin.

[11] Korzybski, A. (1941). *Science and sanity.* New York: Science Press.

[12] Maes, P. (Ed.).(1990). Designing autonomous agents. *Robotics and Autonomous Systems 6*(1,2) 1–196.

[13] Mataric, M., & Brooks, R. A. (1990). *Learning a distributed map representation based on navigation behaviors.* Paper presented at USA-Japan Symposium on Flexible Automation.

[14] Mataric, M. (1991). Behavioral synergy without explicit integration. *Proceedings of the AAAI Spring Symposium on Integrated Intelligent Architectures.*

[15] Maturana, H. R. (1983). What is it to see? *Què es ver?, 16*, 255–269.

[16] Minsky, M. (1986). *The society of mind.* New York: Simon & Schuster.

[17] Newell, A. (1984). The knowledge level. *Artificial Intelligence, 18*(1) 87–127.

[18] Reeke, G. N., & Edelman, G. M. (1988). Real brains and artificial intelligence. *Daedalus, 117*(1) pp. 135–185.

[19] Rosenfield, I. (1988). *The invention of memory: A new view of the brain.* New York: Basic Books.

[20] Schön, D. A. (1979). Generative metaphor: A perspective on problem-setting in social policy. In A. Ortony (Ed.), *Metaphor and Thought* (pp. 254–283). Cambridge, UK: Cambridge University Press.

[21] Steels, L. (1990). Cooperation through self-organization. In Y. Demazeau *Distributed artificial intelligence* (pp.450–468). Amsterdam: North-Holland.

[22] Suchman, L. A. (1987). *Plans and situated actions: The problem of human-machine communication.* Cambridge, UK: Cambridge University Press.

[23] Vygotsky, L. (1986). Thought and language (A. Kozulin Trans.). Cambridge, MA: MIT Press.

[24] Winograd, T., & Flores, F. (1986). *Understanding computers and cognition: A new foundation for design.* Norwood, NJ: Ablex.

9. The Challenge of Autonomous Agents: Pitfalls and How to Avoid Them

ROLF PFEIFER and PAUL VERSCHURE
University of Zurich-Irchel

9.1 Introduction

Traditional symbol processing AI has been criticized on many grounds. Well known criticisms concern, among others, brittleness, lack of learning and generalization capacity, lack of fault and noise tolerance, neural implausibility, and the inability to perform in real time. More recently there has been much discussion about situatedness, grounding, and the frame problem.

The frame problem was pointed out long ago. In the classical sense it refers, in essence, to the problem of how to draw the relevant inferences given a logical description of a changing world [29]. Recently the problem has experienced a renaissance and has been considered in a broader context of (e.g. [21]; see also the complete volume by [47]). In this broader sense the term *frame problem* is used to designate the whole set of problems involved in modeling change when dealing with the *real world* where the real world is complex, constantly changing, and only partially knowable.

The symbol grounding problem refers to the problem of how symbols acquire meaning. Typically in AI the meaning of symbols is defined by how they relate to other symbols and how they are processed by some interpreter (e.g., [48]). The relation of the symbols to the outside world is rarely discussed explicitly. This position is also predominant in linguistics: It is taken for granted that there is some kind of correspondence between the symbols or sentences and the outside world. The study of meaning then relates to the translation of sentences into some kind of logic-based representation whose semantics is clearly defined (e.g., [62], p. 18). This position is acceptable in the area of natural language because there is always a human interpreter, and it can be safely expected that he or she is capable of establishing the appropriate relations to some outside world: The mapping is "grounded" in the system's (the human's) experience of its *interaction* with the real world.

However, if we are dealing with autonomous agents, we have to take into account that the agent needs to interact with the environment on its own, without a human interpreter. Thus, the meaning of the symbols must be grounded in the agent's interaction with the real world. Here it is important that "interaction" be taken to mean perception *and* action. If sensory inputs don't relate to action they don't matter to the agent and their meaning can therefore not be established (see following). Symbolic systems in which symbols only refer to other symbols are not grounded because the connection to the outside world is missing.[1]

Situatedness roughly means the following: Autonomous agents have to act in a real world that is constantly changing, only partially knowable, and intrinsically unpredictable. They have to act in real time because the environment is constantly changing, largely—but not only—because of what other agents do. Now the traditional AI approach to designing agents is to equip them with models of their environment. These models form the basis for planning processes, which in turn are used for deciding on a particular action. But plan-based agents very quickly run into combinatorial problems (e.g., [7]) because in an unpredictable world many alternatives have to be considered. But because the environment is only partially knowable a complete model cannot be built in the first place. But even if only partial models are developed, keeping the models up to date requires a lot of computational resources. Inspection of the problem of taking action in the real world shows that it is neither necessary nor desirable to develop complete and very detailed plans and models for the following reasons (e.g., [1, 55, 62]). Typically, only a small part of an agent's environment is relevant for its actions. A *situated* agent is capable—based on its experience—of determining what is relevant by interacting with the situation: It does not have to rely on elaborate models because the real world is, in a sense, part of the agent's knowledge. The agent can simply "look at it" through its sensors. This capability is necessary if the agent is to act in real time in the real world.

A situated agent can take advantage of a particular situation (i.e., it

[1]As we demonstrate later, the symbol grounding problem is really an artifact of symbol-based systems. It is possible to design systems that do not suffer from the grounding problem. See section entitled "Avoiding the Pitfalls."

can seize opportunities that arise from it). It can also refer to aspects of the situation relative to its own position (e.g., "the direction in which I am going," or "the ice cube in front of me") without having to calculate, for example, which particular ice cube out of all the ice cubes that are represented in the system's world model, which must be processed. These aspects are called *indexical.* They are ambiguous if uttered out of context but unambiguous in a particular situation.

From these considerations it follows that if an autonomous agent is to act intelligently (i.e., in an adaptive and robust way) it must be situated. This contrasts with the traditional view that the behavior of agents be mainly plan-based (which implies that detailed models of the environment be defined and maintained). This is not to say that the concept of plan is not relevant, but that it should be seen in the context of situatedness that pertains to the dynamics of the system-environment interaction.

In order to investigate these problems the development of physically instantiated autonomous agents[2] has been proposed. Now, the idea of building mobile robots for the purpose of studying intelligence has been around in AI for quite some time. A prominent example is Shakey, a robot whose first version was finished around 1969 at SRI [49, 40]. One of the underlying assumptions in Shakey, for example, was that symbolic representations mediate between sensory signals and motor actions. This can be seen as a major paradigm of early approaches and has been characterized by a so-called "sense-think-act" cycle [28]. A situation in the environment is first perceived ("sensing"), then, based on the result of the "sense" phase, reasoning would take place, which includes building a model of the current surroundings, constructing a plan, and deciding on the next action ("thinking"), and finally the action would be performed in the real world ("acting"). There have been a number of other approaches that can roughly be subsumed under the same paradigm for example, Cart [33], Hilare [17], or the FMC robot [23]. It turned out that these robots suffered from a number of problems. The reasons were of a technological and a fundamental nature. The key issues that had been neglected were precisely the frame problem, the problems of situatedness and of grounding. For example, actions to be taken were calculated from global models, which is a computationally intractable problem. Therefore, calculating the next steps would take too much time and the robots could only function in relatively stable environments (i.e., they were not situated). In other words, the robots could not act in real time. Another unresolved problem is to connect the sensory inputs from the environment to the symbols in the internal model (the symbol grounding problem). We will come back to this point when talking about the "representationalist" pitfall.

In order to tackle these fundamental issues the "sense-think-act" paradigm was inappropriate—it is subject to a number of pitfalls, as will be

[2] For the purpose of this chapter we use *robot* and *agent* as synonyms.

shown later. This discussion shows that developing autonomous agents alone will not solve the fundamental problems of situatedness and grounding. But if successful autonomous agents are to be developed, these problems must be solved, and to achieve that goal fundamentally new approaches are needed.

The history of early efforts of building autonomous robots leading up to modern approaches has been outlined by [28], and by [6] and is not be further elaborated here. Only one approach is discussed, namely the subsumption architecture [4]. It has had a significant impact at least on part of the autonomous robot community and can be seen as the precursor of a new paradigm for AI.

Rather than decomposing a robot in terms of functional modules like perception, modeling, planning, task execution, and motor control, in the subsumption architecture it is decomposed in terms of behaviors like object avoidance, wandering, exploring, map building, and so on. Each behavioral module can directly get sensory inputs and produce behavioral outputs without the need to consult a higher level module for planning or execution. [52] and [6] used the term *behavior-based AI* (in contrast to knowledge-based AI) to delineate this approach. The subsumption architecture is one illustration of how coherent behavior can be achieved without having to rely on a sense-think-act cycle, another one is discussed later. We will call the collective efforts in this direction *New AI*.[3]

The problems that we have discussed imply that a revision of traditional AI is needed. The extent of the rethinking that is required is illustrated by pointing out some traps one is likely to fall into if traditional ideas are applied to the development of autonomous agents. In this chapter we first discuss some of the important pitfalls. They have been identified on the basis of literature on robot design, many informal discussions, and our own experience. We then show how these pitfalls can be avoided by discussing a number of recent approaches, including our own, which we have called *distributed adaptive control* (DAC). We also demonstrate how these approaches contribute toward solving some of the fundamental problems of AI.

9.2 Designing Autonomous Agents: Major Pitfalls

Let us assume that we want to design and build an autonomous robot. There are a number of pitfalls to look out for. They are mainly a consequence of employing the principles of the traditional AI paradigm as outlined in [35]. Underlying this traditional approach is the assumption that you can take a physical symbol system (in the sense of [35]) and use

[3]The term *Nouvelle AI* has also been used [5].

it to control a robot.

Even if one is aware of the pitfalls—and this chapter draws attention to them—they are not easily avoided. The list of pitfalls we present is certainly not complete. But it shows some important issues in autonomous agents and serves as a starting point to delineate the paradigm of New AI. We will discuss the following pitfalls: goal directed systems, representationalist, neural network, direct programming, hybrid systems, modularity, and biomimicry.

9.2.1 The Goal-directed System Pitfall

One of the first decisions that will have to be made in designing an autonomous agent concerns what it is supposed to do (i.e., what it is for). It seems very natural that for this purpose the agent will have to be equipped with goals and knowledge that will enable it to derive the appropriate plans. Moreover, the first thing people think about when they talk about behaving systems is goals. Newell [35] argued that intelligent agents need goals, and these goals have to be explicitly represented. We show that this idea is highly problematic. This point needs some elaboration.

McFarland [30] made a distinction between goal-achieving, goal-seeking, and goal directed behavior.[4] A *goal-achieving* system is one that can recognize a goal once it is arrived at. A *goal-seeking* system is one that is designed to seek the goal without the goal being explicitly represented within the system. A *goal directed* system has an explicit representation of the to-be-achieved goal, which is instrumental in guiding the behavior. In AI,the vast majority of systems have been and still are goal directed systems. Famous historical examples are GPS [12], and STRIPS [13], but more modern AI programs, like expert systems are also largely goal directed. An example of a recent goal directed architecture, specifically designed for autonomous agents, is described in [27]. It uses, in essence, a STRIPSlike idea of add and delete-lists, and a controlled spreading-activation mechanism in a network of actions for action selection. The system is goal directed because it employs explicit representations of goals, and they are instrumental in driving the robot's actions.

But there are several problems with the notion of goal directed systems. To discuss this issue we distinguish observation and design. Let us begin by discussing observation. First, a clear distinction must be made between the attributions of an observer and the mechanisms actually driving the agent's actions. Goals are *ascribed* by an observer to an agent and thus only exist in the eye of the observer. They are used to organize an observer's thoughts about an agent in order to come up with some predictions (e.g., about what it will probably do next), or to communicate with others about the agent's

[4] In fact there is another one, intentional behavior, which we will not go into here. The interested reader is referred to an excellent collection of papers on the topic of goals [32].

behavior. Because goals are entirely observer-based descriptions, it is clear that no conclusions can be drawn about the processes within the *agent* that lead to behaviors that the observer describes in these terms.

Second, it is not possible to determine the goal that drives an agent's actions. For example, if someone heads toward the cafeteria early in the morning I can attribute the goal of wanting coffee or tea to the person, and I interpret change in the agent's behavior when the goal is achieved (e.g., drinking the coffee) as confirming evidence for my hypothesis. However, if along the way, the person meets a friend, starts talking, and never ends up in the cafeteria, I have no way of knowing whether the person actually had the goal to go there. Of course, I can ask, but that is highly unreliable and may lead to post-hoc rationalizations [41].

Moreover, the goals attributed to an agent can also be at very different levels. For example, in the cafeteria our agent's behavior can be sensibly described in terms of having the following goals: reducing thirst, wanting coffee, wanting to talk to someone in the cafeteria, wanting to be in good spirits for the exam coming up, wanting to pass the exam, wanting to get a PhD, or wanting to become famous. There is a lot of arbitrariness in attributing goals, and there is no way for an observer to come to a definite decision on which is the right one; there is no experimental procedure.

Similar arguments hold for animal behavior, the difference obviously being that I cannot ask animals about their goals (but, as pointed out already, that would not really make a difference). In order to support a particular choice of a goal (as a hypothesis for explaining the behavior of an agent) one might want to find additional evidence to the purely behavioral one, namely in physiology and biology. However, and this is the third point, there is no physiological evidence for explicit goal representations from animal studies and perhaps never will be [30].

To illustrate this point let us look at a simple example, the classical navigation problem: How does an agent get from location A to location B? Studies in animal navigation (e.g., [3, 42, 56]) show that sometimes animals can travel long distances from one location to another. For example, certain types of fish (salmon, eel) can travel back to their place of birth over thousands of miles. Their behavior can be described sensibly by attributing to them the goal of being at the place where they came from (location B). But there is no basis to assume that the fish have an explicit representation of the goal of being at location B. But, of course, there are physiological mechanisms responsible for this behavior. The fish seem to be following a concentration gradient of some chemicals, at least once they are back in fresh water [20], and in combination with a rheotactic response (a tendency to orient against the direction of water flow—[19]) this leads to the observed behavior.

In other words, the behavior of the fish can be explained on the basis of purely local mechanisms, without the need to resort to global goal representations. A behavioral program is triggered by some physiological variables and is shut off again when certain conditions obtain, again on the basis of some physiological mechanism. This mechanism, in a sense, could be described as recognizing when the behavior should change. In this perspective the fish is a goal-achieving system. But the goal does not really pertain to a particular location, as we, observers define it in the navigation problem. Because within the agent (the fish) everything is predetermined just as in the case of an automaton, we could also call the system goal seeking: A behavioral program is triggered by certain combinations of values of variables, is executed, and shut off again. A more detailed analysis of the navigation problem is given in [44].

The attribution of global goal representations implies that the system possesses a model of the world whose scope goes beyond direct sensory input. This contrasts with an explanation founded on local mechanisms where only the immediate system–environment interaction is relevant: Because the gradient of chemical concentration is already in the environment, there only needs to be a mechanism for locally following a gradient. This mechanism has the same status as any other reflex in the fish.

Now about designing agents: What we have shown so far is that behavior that can be well described by using the idea of goals does not necessarily imply that the system is goal directed. However, we have not yet demonstrated that when designing a system, it would be inappropriate to design a goal directed system. The fact that animals presumably don't have explicit goal representations (or at least, there does not seem to be much evidence in favor) does not imply that artifacts should not be goal directed. There are four main points why building goal directed systems might not be the best way of designing autonomous agents. First, when defining goals explicitly the current situation and the goal situation need to be represented. One runs into the representationalist pitfall (see next pitfall). Second, autonomous agents working on the basis of explicit goal representations have apparently had only limited success (see, e.g., [28]). Third, systems based on static designer-defined ontologies—and such ontologies are needed when explicitly representing goals—tend to be less adaptive (see representationalist pitfall). Fourth, there are highly efficient alternatives that work very well in nature (see examples) and are very adaptive.

But if goals are not the right way of modeling an agent's behavior, how then is it possible to tell the agent what to do, say to go from A to B, in the first place? It seems very hard *not* to think of goals. There is no definite answer yet, but we discuss some pertinent ideas in the following (see section "Avoiding the Pitfalls").

Not only is it hard not to describe behavior in terms of goals, but we also have a hard time not thinking of our environment in terms of distinct objects. But thinking of the world in terms of identifiable objects leads us to suspect that they are represented in the "mind" of the agent in terms of memory structures or representations that somehow mirror the descriptions of the objects as we see them ourselves. This point is illustrated by our discussion of goals where it is assumed that the *internal representations* somehow "mirror" our *descriptions* of the world. In this sense the goal directed systems pitfall is a special case of the more general representationalist pitfall, which we turn to next.

9.2.2 The Representationalist Pitfall

The literature on representation in AI, cognitive science, and philosophy is vast and cannot be possibly covered here. We adhere, in essence, to the original position of Newell and Simon, as outlined in their seminal paper on the physical symbol systems hypothesis ([39], see also [35]). Representations in the sense used here must obey the *representation law* as proposed by Newell [38]. It is illustrated in Fig.9.1. By a representationalist position we mean one which is, in essence, based on the assumption that in order to approximate a knowledge-level description [35], knowledge must be represented explicitly at the symbol level [37].

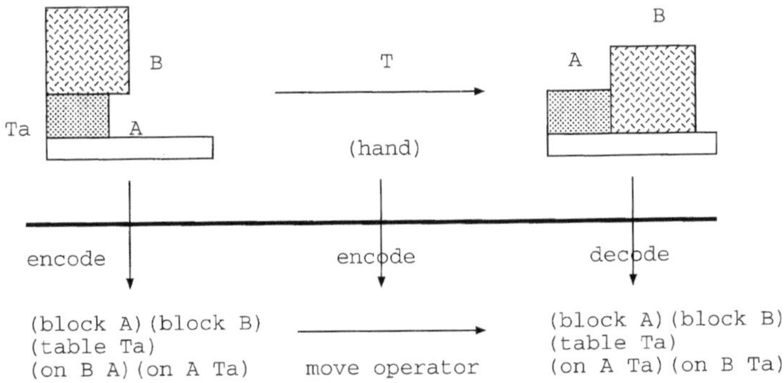

Fig. 9.1: Schematic illustration of the representation law.

To be more concrete, when a representationalist designs an AI system, one of the first questions to ask is what the best means of representing knowledge about the task domain would be and what would have to be represented: What are the classes, the objects, the relations, the events, and the actions? In other words, the domain ontology has to be defined. However, when designing autonomous agents, there is a fundamental problem with this view (e.g., [10]). For example, the fact that an agent can navigate in an environment does not necessarily imply that it has to be able to recognize the objects (e.g., blocks, other agents) around which it navigates: It only needs to respond in appropriate ways to the sensory inputs. Put differently, to not walk into a tree there is no need to identify it as a tree: It is sufficient to recognize that something is there that must be avoided.

The fact that we, as humans, with our extremely sophisticated sensors (like eyes) can recognize objects or walls does not imply that the robot will need to recognize them in a similar way to perform a particular task. Even humans do not always first identify objects before taking action. For example, when an object rapidly approaches, we duck long before recognizing the object. The traditional point of view is that there is an internal representation of an object in terms of a symbol structure onto which the sensory inputs are to be mapped. There are several problems with this view.[5]

First, static models which "mirror" some parts of the outside world (e.g., certain objects) do not take into account that the world continuously changes, and sensory input is continuously reinterpreted. Potentially relevant objects cannot be forseen, such as particular environmental regularities, for example, where food can be found. These regularities can appear in so many different ways in the environment that it is highly unlikely that they can be predefined in terms of distinguishable objects. If the agent is to be adaptive the interpretation of sensory input must also change continuously and be sensitive to context [11]. This dynamic, continuous reinterpretation cannot be achieved using static models. There have been systems that acquire, in a sense, their own models of the environment, for example, induction systems [31] or unsupervised classification networks [22], but they both rely on a preclassification of the environment in terms of features (see later, the neural network pitfall).

Second, the objects are defined from a designer's perspective. The definitions therefore reflect the designer's intuitions about the appropriate basic categories, his domain ontology. A domain ontology is a classification of the world in terms of high-level symbolic categories such as blocks, walls, moving, and so on. Whenever we are defining symbolic categories for autonomous agents (i.e., artifacts that have to interact with the real world without the mediation of a human interpreter) we are confronted with the symbol grounding problem. But the symbol grounding problem only exists because of this particular way of describing agents, namely in terms of symbol structures.

However, when designing autonomous agents there is always a general grounding problem: The structures—we might also want to call them knowledge—that guide the agent's behavior must either relate directly to sensors and effectors or they must be built on top of already grounded knowledge (i.e., they must be acquired or learned).[6] But if they are ac-

[5]It is clear that we cannot give a comprehensive account of problems involved in representation—there is a vast literature on the topic. We restrict ourselves to what has been and is important to the practice of AI in designing autonomous agents.

[6]In the next chapter we show how agents whose knowledge is fully grounded in this general sense can be built.

quired by the agent itself, rather than defined by the designer, it is no longer possible for the designer to predefine what actions will be appropriate for the agent, because what the agent will learn depends on the particular properties of the environment, which in turn cannot be forseen.[7] If an agent is to behave sensibly its knowledge must be fully grounded, otherwise—because it will not be able to make sense of its inputs—it will not be able to take appropriate action (i.e., its actions will not relate to the current situation).

Third, the predefinition of objects implies that sensory states will have to be mapped onto internal models, a task that has turned out to be extremely difficult to do, as the field of computer vision teaches us [28]. In our discussion of situatedness we showed that input processing must be driven by the context (i.e., the action the agent is currently involved in). Input will only be processed to the extent needed to take a suitable action. The postulate of models onto which sensory inputs are to be mapped can be related to the sense-think-act cycle. As argued earlier, systems based on the sense-think-act paradigm have problems acting in real time.

A truly hard problem (discussed earlier) imported by a representationalist view is the one of maintaining a world model. Indexical aspects pose formidable computational problems, especially if the agent moves around. The relations between the objects change continuously as the agent moves. All these relations need to be continuously updated. But the need to maintain elaborate world models can be dramatically reduced by appropriate designs. Work in the field of new AI shows that it is entirely possible to achieve well-organized behavior without any strong notion of representation, which, given a traditional view, is difficult to imagine (e.g., [6, 43, 60]; see also next section).

The representationalist pitfall is an obstinate one. Especially from an AI point of view it is hard to see how an agent could be made intelligent without explicitly representing knowledge in the agent about its environment and about how to act in particular situations. Connectionism seemes to be able to deal with these problems. However, this has lead to another pitfall, the neural network pitfall.

9.2.3 The Neural Network Pitfall

Connectionism was proposed as a paradigm that would allow us to develop brainlike nonsymbolic theories of cognition. However, it can be shown that neural networks as they are often used are just as symbolic as traditional AI models [58]; they are just as representationalist. For example, in the famous NETTalk model [51] the encoding in the input layer is in the form of letters (i.e., symbolic) and the encoding in the output layer is in terms of phoneme features. Phoneme features are designer-defined categories and thus the

[7] This point relates to the direct programming pitfall.

respective sound encodings are also symbolic. The symbolic encoding of the examples (i.e., how the letters are mapped onto the phonetic features) forces the system to distinguish vowels from consonants. Therefore, this distinction cannot be called emergent. Thus, employing neural networks per se does not automatically get us out of the representationalist pitfall. This is what we call the neural network pitfall, namely assuming that neural networks will automatically solve, for example, the fundamental problems of grounding.

NETTalk uses a supervised learning procedure (back propagation). But even in nonsupervised schemes like the one of [22] the input layer typically consists of symbolically interpretable categories (like the channel number of a multichannel analyzer, as they are used in speech processing). There have also been approaches where the inputs to the neural network are simply pixels that are either on or off. In those cases the problem is not so much one of precategorization but one of knowing when and what to learn (see later, the modularity pitfall). What *is* needed is an appropriate embedding of neural networks in a physically instantiated agent [45].

9.2.4 The Direct Programming Pitfall

An important step in designing a robot is, of course, the specification of its physical set-up, its body, its sensors, and effectors. The sensors and effectors rules that specify the robot's response (its motor behavior) to a particular sensory input pattern can be defined in terms of sense-act rules. An example would be if the left bumper sensor is on, then reverse and turn right.

Physical events in the real world are translated by the sensors into internal states. For example, if a bumper sensor is turned on (because of hitting) this event will cause a change in the agent's internal state. The internal states that are directly affected by the sensors are called the *input space* [25]. If the input space is simple—if there are only a few sensors and they affect the internal state only in simple ways (in a binary manner as, for example, simple IR sensors—it is *relatively* straightforward to supply a set of sense-act rules (also called *reflexes*). We use the term *relatively* straightforward because on the one hand it can be done, at least in some cases. For example, the set of augmented finite state machines in the subsumption architecture can be defined and leads to working systems [6]. On the other, even in really simple cases there are very many sensory states and the definition of appropriate actions is by no means trivial or straightforward (T. Smithers, 1990, September, personal communication).

Even if there may be difficulties involved, at this basic level the agents can be directly programmed, in fact they *must* be directly programmed if the agents are to behave at all.[8] Moreover, these basic sense-act rules are

[8] For the purposes of the current discussion we are leaving out evolutionary considerations.

by definition grounded because they relate directly to the physical set-up of the agent.

But if the input space is more complex, only a subspace—typically a very small one—of the whole input space will be relevant to the agent. For example, if the agent is equipped with high resolution range finders or visual sensors, the input space can become awesomely large. This implies that the designer has to specify which patterns in the input space are relevant, which will trigger a certain action. In other words, the designer must have hypotheses about what events in the real world will be relevant (e.g., the appearance of an obstacle) and how these events will affect the input space: The designer will need a *domain ontology* and a way to relate elements in this ontology to states in the input space.

If we are dealing with the real world in which every environment will contain novel items and show variation, it is not possible to specify a (static) domain ontology once and for all, as we have already argued. Thus the system must be able to form its own categories in relation to variation in the environment. To put it differently, if the agent is to adapt to a variety of environments, and if these environments are continuously changing, not all behavior of the agent can be *programmed directly*; some of it must be learned by the agent.

The issue of direct programming relates back to representations. The more predefined categories, the more will have to be programmed directly. Clearly, there are always ontological commitments that have to be made by the designer of an agent. The design of the sensors, the motor actions, and how they relate (i.e., the basic reflexes) are examples of designer commitments. They are based on the designer's intuitions about what might be useful for a robot in a particular environment (e.g., touch sensors, range finders, turning away when touching). Experience in robot building shows that these basic intuitions are often inappropriate and continuously need to be revised—even in static environments. But we are interested mostly in changing environments because the real world is continuously changing, and intelligence is only required in changing environments. Thus, we do not want to—and we cannot—decide beforehand everything the robot should do as it gets particular patterns of sensory input (indicating, in our observer's perspective, that the robot is near an object) because what will be the best thing for the agent to do depends on the particular environment (large or small objects, density of objects, speed, etc.). It is neither desirable nor possible to make too many initial commitments.[9]

In this context it is interesting to note that in nature the genotype does not preprogram the complete individual with all its knowledge (e.g., [8, 11]). The final form of the organism, the phenotype, is the result of the interaction of the initial cell with its environment in the process of

[9] To investigate this set of issues has been one of the goals of the Really Useful Robots (RUR) project of the University of Edinburgh [34].

development. Moreover, while it may be preprogrammed how food can be sensed, its presise location in the environment cannot because that depends on the particular circumstances.

On the other hand, making too few commitments would be as severe a mistake. As we show in Section 9.3, the process of adaptation must be constrained: There must be a number of suitable reflexes that endow the agent with a set of basic ways of acting in the environment. It is these basic reflexes on top of which the complete behavior of the agent will evolve. Thus, in a sense, this repertoire constrains all potential behaviors. But there is an additional point to be made. When designing an agent, in addition to defining the physical set-up and the basic reflexes, the control architecture has to be designed. This in turn implies that certain additional ontological commitments have to be made. For example, the variables of the dynamical system or neural network that implements the control architecture and the internal processes for learning and action selection have to be determined. There are many constraints in the environment; because the environment is physical, it has certain properties of continuity. If an agent is to function in a particular environment, it is generally a good idea to exploit environmental constraints in designing the architectures. For example, it has been shown that by taking into account the fact (or rather, the hypothesis) that letter perception proceeds via successive levels of integration of local features, which exploit certain regularities of the way they are materialized, the computing times of general back propagation networks could be reduced by orders of magnitude [26]. In conclusion, a compromise between commitments and flexibility has to be found. Whereas low-level behaviors must be programmed, high-level ones should be achieved indirectly via learning processes. This is called the direct/indirect design trade-off: The more the characteristics of a particular environment are taken into account in the architecture (i.e., directly programmed) the better it can exploit them, but the less it will be able to adapt flexibly to other, unforseen environmental properties. The less there is defined directly and the more there is left to general learning mechanisms, the more adaptable the agent will be, but the less efficient its behavior in any one particular environment.

9.2.5 The Hybrid Systems Pitfall

In the last section we argued that the number of predefined categories should be minimal even though the architecture has to be constrained to fit a particular type of environment. In a symbol processing framework an important part of the task of developing a system is to come up with the appropriate domain ontology: Symbols are assigned to objects, actions, relations between objects, and so on. In the case of classical AI systems (e.g., expert systems, language systems, goal directed systems) it has proven useful to work with symbol systems, and, one way or other, the robots will have to be told what to do. So it seems natural to use goal, object, and plan representations for this purpose, as discussed before. Now these internal representations will have to be connected to the physical set-up (i.e., the sensory and motor outfit as the latter relate to the outside world). For controlling the low-level mechanisms of robots it has proven useful to employ neural networks. Examples are problems of hand–eye coordination ([24, 50]). Now the task is to combine the high-level symbolic part with the low-level dynamical one, which means developing a hybrid system. An often-heard slogan is "getting the best of both worlds." Although from a pragmatic point of view there is a lot of power to be gained by developing hybrid systems (e.g., [18]), this is not the case from a cognitive science perspective or from a perspective of building autonomous systems. If there is, on the one hand, a designer-defined ontology (which leads to the representationalist pitfall) and on the other, a physical set-up of the robot equipped with mechanisms for building categories of its own, there will always be a significant mismatch between what has been learned and prespecified. If the environment is sufficiently complex, if it is unpredictable, and if the category formation depends strongly on the kind of environment, then what categories will develop cannot be predicted in principle. This is the very reason, as discussed before, why a robot cannot be fully programmed directly. Thus, it is doubtful whether a hybrid systems approach will be suitable for autonomous agents.

9.2.6 The Modularity Pitfall

Underlying hybrid systems there is the idea of components or modules: There is a module for symbolic processing and one for nonsymbolic processing. Similarly, it has been suggested that there are separate functional modules for perception, memory, planning, decision making, motor control, language, and so on. In fact, much of psychology is organized along such modular decompositions. The assumption is, that although there is a certain dependence among the modules, they can, in essence, be modeled independently. This view, however, has lead to ever more difficult problems. An example is natural language processing where the assumption of a separate language faculty [9, 14] has lead to a syntax-dominated view of language. Without going into details, it has become obvious that semantics cannot be appropriately dealt with within this syntactical framework [54]. Another example of a modular view is the one of a delineable and measurable entity called *intelligence* (e.g., [16]). This view is implicitly underlying the logic-oriented view of intelligence because it assumes that there is a kind of intelligence module that can be modeled in separation of the rest of the agent. The modularity assumption underlying logic-based AI has lead to a logic-dominated view of intelligence. But as mentioned earlier, implementing a logic-based module into a behaving system leads to the fundamental problems we have discussed under the heading of the representationalist pitfall—for example, the one of grounding.

Perhaps more pertinent to autonomous agent design is the hypothesis that there is a separate functional module for visual perception. In this traditional view this module enables the agent to recognize objects. Based on the result of this process the agent can then act appropriately. However, we already saw that the domain ontology of an autonomous agent cannot be defined by the designer. Therefore what will have to be recognized cannot be determined in advance but should be acquired by the agent. This process should somehow be directed because there are always multiple ways in which a classification can be performed. The most appropriate way of constraining classification is by taking the consequences of the agent's actions into account. It follows that perception cannot be separated from action in the first place; the two cannot be considered as separate modules.

This point is illustrated by the research on computer vision. Much work has been invested on developing vision systems in isolation. But given the large efforts expended, the successes have not been overwhelming [28]. However, if vision is assumed to be part of a larger system—for example, one that can move—certain problems become much easier because of the additional constraints provided by the combination. For example, motion provides systematically correlated sensory inputs. What affects the sensors are continuously changing physical events, which will normally not lead to significant jumps in the states in the input space. This continuity can be exploited by the architecture (focus on correlations between neighboring points in the input space). Moreover, these inputs are also systematically correlated to what the agent is currently doing (e.g., direction and speed of motion). This implies that the inputs are always relevant to action. It is this tight connection to action that provides the basic motivation for processing input in the first place.

To avoid misunderstandings, it should perhaps be mentioned that functional modules are different from physical devices. Physical devices, such as sensors are needed. But the fact that there is, for example, a visual sensor does not imply that this constitutes the perception module. For purposes of perception, the visual sensor must be viewed as part of the complete agent, as discussed previously.

In conclusion, although for descriptive purposes it may be helpful to talk about different modules, in designing autonomous agents, it is of utmost importance to keep the complete agent in mind from the very beginning. A number of problems turn out to be artifacts of the isolation of a particular module. For example, many of the problems involved in interpreting static camera images disappear when motion is introduced. The importance of developing complete systems has not only been pointed out by roboticists but also by psychologists [57].

9.2.7 The Biomimicry Pitfall

The biomimicry pitfall is somewhat different from the previous ones because it is not a direct consequence of applying a traditional AI approach to robot design. But the relation to biology has attracted a lot of attention recently so that we include it as a separate pitfall.

In the past few years an idea has experienced a renaissance [2]. The space of possible designs for autonomous agents is so enormous that a crucial aspect in the design process consists in finding appropriate constraints. One source of constraints comes from observing good designs in existing natural autonomous agents. So, drawing inspiration from the animal world seems to be very natural. The biomimicry pitfall is that *unreflected* mimicking of biological systems is not an appropriate strategy for robot design.

Here are some reasons why simply mimicking biological systems is problematic. Frequently in the animal world, the particular mechanisms observed represent highly specialized solutions, which only work in the particular ecological niche the animal lives in. It is normally far from obvious to determine the general class of mechanisms of which a particular one is an instance. Biologists use considerations across species as well as evolutionary theory to achieve generality. Implementing the mechanisms observed in the animal world, such as trying to model a particular insect on the basis of hypotheses about the real insects' mechanisms, can lead to fruitful insights if it is embedded in an appropriate research strategy.[10] But it does not necessarily follow that the robots designed in this way will be good ones from an engineering point of view. What we *are* interested in is general principles so that they can be applied to a variety of environments that may be natural or artificial, and this generality is not achieved only by mimicking nature.

It should also be noted that when we talk about mechanisms at the biological level we are talking about *models*. They are no more or no less "true" than any other kind of model, but the nature of the constraints they implement is different. This latter property is why we are interested in them.

Another aspect of the biomimicry pitfall is the fact that biological-control architectures are erroneously seen as exclusively designed for information processing purposes. However, nervous systems also support a lot of other processes; for example, they have to sustain their own metabolism [46].

What is needed is a nonnaive way of including biological insights. We believe that there are currently no generally accepted strategies available for how to best structure the interaction between robot design and biology. An interesting one has been applied by Franceschini and his collaborators [15], who built a robot on the basis of a model of the visual system of the fly. This endeavor has lead to important additional insights about

[10] A successful example of such a strategy is described in Franceschini [15].

fly navigation and about robot navigation. Another one is applied in our own research where the focus is on including biological constraints at an abstract level (see next section). Of course, working out the relationship between the disciplines will require an interdisciplinary dialogue, which, alas, is very hard to achieve.

This list of potential pitfalls could be continued almost indefinitely, but it should suffice to make our point that applying the paradigm of traditional artificial intelligence to the design of autonomous robots leads to significant problems.

9.3 Avoiding the Pitfalls

So far we have been outlining ways of proceeding and attitudes one should try to avoid when building autonomous agents, but we have said very little about what one should do. It would be premature to propose a complete methodology. For this the time is simply not right—the field has not yet sufficiently matured.

We briefly enumerate the pitfalls and for each suggest how they can be avoided. One of the architectures we discuss is distributed adaptive control (DAC) [43, 61]. In our view, it takes care of most of the problems discussed in this chapter; it avoids the pitfalls discussed to a certain extent. But we will also use other approaches to illustrate certain points.

The basic idea of DAC is as follows: The agent is a simple mobile robot equipped with a number of sensors (collision detector, range finder, target detector) and can move forward, reverse, and turn. The essential ingredient is a so-called *value scheme*, which encodes the agent's basic needs (e.g., to maintain a certain energy level,[11] to keep moving), reflexes (e.g., if a collision on the left is registered, reverse and turn right), parameter settings, and properties of the sensors. The agent has a neural network-based architecture, derived from a model of classical conditioning [58], which enables it to integrate the basic reflexes with more sophisticated sensors (e.g., a range finder). (see Fig. 9.2)

There are four layers of neurons (command, collision detection, target detection, range finder). The connections in the upper half of Fig. 9.2 are hardwired, the ones in the lower half, modifiable. Moreover, the layer activated by the collision detector inhibits the layer activated by the target detector. The integration of the basic reflexes (e.g., if collision on left, reverse and turn right) with the range finder (the more sophisticated sensor) is achieved by an associative Hebbian learning process with *active forgetting*. Active forgetting means that forgetting only takes place if something

[11] In this example, the only basic "need" is to keep moving.

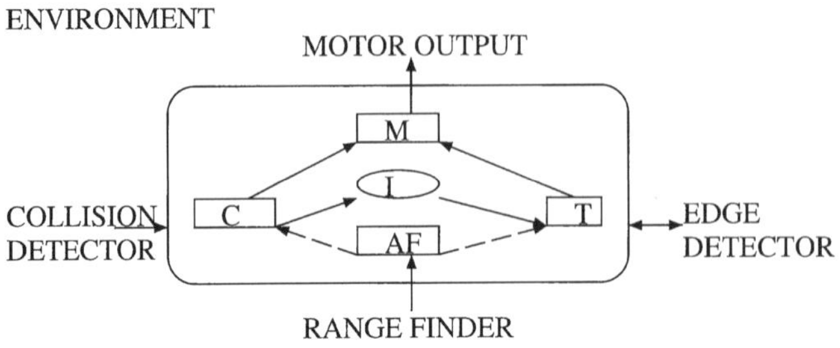

Fig. 9.2: Neural network architecture of Distributed Adaptive Control.

is learned. As the agent moves around in the environment—its basic motivation is to keep moving—it will first hit obstacles, but after a while it will avoid them because it has learned to use range-finder input to control its actions. In a sense, it starts *anticipating* obstacles, which enables it to turn away before it is hitting.

The target detector can be thought of as a kind of nose. There is a basic reflex that can be described as "if a target is detected, turn toward target". In one experiment targets were always put behind holes in walls. In this environment the agent acquired a behavior that one might call "wall-following." It is interesting to note that wall-following is only observed if there is this particular regularity of targets in the environment. If the agent moves around, it will after some time start following walls, and if somewhere in the wall there is a hole with a target, it will turn into the hole toward the target. To an outside observer this looks as if the agent were pursuing a goal, namely to seek targets. It is clearly not goal directed because there is no explicit representation of the goal to be at the target location. Rather it is goal achieving if we consider maintaining internal physiological conditions to be goals; otherwise it is goal seeking because the behavioral programs are automatically triggered and later shut off.

Another example, which was mentioned earlier, the subsumption architecture [4], will also be used for purposes of illustration. Instead of specifying a set of goals, the specification consists of a set of behaviors. Each of these behaviors, implemented by some kind of augmented finite state machine, can respond directly to inputs without having to consult a central controller or homunculus and without having to represent the whole environment internally. For example, obstacles can be avoided without having been identified as blocks or pyramids. To the outside observer, Brooks' robots seem to behave in purposive manners. However, they are not goal directed systems; there are no explicit representations of goals that drive the robot's behavior.

DAC and subsumption architecture-based agents demonstrate that seemingly purposeful behavior can be achieved without the need to explicitly represent goals. This leads us back to a question we asked before: How can the agent be told what to do, if not by defining its goals? This problem is discussed in detail in the following.

Just as goals, other items (physical objects, events, and actions) need not be explicitly represented, to achieve coherent behavior. This was demonstrated convincingly by [6] and by DAC. If no domain ontology needs to be explicitly represented, the approach is not subject to the representationalist pitfall.

One experiment we did with the DAC architecture was to propagate activation from a node in the motor layer, for example, the one for reverse and turn left, back to the range-finder layer. This leads to a kind of prototypical pattern, prototypical for situations in which the agent should reverse and turn right. We, as observers, might want to call these prototypical patterns, representations of action relevant situations that the agent can potentially exploit.[12] But these representations are not designer defined. Rather they are acquired by the robot over time and are tied to the agent's actions. It is important to note that they would be different for different environments and for different learning experiences.

One of the keys to achieving coherent behavior without explicit representations is not to process inputs in separation but to tie input processing to action. In other words, the idea is not to try to map inputs onto some sort of internal representation and then to decide on a particular action. Rather, the input will only be processed to the extent that it matters for the execution of appropriate actions. This principle leads to significant reductions in processing requirements. This is illustrated by an example that we have already discussed: Obstacle avoidance can be achieved without having to identify the object.

Earlier we mentioned that not all behavior of the agent can be programmed beforehand and argued that there must be learning involved (see direct programming pitfall). But there is another way in which an agent can display behavior that has not been directly programmed, namely through the interaction of several behaviors. In both cases the term *emergent behavior* has been used because, in some sense, the resulting behavior is more than the sum of its parts. It has been proposed that one should design for emergence in order to achieve robust behavior, the prominent example being wall-following [40]. Rather than putting a component into the system that exclusively deals with this behavior (such as the following rule "if there is a wall, follow the wall") the behavior should emerge out of the interaction of several behaviors (such as being attracted to wall, and being repelled by wall). In this sense the resulting behavior is no longer directly programmed. The potential of this way of emergent design still has to be explored. What can be said at this point is that finding the right primi-

[12] A detailed account of the problem of representation and of action prototypes is given in Pfeifer and Verschure [44].

tives and putting them together appropriately is the crucial problem to be addressed.

Let us go back to the problem of how the agent can be told to do something, say to go from location A to location B, without specifying a global goal representation. When we talk about telling the robot to go from A to B we normally mean that the designer will define for a particular situation what A and B mean. But if this is done by the designer then the specific descriptions will have to be supplied to the agent, and we are back to the goal directed systems and the representationalist pitfall. A possible solution is through provision in the value scheme, for example, by relating some actions to a particular drive or several drives. Assuming that the agent is in location A, it must somehow get an advantage out of going to B; otherwise it will not do it.

To make things concrete, let us use the same simulation example we described before: If there are target sources behind holes in walls in the environment, the agent will eventually learn to follow walls. After having acquired this wall-following behavior, if the agent is released anywhere in the environment (let's call this location A), it will move straight while avoiding obstacles, until it gets near a wall. It will then follow the wall until there is indeed a target source behind a hole in the wall. If we take this to be our target location B we do indeed have a robot that will go from location A, which is the agent's current location, to location B, which is defined by the designer. The path will not be the shortest one the system could take, but it will be much better than random search if there is this particular regularity in the environment. There is no explicit representation of the goal to be at location B. There is only an internal variable that shuts off the moving behavior. In this sense the agent is probably best described as a goal-seeking system. In other words we have designed a robot that will go from A to B without having to introduce goals. This avoids the goal directed systems pitfall.

The learning is essential because the particular regularities of the environment cannot be fully anticipated, and therefore the target location cannot be predefined. Thus, having a learning system avoids to a certain extent the direct programming pitfall. But, of course, the issues of how much should be predefined and how much should be acquired remains largely open.

This view, of course, also implies that a hybrid systems perspective would be inappropriate because this would imply defining goals at some level leading to the problems discussed earlier. If a strict bottom-up approach, as DAC, is adopted there is no danger of falling into the hybrid systems trap because all the knowledge of the agent will be built on top of other knowledge, which is grounded in its physical set-up (in the general sense discussed earlier): There is no need to make any commitments at the symbol level; symbols can be omitted altogether. By the way the neural network is integrated with sensors and the motor system, the neural networks pitfall is avoided because the network gets its input directly from the transducers, and there is no precategorization of the environment in terms of specific objects or events.

The previous discussion shows how the first five pitfalls can, at least to some extent, be avoided. Let us briefly discuss the last two, which concern modularity and biomimicry. An important consideration is that reflexes should be the starting point rather than sensory inputs and motor outputs, because, as pointed out earlier, perceptual processing must be tied to action. The role of these reflexes is not so much prespecifying optimal sense-act relations but rather constraining the learning process, in particular the ways in which sophisticated sensors are integrated with action. The choice of the most appropriate set of reflexes is again an open problem. What we want to stress is that reflexes are the right *sorts* of primitives because they, on the one hand, can be naturally used to drive the learning process. On the other, a tight coupling of the whole system with the environment is achieved: Perceiving, acting, and learning are no longer individual modules but views on the complete system. Using sensory inputs or motor outputs would not be adequate, because it would lead to a modularization in terms of perception and action. The problems with this perspective have been outlined earlier. We conclude that the modularity pitfall can be largely avoided.

It is hard to say how to avoid the biomimicry pitfall, and the relation between biology and autonomous agent design needs to be elaborated in much more detail. Let us only mention that biological insights can be used to constrain the space of possible designs. Examples of biological constraints we have applied are the restriction to pure local processes in the network (Hebbian learning), the idea of a value scheme that includes the drives and the basic reflexes, as well as the requirement that there be no distinction between a learning and a performance phase. Although we do think that these constraints are sensible ones and well founded, this is essentially a matter of taste.

Contributing to AI: So far we have shown how to avoid some of the pitfalls in autonomous agent design. However, we have not discussed the contribution toward solving the problems of traditional AI mentioned initially. Agents developed by avoiding the pitfalls will be more robust, they obviously have the capacity to learn and generalize, and they have at least a certain biological plausibility. If the agent is built on principles of learning, it will have the capacity to generalize to new situations and to adapt to different types of environments. This will have the effect that the knowledge we might want to attribute to the agent is fully grounded in its experience. The physical set-up and the reflexes are by definition grounded, as mentioned earlier. The agent is also situated: It can exploit the sensory inputs from a particular situation. But their interpretation is mediated by the traces of its own experience and thus changes continuously. The agent performs and reacts appropriately without having to maintain sophisticated world models, and can therefore act in real time. Acting in real time is especially important for autonomous systems because they might be physically hurt if they take too long, and there is always time pressure in real-world environments. It follows that this approach does indeed contribute to the basic problems of AI; at least it represents a first step.

9.4 Conclusions

We have argued for radical change. But is our approach indeed so different from traditional ones? Are we really talking about a new paradigm for artificial intelligence or are we doing something entirely different, asking completely different questions? After all, wall-following is very different from doing medical diagnosis. We can only talk about a new paradigm if there is significant overlap between the questions we are asking now and those we were asking before; otherwise it would be simply a different field. We do believe that we are trying to answer partly the same questions as traditional AI. For example, a fundamental issue is the design of systems that we want to call intelligent. Another one is the search for systems that are grounded (in the general sense), situated, and robust. Whether the proposed bottom-up approach will eventually scale up to the kinds of tasks we attempted to do in the traditional line of research is essentially an empirical question. We do believe it to be the case, although it may turn out that the kinds of activities we want autonomous agents to do will not sensibly be the ones of troubleshooting, scheduling, and configuration: The notion of tasks may have to be revised. For example, if we are thinking of building an autonomous agent for picking up ping-pong balls, the design of it might involve so many skills (e.g., visual/tactile-motor coordination, sophisticated modes of locomotion), and thus make the agent so extremely expensive that it would be highly inappropriate to attempt to design only for this particular task. Thus, tasks can no longer be as arbitrarily chosen as, for example, in the classical expert systems domain.

In conclusion, we have argued for a new AI. To develop this paradigm we should try to keep clear of the pitfalls that are a consequence of transferring traditional ways of thinking to the domain of autonomous agent design. If the pitfalls can be avoided, new AI not only promises to be an exciting and productive field of research, but will also contribute significantly to the understanding of intelligent behavior and the ambition to build intelligent machines.

References

[1] Agre, P. E., & Chapman, D. (1987). Pengi: An implementation of a theory of activity. *Proceedings of AAAI-87*, Los Angeles: Morgan Kaufmann. pp. 268–272.

[2] Ashby, W. R. (1952). *Design for a brain.* London: Chapman & Hall.

[3] Baker, R. R. (1973). *The evolutionary ecology of animal migration.* London: Hodder & Stoughton.

[4] Brooks, R. (1986). A robust layered control system for a mobile robot. *IEEE Journal of Robotics and Automation, RA-2,* 14–23.

[5] Brooks, R. (1990). Elephants don't play chess. *Robotics and Autonomous Systems, 6,* pp. 3–15.

[6] Brooks, R. (1991). Intelligence without representation. *Artificial Intelligence, 47,* 139–160.

[7] Chapman, D. (1987). Planning for conjunctive goals. *Artificial Intelligence, 32,* 333–377.

[8] Changeux, G. P. (1985). *Neuronal man: the biology of mind.* Oxford, UK: Oxford University Press.

[9] Chomsky, N. (1957). *Syntactic structures.* The Hague, Netherlands: Mouton.

[10] Clancey, W. J. (1989). The frame-of-reference problem in cognitive modeling. *Proceedings of the Cognitive Science Society* (pp. 107–114). Hillsdale, NJ: Lawrence Erlbaum Associates.

[11] Edelman, G. (1989). *The remembered present: a biological theory of consciousness.* New York: Basic Books.

[12] Ernst, G., & Newell, A. (1969). *GPS: A case study in generality and problem solving.* New York: Academic Press.

[13] Fikes, R. E., & Nilsson, N. J. (1971): STRIPS: A new approach to the application of theorem proving to problem solving. *Artificial Intelligence, 2,* 189–208.

[14] Fodor, J. (1983). *The modularity of mind.* Cambridge, MA: MIT Press, Bradford Books.

[15] Franceschini, N., Pichon, J. M., & Blanes, C. (1991). Real time visuomotor control: from flies to robots. In *Proceedings of IEEE Fifth International Conference on Advanced Robotics* (pp. 91–95).

[16] Gardner, H. (1985). *Frames of mind—The theory of multiple intelligences.* New York: Basic Books.

[17] Giralt, G., Chatila, R., & Vaisset, M. (1984). An integrated navigation and motion control system for multisensory robots. *Robotics Research, 1,* 191–214.

[18] Gutknecht, M., Pfeifer, R., & Stolze, M. (1991). Cooperative hybrid systems. *Proceedings of International Joint Conference on Artificial Intelligence-91,* (pp. 824–829).

[19] Hara, T. J. (1971). Chemoreception. In W. S. Hoar & D. J. Randall (Eds.), *Fish physiology. Volume V: Sensory systems and electric organs* (pp. 79–120). New York: Academic Press.

[20] Hasler, D. A., Scholz, A. T., & Horall, R. M. (1978). Olfactory imprinting and homing in the salmon. *American Scientist, 66*, 347–355.

[21] Janlert, L. E. (1989). Modeling change—The frame problem. In Z. Pylyshyn (Ed.), *The robot's dilemma. The frame problem in artificial intelligence* (pp. 1–40). Norwood, NJ: Ablex.

[22] Kohonen, T. (1988). *Self-organization and associative memory.* Berlin: Springer.

[23] Kuan, D., Phipps, G., & Chuan Hsueh, A. (1988). Autonomous robot vehicle road following. *IEEE Transactions on Pattern Analysis and Machine Intelligence, 10,* London: IEEE. pp. 55–87.

[24] Kuperstein, M. (1988). Neural network model for adaptive hand–eye coordination for signal postures. *Science, 239*, 1308–1311.

[25] Lamberts, K., & Pfeifer, R. (1993) Computational models of expertise: Accounting for routine and adaptivity in skilled performance. In K. Gilhooly & M. Keane (Eds.), *Advances in the psychology of thinking* (pp. 114–167). New York: Simon & Schuster.

[26] Le Cun, Y. (1989). Generalization and network design strategies. In R. Pfeifer, Z. Schreter, F. Fogelman-Soulié, & L. Steels (Eds.), *Connectionism in perspective.* Amsterdam: Elsevier. pp. 143–157.

[27] Maes, P. (1990). Situated agents can have goals. *Robotics and Autonomous Systems, 6*, 49–70.

[28] Malcolm, C. A., Smithers, T., & Hallam, J. (1989). An emerging paradigm in robot architecture. In T. Kanade, F. C. O. Groen, & L. O. Hertzberger (Eds.), *Proceedings of Intelligent Autonomous Systems, 2,*(pp. 284–293).

[29] McCarthy, J., & Hayes, P. J. (1969). Some philosophical problems from the standpoint of artificial intelligence. In B. Meltzer, & D. Michie (Eds.), *Machine intelligence, 4,* 463–502.

[30] McFarland, D. (1989). Goals, no goals and own goals. In A. Montefiore, & D. Noble (Eds.), *Goals, no-goals, and own goals. A debate on goal directed & intentional behavior* (pp. 39–57). London: Unwin Hyman.

[31] Michalski, R. (1983). A theory and methodology of inductive learning. *Artificial Intelligence, 20,* 111–161.

[32] Montefiore, A., & Noble, D. (Eds.), (1989). *Goals, no-goals, and own goals. A debate on goal directed and intentional behavior.* London: Unwin Hyman.

[33] Moravec, H. P. (1982). The Stanford cart and the CMU rover. In *Proceedings of the IEEE, 71,* 872–884.

[34] Nehmzow, U., Hallam, J., & Smithers, T. (1989). Really useful robots. In *Proceedings of Intelligent Autonomous Systems, 2,*

[35] Newell, A. (1981). The knowledge level. *AI Magazine, 2,* 1–20.

[36] Newell, A. (1980). Physical symbol systems. *AI Magazine,* 1–20.

[37] Newell, A. (1986). The symbol level and the knowledge level. In Z. W. Pylyshyn & W. Demopulos (Eds.), *Meaning and cognitive structure* (pp. 31–54). Norwood, NJ: Ablex.

[38] Newell, A. (1990). *Unified theories of cognition.* Cambridge, MA: Harvard University Press.

[39] Newell, A., & Simon, H. A. (1976). Computer science as empirical inquiry: symbols and search. *Communications of the ACM, 19,* 113–126.

[40] Nilsson, N. (Ed.).(1984). Shakey the robot. (Tech. Rep. No. 323). Menlo Park: SRI International, AI Center.

[41] Nisbett, R. E., & Wilson, T. D. (1977). Telling more than we can know: Verbal reports on mental processes. *Psychological Review, 84,* 231–259.

[42] Orr, R. T. (1970). *Animals in migration.* London: McMillan.

[43] Pfeifer, R., & Verschure, P. (1992). Distributed adaptive control: a paradigm for designing autonomous agents. In *First European Artificial Life Conference Proceedings* (pp. 21–30). Cambridge, MA: MIT Press.

[44] Pfeifer, R., & Verschure, P. Designing efficiently navigating nongoal directed robots. In J. A. Meyer, H. Roitblat, & S. Wilson (Eds.), *From animals to animates, Proceedings of SAB-92.* Cambridge, MA: MIT Press.

[45] Pfeifer, R., & Verschure, P. (1993). Beyond rationalism: Symbols, patterns, and behavior. *Connection Science.*, [special Issue on Philosophy]. Vol 5 (1), pp. 15-25.

[46] Purves, D. (1988). *Body and brain.* Cambridge, MA: Harvard University Press.

[47] Pylyshyn, Z. W. (Ed.) (1987). *The robot's dilemma: The frame problem in artificial intelligence.* Norwood, NJ: Ablex.

[48] Quillian, R. (1968). Semantic memory. In M. Minsky (Ed.), *Semantic information processing.* Cambridge, MA: MIT Press. pp. 227-271.

[49] Raphael, B. (1976). *The thinking computer. Mind inside matter.* San Francisco: Freeman.

[50] Ritter, H., & Kohonen, T. (1989). Self-organizing semantic maps. *Biological Cybernetics, 61,* 241–254.

[51] Sejnowski, T., & Rosenberg, C. (1987). Parallel networks that learn to pronounce English text. *Complex Systems, 1,* 145–168.

[52] Steels, L. (1989). Connectionist problem solving—An AI perspective. In R. Pfeifer, Z. Schreter, F. Fogelman-Soulié, & L. Steels (Eds.) *Connectionism in perspective* (pp. 215-229). Amsterdam: Elsevier.

[53] Steels, L. (1991). Towards a theory of emergent functionality. In J. A. Meyer, & S. W. Wilson (Eds.). *From animals to animates* (pp. 451–461). Cambridge, MA: MIT Press.

[54] Stich, S. (1983). *From folk psychology to cognitive science.* Cambridge, MA: MIT Press, Bradford Books.

[55] Suchman, L. A. (1987). *Plans and situated actions.* Cambridge, MA: Cambridge University Press.

[56] Swingland, J. R., & Greenwood, P. J. (1983). *The ecology of animal movement.* Oxford, UK: Clarendon Press.

[57] Toda, M. (1982). Man and the fungus eater. In M. Toda (Ed.), *Man, robot and society* (pp. 89–99). The Hague, Netherlands: Nijhoff.

[58] Verschure, P. (1991). Taking connectionism seriously: The vague promise of subsymbolism and an alternative. *Proceedings of the Fourteenth Annual Conference of the Cognitive Science Society* (pp. 653–658). Hillsdale, NJ: Lawrence Erlbaum Associates.

[59] Verschure, P., & Coolen, A. (1991). Adaptive fields: Distributed representations of classically conditioned associations. *Network, 2,* 189–206.

[60] Verschure, P., Krose, B. J. A., & Pfeifer, R. (1992). Distributed adaptive control: The self-organization of structured behavior. *Robotics and Autonomous Systems, 9,* 191–196.

[61] Verschure, P., & Pfeifer, R. (1992). Categorization, representatons, and the dynamics of system–environment interaction: a case study in autonomous systems. In J. A. Meyer, H. Roitblat, & S. Wilson (Eds.), *From animals to animates, Proceedings of SAB-92.* Cambridge, Ma: MIT Press. pp. 210–217.

[62] Winograd, T., & Flores, F. (1986). *Understanding computers and cognition.* Reading, MA: Addison-Wesley.

10. The Importance of Being Adaptable

LESLIE PACK KAELBLING
Teleos Research

10.1 Introduction

This chapter addresses the engineering problem of creating robotic agents that perform tasks in an environment. One motive for making artificial agents adaptable is that many natural agents are adaptable, and there is a strong analogical similarity between natural and artificial agents. For engineering purposes, however, we must only adopt techniques of agent design that either simplify the design and construction of artificial agents or cause the agents to ultimately perform better. We argue that it is crucial for artificial agents to be capable of adapting their behavior to their environments.

The designer of an agent is given a specification of an environment or a class of environments in which the agent must work and a specification of the task the agent is to perform. The environment description may include the physical morphology and primitive sensorimotor capabilities of the agent, or those may be left to vary as part of the design. The word *task* is used very broadly here: A task could be as simple as keeping moving without bumping into things or as complex as to research the geological make-up of an unexplored planet. Because we're interested in agents that have a long-term interaction with an environment, tasks will not be specifications of short-term achievement goals that terminate before the end of the agent's "life."

It is theoretically possible, given complete specifications of the task and the environment, to design an agent that optimally carries out the task in the environment. However, this strict prerequisite is rarely, if ever, satisfied. When the environment is not completely known to the designer ahead of time, the agent must itself be designed to adapt to its environment.

The dictionary [12] defines adapt as "to adjust to a specified use or situation." We use the term *adaptation* rather than *learning* in order to focus attention on the improvement of behavior by making it more appropriate for the environment in which the agent is situated. The term *learning* has been used for a much wider variety of processes, including so-called symbol-level learning, [4] in which no information is gained, but the internal processes of the agent are made more efficient.

We must make our agents adaptable when the specification of the environment and the agent's sensorimotor capabilities is incomplete, incorrect, or simply at an inappropriate level of abstraction. Here is a motivational story:

I once spent a long time trying to program a mobile robot to use ultrasonic sensors to navigate down the hallway. I had a physical specification of the environment (it was the hallway I was sitting in) and fairly accurate manufacturers' specifications for the sensors and motors of the robot. Theoretically, I had enough knowledge to write the correct program and be done with it. However, the specifications of the abilities of the robot and of the properties of the environment were impossible for me to translate directly into the correct program. So, I worked in a debugging cycle that went like this:

- Write a program for the robot;
- Run it on the robot and it drives into a wall;
- Analyze the behavior of the robot and see where the program was mistaken;
- Fix the problem in the program;
- Run it on the robot and it drives into a wall (this time for a different reason!);

and so on. The result of this cycle was that I learned a good deal about the nature of the interaction between the robot's sensors and the physical environment. Using this information, I *adapted* the robot's behavior so that it would perform its task correctly. A much more efficient strategy would have been for me to design a behavior for the robot that would *itself* adapt to the environment it was in.

The need for adaptability is even more pronounced when the specification of the environment is quite weak, allowing for a variety of different types of environments or even environments whose characteristics change over time. In that case, no amount of off-line learning on the part of the designer will allow a correct fixed strategy to be obtained, because the correct behavior will vary from run to run and even from time to time during the course of a single run.

It is difficult to give a concrete computational definition for adaptability. There are many agent programs that have internal state changes that we would not necessarily wish to term adaptable. Consider the following examples of agents adapting to their environments:

1. A robot is programmed to move along the wall to its left by first orienting itself parallel to the wall, then staying parallel to it as it goes.

2. A robot is programmed to deliver items from office to office as efficiently as possible; in its first attempts, it searches exhaustively for an office it is looking for, but eventually it goes directly to its destinations.

In case 1, the robot can work in most environments that involve being near a wall, but it must determine where it is with respect to the wall and specialize its wall-following program accordingly. The robot might be said to have *perceived* where the wall is.

In case 2, the robot will again have to specialize its general program, this time by determining the layout of the offices in its environment. In this case, the robot might be said to have *learned* where the offices are and *adapted* its behavior accordingly.

But is there any qualitative difference in the state changes in the two scenarios? It is certainly more difficult for the robot in the second scenario to gain the information necessary to specialize its program to its environment, but there are many tasks of intermediate difficulty. In our natural language use of the terms *perception* and *learning* or *adaptativity* we tend to make the distinctions shown in Fig.10.1.

	perception	adaptivity
Information gained is:	... easy to acquire ... dynamic ... specific	... hard to acquire ... static ... general

Fig. 10.1: The perception–learning spectrum

Each of these represents different extremes of a property with many intermediate degrees. We conclude that there is a spectrum of situations of information gain, ranging from what is commonly described as perception to what is commonly described as learning or adaptivity. In the remainder of this chapter, we focus on the long-term adaptation of behavior to suit general properties of the embedding environment.

10.2 Reinforcement Learning

One way to view the problem of constructing adaptable behaviors for agents is as a *reinforcement learning* problem. In reinforcement learning, the goal of the agent's designer is for the agent to learn what actions it should perform in which situations in order to maximize an external measure of success. All of the information the agent has about the external world is contained in a series of inputs that it receives from the environment. These inputs may encode information ranging from the output of a vision system to a robot's current battery voltage. The agent can be in many different states of information about the environment, and it must map each of these information states, or situations, to a particular action that it can perform in the world. The agent's mapping from situations to actions is referred to as an *action map*. Part of the agent's input from the world encodes the agent's *reinforcement*, which is a scalar measure of how well the agent is performing in the world. The agent should learn to act in such a way as to maximize the total reinforcement it gains over its lifetime.

As a concrete example, consider a simple robot with two wheels and two photosensors. It can execute five different actions: stop, go forward, go backward, turn left, and turn right. It can sense three different states of the world: The light in the left eye is brighter than that in the right eye, the light in the right eye is brighter than that in the left eye, and the light in both eyes is roughly equally bright. Additionally, the robot is given high values of reinforcement when the average value of light in the two eyes is increased from the previous instant. In order to maximize its reinforcement, this robot should turn left when the light in its left eye is brighter, turn right when the light in its right eye is brighter, and move forward when the light in both eyes is equal. The problem of learning to act is to discover such a mapping from information states to actions.

Thus, the problem of learning to act can be cast as a function-learning problem: The agent must learn a mapping from the situations in which it finds itself, represented by streams of input values, to the actions it can perform. In the simplest case, the mapping will be a pure function of the current input value, but in general it can have state, allowing the action taken at a particular time to depend on the entire stream of previous input values.

In the past few years there has been a great deal of work in the artificial intelligence (AI) and theoretical computer science communities on the problem of learning pure Boolean-valued functions [6, 10, 11, 14, 17]. Unfortunately, this work is not directly relevant to the problem of reinforcement learning because of the different settings of the problem. In the traditional function-learning work, often referred to in the AI community as concept learning, a learning algorithm is presented with a set or series of input–output pairs that specify the correct output to be generated for that particular input. This setting allows for effective function learning, but differs from the situation of an agent trying to learn an action map. The agent, finding itself in a particular input situation, must generate an action. It then receives a reinforcement value from the environment, indicating how valuable the current world state is for the agent. The agent cannot, however, deduce the reinforcement value that would have resulted from executing any of its other actions. Also, if the environment is noisy, as it will be in general, just one instance of performing an action in a situation may not give an accurate picture of the reinforcement value of that action.

Reinforcement learning reduces to concept learning when the agent has only two possible actions, the world generates Boolean reinforcement that depends only on the most recently taken action, there is exactly one action that generates the high reinforcement value in each situation, and there is no noise. In this case, from performing a particular action in a situation, the agent can deduce that it was the correct action if it was positively reinforced; otherwise it can infer that the other action would have been correct.

Reinforcement learning has its name because of its similarity to models used in psychological studies of behavior learning in humans and animals [5]. It is also referred to as "learning with a critic," in contrast with the "learning with a teacher" of traditional supervised concept learning [20].

10.3 Issues in Reinforcement Learning

Within the general framework of reinforcement learning, there are a variety of issues that must be addressed. Some of these have been active research topics; others are important directions for future research.

10.3.1 Exploration Strategies

One of the most interesting facets of the reinforcement-learning problem is the tension between performing actions that are not well understood in order to gain information about their reinforcement value and performing actions that are expected to have good results in order to increase overall reinforcement. If an agent knows that a particular action works well in a certain situation, it must trade off performing that action against performing another one that it knows nothing about, in case the second action is even better than the first. Or, as Ashby [1] put it:

> The process of trial and error can thus be viewed from two very different points of view. On the one hand it can be regarded as simply an attempt at success; so that when it fails we give zero marks for success. From this point of view it is merely a second-rate way of getting to success. There is, however, the other point of view that gives it an altogether higher status, for the process may be playing the invaluable part of *gathering*

> *information*, information that is absolutely necessary if adaptation is to be successfully achieved (p. 34).

The longer the time span over which the agent will be acting, the more important it is for the agent to be acting on the basis of correct information. Acting to gain information may improve the expected long-term performance although causing short-term performance to decline.

Another important aspect of the reinforcement-learning problem is that the actions that an agent performs influence the input situations in which it will find itself in the future. Rather than receiving an independently chosen set of input-output pairs, the agent has some control over what inputs it will receive and complete control over what outputs will be generated in response. In addition to making it difficult to make distributional statements about the inputs to the agent, this degree of control makes it possible for what seem like small experiments to cause the agent to discover an entirely new part of its environment.

10.3.2 Input Generalization

Many of the early algorithms for reinforcement require an enumeration of all possible inputs to the agent. For interesting real-world agents, the number of inputs can become enormous, causing a combinatorial explosion in the run-time and space requirements for the algorithms. In addition, such algorithms completely compartmentalize the information they have about individual input situations. If they learn to perform a particular action in a particular input situation, that has no influence on what they will do in similar input situations. In realistic environments, an agent cannot ever expect to encounter all of the input situations, let alone have enough experience with each one to learn the appropriate response. Thus, it is important to develop algorithms that will generalize across input situations.

It is important to note, however, that in order to find algorithms that are time and space efficient and that have the ability to generalize over input situations, we must give up something. What we will be giving up is the possibility of learning any arbitrary action mapping. In the worst case, the only way to represent a mapping is as a complete look-up table, which is what the early reinforcement-learning algorithms do. There are many useful and interesting functions that can be represented much more efficiently, and the continuing research in this area must rest on the hope and expectation that an agent can learn to act effectively in interesting environments without needing action maps of pathological complexity.

Input generalization can be added to reinforcement-learning algorithms by adopting function-approximation methods, such as radial-basis functions, CMAC, back propagation, and so on. A more directly statistical approach, which creates a decision tree by finding the most "relevant" input bits, was taken by Chapman and Kaelbling [3].

10.3.3 Structural Credit Assignment

It is often convenient to think of the output of an agent as being divided up into a number of independently calculated fields. These fields could correspond to different actuators of the robot or to individual bits that make up some arbitrary encoding of actuator commands. Once the output is divided into fields, the agent can learn to generate values for the fields independently. This can be useful because, in many situations, generalization can take place across the choice of output values; the agent may learn how to calculate the first bit independently, without having to consider it in combination with all the other bits. This division can also lead to great improvements in computational complexity.

Once the problem is broken down into several parallel learning problems, there is a question of *structural credit assignment*, or how the reinforcement should be distributed. The naive method, called *team learning* [13], is simply to distribute the reinforcement signal from the world directly to all the learners. The team method works in only a very restricted set of cases because, the vast majority of the time, most of the learning modules are getting erroneous reinforcement. Consider the case in which there are 10 learners each learning a single bit of the output in parallel. If just one of the learners generates the incorrect output bit, *all* of the learners will be punished. Kaelbling developed a method for structural credit assignment that works by conditioning the outputs of some components on the output of other components [7].

10.3.4 Temporal Credit Assignment

In many realistic environments, an agent will have to carry out a number of actions before arriving at a state that has high reinforcement value. How can that reinforcement be propagated backwards in order to reward temporally distant decisions? This question is referred to as the problem of *temporal credit assignment* or sequential decision making. It was originally solved in the context of dynamic programming, with complex iterative algorithms that run after a complete state-transition model of the world has been built. More recent methods [2, 16, 18] allow credit to be propagated backwards incrementally during the activity of the agent. Watkins' *Q-learning* method works quite reliably, but must be carefully coupled with a good exploration strategy.

10.3.5 Mappings with State

So far, we have considered learning only action maps that are pure, instantaneous functions of their inputs. It is more generally the case, however, that an agent's actions must depend on the past history of input values in order to be effective. By storing information about past inputs, the agent is able to induce a finer partition on the set of world states, allowing it to make more discriminations and to tailor its actions more appropriately to the state of the world.

Perhaps the simplest way to achieve this finer-grained historical view of the world is to remember all input instances from the last k time steps and present them in parallel to the behavior-learning algorithm. This method has two drawbacks: It is not possible for actions to depend on conditions that reach back arbitrarily far in history, and the algorithmic complexity increases considerably as the length of the available history is increased.

There have been no convincing alternative approaches. One suggestion, made by Kaelbling and implemented with limited success, is to learn mappings described by sequential Boolean networks, containing delay operators (and possibly feedback). This approach is difficult, because there seem to be no good heuristics to drive the construction of candidate networks. Another candidate approach is discussed in the context of building world models.

10.3.6 Using a priori Information

Tabula rasa learning, as reinforcement-learning has typically been carried out, may not be a sufficient method for creating intelligent embedded agents. However, the methods of reinforcement learning may be used in concert with other information provided in different forms by a human programmer or through evolutionary processes, in order to construct agents that start with a useful base of information and can improve upon it. A priori information might be provided in a number of different forms.

One of the simplest kinds of information that would improve the performance of reinforcement-learning algorithms is the expected reinforcement of the optimal policy. An agent that has this information can use it to make more informed trade-offs between acting to gain information and acting to gain reinforcement. The agent will be able to tell when it has found the best policy and need not experiment further.

Russell [15] introduced the idea of using *determinations* to bias learning. Determinations are, essentially, descriptions of which input values the outputs depend on. We might also start from a complete or partial program specified in terms of condition-action rules. An interesting research direction would be to develop representations of programs that are amenable to adjustment using reinforcement-learning methods.

The promising approach of Brooks and Maes [9] was to endow the agent with a set of primitive behaviors and for the agent to learn to switch between them. This notion might be extended into a sort of hierarchical learning of behaviors in which the learned composite behaviors become primitives for a similar learning process at a higher level.

10.3.7 Teaching and Observation

Many natural agents learn by observing other agents in the same environment or by being taught how to behave. The processes of observation and teaching may be important in the construction of artificial agents as well. There has been some preliminary work in this area [19], but there is a great deal of room for further inquiry. Interesting questions arise having to do with the fact that a collection of agents does not necessarily all have the same sensorimotor abilities, so that the optimal strategy for one might be very different from that for another. Does that mean agents have to be identical to learn from one another's experience? Teaching by example seems the most relevant to behavior learning. It amounts to a special kind of observation of an agent that is likely to be behaving very well in the environment.

10.3.8 Building World Models

Most approaches to reinforcement learning attempt to learn the action strategy directly. Another method is to learn some independent description of the way the world works, or a *world model*, then use the model to calculate what the correction action strategy should be.

One conjecture, made by Sutton and others, is that the model-learning approach will work better in many cases, because the model can be used for off-line calculation of the policy, which prevents the agent from having to make mistakes in the world. Empirical trials [8] have not yet clearly demonstrated this to be the case, because of the number of mistaken actions the agent must take in the course of learning the model.

Another motivation for learning a model is to make exploration more directed. It might take a very long time for an agent to reach a particular region of a complex state space through random exploratory strategies. If the agent has a rough model of the effects of its actions, it can take actions that will lead it to parts of the space it has never seen before, allowing it potentially to discover the optimal strategy sooner.

10.4 Conclusion

It is crucial for artificial as well as natural agents to adapt to the environments in which they operate. A useful framework, for viewing this process of adaptation is reinforcement learning. There is increased interest in the area of reinforcement learning, but there are many important issues that can serve as directions for future research.

References

[1] Ashby, W. R. (1960). *Design for a brain: The origin of adaptive behaviour (2nd ed.).* New York: Wiley.

[2] Barto, A. G., Sutton, R. S., & Watkins, C. J. C. H. (1989). *Learning and sequential decision making.* (Tech. Rep. No. 89–95). Amherst, MA: Department of Computer and Information Science, University of Massachusetts.

[3] Chapman, D., & Kaelbling, L. P. (1991). Input generalization in delayed reinforcement learning: An algorithm and performance comparisons. *Proceedings of the International Joint Conference on Artificial Intelligence* (pp. 599–603). Los Angeles: Morgan Kaufmann.

[4] Dietterich T. G. (1986). Learning at the knowledge level. *Machine Learning, 1*(3) 287–315.

[5] Estes, W. K (1950). Toward a statistical theory of learning. *Psychological Review, 57*, 94–107.

[6] Haussler, D. (1988). Quantifying inductive bias: AI learning algorithms and Valiant's learning framework. *Artificial Intelligence, 36*(2) 177–222.

[7] Kaelbling, L. P. (1990). *Learning in embedded systems.* Unpublished doctoral dissertation. Stanford, CA: Stanford University.

[8] Lin, Long-Ji (1991). Self-improving based on reinforcement learning, planning, and teaching. In *Proceedings of the Eighth International Workshop on Machine Learning.* Los Altos, CA: Morgan Kaufmann.

[9] Maes, P., & Brooks, R. A. (1990). Learning to coordinate behaviors. In *Proceedings of the Eighth National Conference on Artificial Intelligence.* Los Altos, CA: Morgan Kaufmann.

[10] Michalski, R. A. (1983). A theory and methodology of inductive learning. In R. S. Michalski, J. G. Carbonell, & T. M. Mitchell, (Eds.), *Machine learning: An artificial intelligence approach,* (pp. 239–260). Palo Alto: Tioga.

[11] Mitchell, T. M. (1982). Generalization as search. *Artificial Intelligence, 18*(2), 203–226.

[12] Morris, W. (1969). (Ed.). *The American Heritage dictionary of the English language.* Boston: American Heritage Publishing & Houghton Mifflin.

[13] Narendra, K., & Thathachar, M. A. L. (1989). *Learning automata: An introduction.* Englewood, NJ: Prentice-Hall.

[14] Quinlan, J. R. (1983). Learning efficient classification procedures and their application to chess end games. In R. S. Michalski, J. G. Carbonell, & T. M. Mitchell, (Eds.), *Machine learning: An artificial intelligence approach.* Tioga.

[15] Russell, S. J. (1989). *The use of knowledge in analogy and induction.* London: Pitman.

[16] Sutton R. S. (1988). Learning to predict by the method of temporal differences. *Machine Learning, 3*(1), 9–44.

[17] Valiant, L. G. (1984). A theory of the learnable. *Communications of the ACM, 27*(11), 1134–1142.

[18] Watkins, C. (1989). *Learning from delayed rewards.* Unpublished doctoral dissertation. Cambridge, UK: Cambridge University.

[19] Whitehead, S. (1991). Complexity and cooperation in q-learning. In *Proceedings of the Eighth International Workshop on Machine Learning.* Los Altos, CA: Morgan Kaufmann.

[20] Widrow, B. N., Gupta, K., & Maitra, S. (1973). Punish/reward: Learning with a critic in adaptive threshold systems. *IEEE Transactions on Systems, Man, and Cybernetics, SMC-3*(5), 455–465.

11. Grounding Symbolic Capacity in Robotic Capacity

STEVAN HARNAD
Universite d'Aix Marseille II

According to computationalism [5, 35, 36], mental states are computational states, so if one wishes to build a mind, one is actually looking for the right program to run on a digital computer. A computer program is a semantically interpretable formal symbol system consisting of rules for manipulating symbols on the basis of their shapes, which are arbitrary in relation to what they can be systematically interpreted as meaning. According to computationalism, every physical implementation of the right symbol system will have mental states.

Artificial intelligence is the branch of computer science that is concerned with designing symbol systems that have performance capacities that are useful to human beings. Cognitive science includes AI as well as mind modeling (MM), which is concerned with building systems that are not only useful to people with minds, but that *have* minds of their own. According to computationalism, AI can do both these things, and for several decades it was hoped that it would. AI's advantages in this regard were the following:

AI could indeed (a) generate performance that ordinarily requires human intelligence and that, unlike behavioral psychology [3, 13, 14, 15, 16], for example, it could explain the functional and causal basis of that performance.

There was also (b) reason to be optimistic about scaling up the performance of AI's initial toy models to human-scale performance because of formal results on the power and generality of computation; according to one construal of the Church-Turing Thesis, computation captures everything we mean by being able to "do" just about *anything*, whether formally or physically [6]. Hence, a computer can do anything any physical system can do—or, conversely, every physical system is really a computer.

The last of the initial reasons for optimism about AI for MM was (c) the apparent capacity of the software/hardware distinction to solve the mind/body problem: If computationalism is correct, and mental states are just implementations of certain symbolic states, then the persistent difficulty that philosophers have kept pointing out with equating the mental with the physical is resolved by the independence of a physical symbol system's formal, symbolic level (the software level) from its physical implementation (the hardware level). A symbol system is implementation independent, and so is the mind.

Unfortunately, problems arose for AI, and not just when it tried to do MM. AI systems have so far not proven to scale up readily, not only for the human-scale performance necessary for MM, but even for the kinds of performance that were merely intended to be useful to people, such as pattern recognition and robotics. Rival approaches began to appear, among them (a) robots that made minimal use (or none at all) of internal symbol systems [7]; (b) neural networks, which were systems of interconnected units whose parallel distributed activity likewise did not seem to have a structured symbolic level [12]; and (c) nonlinear dynamical systems in general, including continuous and chaotic ones that were not readily covered by the Church-Turing Thesis [34].

In addition, conceptual challenges were posed to the computationalist thesis that had made it seem that AI would be capable of doing MM in the first place. Two such challenges were Searle's [38] Chinese Room Argument and my own Symbol Grounding Problem [19]. Searle pointed out that the tenets of computationalism ("Strong AI") amounted to three hypotheses: (a) mental states are implementations of symbolic states; (b) all physical implementational details are irrelevant (because any and all implementations of the right symbol system will have the same mental states, hence the differences between them are all inessential to having a mind) and (c) performance capacity is decisive (and hence the crucial test for the presence of a mind is the Turing Test (T2), which amounts to the capacity to interact with a person as a lifelong penpal, indistinguishable in any way from a real person (note that this test is purely symbolic). Searle then pointed out that if there were a computer that could pass T2 in Chinese, he [38] could become another implementation of the same symbol system it was implementing (by memorizing all the symbol manipulation rules and then performing them on all the symbols received from the Chinese penpal), yet he would not thereby be understanding Chinese, hence neither would the computer that was doing the same thing. In other words, there was something wrong with hypotheses (a) through (c): They couldn't all be correct, yet computationalism depended on the validity of all three of them.

Searle's [38, 39] recommended alternative to computationalism and AI for those whose real interest was MM was to study the real brain, for only systems that had its "causal powers" could have minds. The only problem was that this left no way of sorting out which of the brain's causal powers were and were not relevant to having a mind [24]. We now knew (thanks in part to Searle) that the relevant causal powers were not exclusively the symbolic ones, but we did not know what the rest of them amounted to; and to assume that every physical detail of the real brain—right down to its specific gravity—was relevant and indeed essential to MM was surely to take on too much. A form of functionalism that sought to abstract the relevant causal powers of the brain already motivated AI: The relevant level was the symbolic one, and once that was specified, every physical implementation would have the relevant causal powers. Searle showed that this particular abstraction was wrong, but he did not thereby show that there could be no way to abstract away from the totality of brain function and causal power.

The symbol grounding problem pointed out another functional direction in which the causal powers relevant to having a mind may lie: The symbols in a symbol system are systematically interpretable as meaning something; however, that interpretation is always mediated by an external interpreter. It would lead to an infinite regress if we supposed the same thing to be true of the mind of the interpreter: that all there is in in his head is the implementation of a symbol system that is systematically interpretable by yet *another* external interpreter. My thoughts mean what they mean intrinsically, not because someone else can or does interpret them (e.g., Searle understands English and fails to understand Chinese independently of whether the English or Chinese symbols he emits are systematically interpretable to someone else). The infinite regress is a symptom of the fact that the interpretation of a pure symbol system is ungrounded. I think the "frame problem," which keeps arising in pure AI—what changes and what stays the same after an action? [29, 37]—is another symptom of ungroundedness.

Another way to appreciate the symbol grounding problem is to see it as analogous to trying to learn Chinese as a second language from a Chinese dictionary alone: All the definientes and definienda in such a dictionary are systematically interpretable to someone who already knows Chinese, but they are of no use to someone who does not, for such a person could only get on a merry-go-round passing from meaningless symbols to still more meaningless symbols. Perhaps with the aid of cryptography there is a way to escape from this merry-go-round [26, 30], but that clearly depends on being able to find a way to decode the dictionary in terms of a first language one already knows. Unfortunately, however, what computationalism is really imagining is that the substrate for this first language (whether English or the language of thought) [10] would likewise be just more of the same: ungrounded symbols that are systematically interpretable by someone who already knows what at least some of them mean.

So the problem is that the connection between the symbols and what they are interpretable as being about must not be allowed to depend on the mediation of an external interpreter—if the system is intended as a model of of what is going on in the external interpreter's head too, as MM requires. One natural way to make this connection direct is to ground the symbols in the system's own capacity to interact robotically with what its symbols are about: It should be able to discriminate, manipulate, categorize, name, describe, and discourse about the real-world objects, events, and states of affairs that its symbols are about; it should be able to do so Turing indistinguishably from the way we do. (I have called this the Total Turing Test or T3 [18, 23, 24]. In other words, T2 and computationalism (symbolic functionalism) are ungrounded and hence cannot do MM, whereas T3 and robotic functionalism, grounded in sensorimotor interaction capacity, can.

In my own approach to symbol grounding I have focused on the all-important capacity to categorize (sort and name) objects [17, 22]—initially concrete categories, based on invariants (learned and innate) in their sensory projections, and then abstract objects, described by symbol strings whose terms are grounded bottom up in concrete categories. (For example, if *horse* and *striped* are grounded directly in the capacity to sort and name their members based on their sensorimotor projections, then *zebra* can be grounded purely symbolically by binding it to the grounded symbol string *striped horse*: A robot that could only sort and name horses and striped objects before could then sort and name zebras too). What is important to keep in mind in evaluating this approach is that although all the examples given are arbitrary fragments of our total capacity (and the initial models, e.g. [31, 32], are just toys), the explicit goal of the approach is T3-scale capacity, not just circumscribed local toy capacity. In my own modeling I use neural nets to learn the sensorimotor invariants that allow the system to categorize, but it is quite conceivable that neural nets will fail to scale up to T3-scale categorization capacity, in which case other category-invariance learning models will have to be found and tried. On the other hand, rejecting this approach on the grounds that it is already known that bottom-up grounding in sensorimotor invariants is not possible [8, 9] is, I think, premature (and empirically ungrounded) [28].

The symbol grounding approach to MM can be contrasted with other approaches that prefer to dispense with symbols altogether. I will consider two such approaches here. One is pure connectionism (PC), which replaces the computationalist hypothesis that mental states are computational states with the connectionist hypothesis that mental states are dynamical states in a neural net [12]. The crucial question for connectionists, I think, is whether the critical test of the PC hypothesis is to be T2 or T3. (I think it is a foregone conclusion that mere toy performance demonstrates nothing insofar as MM is concerned.) If it is to be T2, then I think PC is up against the same objections as AI, if for no other reason than because connectionist systems can be simulated by symbol systems without any real parallelism or distributedness, and if those too can pass T3, then they are open to Searle's argument and the symbol grounding problem [24, 39]. On the other hand, if the target is to be T3, and PC can manage to do it completely nonsymbolically, I, for one, would be happy to accept the verdict that it was not necessary to worry about the problem of grounding symbols, because symbols are not necessary for MM. On the other hand, there do exist prima facie reasons to believe that a PC approach would fail to capture the systematicity that is needed to pass the T2 (a subset of T3) in the first place [11, 20], so perhaps it is best to wait and see whether or not PC can indeed go it alone.

There is a counterpart to PC in robotics—let's call it *pure nonsymbolic robotics* PNSR [7]—that likewise aspires to go the distance without symbols, but this time largely by means of internal sensorimotor mechanisms—sometimes neurally inspired ones, but mostly data-driven ones, driven by the contingencies a robot faces in trying to get around in the real world. Such roboticists tend to stress situatedness and embeddedness in the world of objects, which they take to be grounding without symbols, rather than symbol grounding. PNSR places great hope in internal structures that will emerge to meet the bottom-up challenges of navigating and manipulating its world; much has been made, for example, of a wall-following rule that emerged spontaneously in a locomoting robot that had been given no such explicit rule [40]. As with PC, however, it remains to be seen whether such emergent internal structures and rules, driven only by bottom-up contingencies, can scale up to the systematicity of natural language and human reasoning [11] without recourse to internal symbols.

My own work on categorical perception [17], which is pretty low in the concrete/abstract scale leading from sensorimotor categories to language and reasoning, already casts some doubt on the possibility of scaling up to T3 without internal symbols, as PNSR hopes to do. A category name, after all, is a symbol, and we all use them. Categorical perception occurs when the analog space of interstimulus similarities is warped by sorting and naming objects in a particular way, with the result that within-category distances (the pairwise perceptual similarities between members of the same category, bearing the same symbolic category name) are compressed and between-category distances (the similarities between members of different categories, bearing different symbolic category names) are dilated. This seems to occur because after category learning, the sensorimotor projections of objects are filtered by invariance detectors that have learned which features of the sensory projection will serve as a reliable basis for sorting and labeling them correctly (and the warping of similarity space seems to be part of how back propagation, at least, manages to accomplish successful categorization [31, 32]. The next stage is to combine these grounded symbols into propositions about more abstract categories (e.g., zebra = striped horse). It is hard to imagine how this could be accomplished by a data-driven emergent such as wall-following. It seems more likely that explicit internal symbolization is involved.

Such internal symbols, unlike those of AI's pure symbol systems, inherit the constraints from their grounding. In a pure symbol system the only constraints are formal, syntactic ones, operating rulefully on the arbitrary shapes of the symbols. In a grounded symbol system, symbol shapes are no longer arbitrary, for they are constrained (grounded) by the structures that gave the system the capacity to sort and name the members of the category the symbol refers to, based on their sensorimotor projections: The shape of horse is arbitrary, to be sure, but not that of the analog sensory projections (see [4, 29, 33]) of horses nor of the invariants in those sensory projections that the nets have detected and that connect the horse symbol to the projections of the objects it refers to. All further symbolic combinations that horse enters into (e.g., zebra = striped horse) inherit this grounding. Think of it as the warping of similarity space as a consequence of which things no longer look the same (from color sorting [2], where warping is innate, to chicken-sexing, where it is learned) after you have learned to sort and name them in a certain way. All further symbol combinations continue to be constrained by the invariance detectors and the change in appearance that they mediate.

So I am still betting on internal symbols, but grounded ones. In my view, robotic constraints play three roles in MM: (a) They ease the burden of trying to second-guess T3 constraints a priori, with a purely symbolic oracle: Instead of just simulating the robot's world, it makes more sense to let the real world exert its influence directly [25]. More important than that, (b) the robotic version of the Turing Test, T3, is just the right constraint for the branch of reverse engineering that MM really is. T2 clearly is not (because of Searle's argument and the symbol grounding problem), whereas Searle's preferred candidate, T4 (total neurobehavioral indistinguishability from ourselves) is overconstraining, because it includes potentially irrelevant constraints. Finally, (c) robotic capacity looks like just what one would want to ground symbolic capacity in, given that symbols cannot generate a mind on their own.

Depite these considerations in favor of symbol grounding, neither PC nor PNSR can be counted out yet, in the path to T3. So far only computationalism and pure AI have fallen by the wayside. If it turns out that no internal symbols at all underlie our symbolic (T2) capacity, if dynamic states of neural nets alone or sensorimotor mechanisms subserving robotic capacities alone can successfully generate T3 performance capacity without symbols, that is still the decisive test for the presence of mind as far as I'm concerned, and I'd be ready to accept the verdict. For even if we should happen to be wrong about such a robot, it seems clear that no one (not even an advocate of T4, or even the Blind Watchmaker who designed us, being no more a mindreader than we are) can ever hope to be the wiser [14, 16, 21, 23].

References

[1] Andrews, J., Livingston, K., Harnad, S., & Fischer, U. (in preparation). *Learned categorical perception in human subjects: Implications for symbol grounding.*

[2] Bornstein, M. H. (1987). Perceptual categories in vision and audition. In S. Harnad (Ed.), *Categorical perception: The groundwork of cognition.* New York: Cambridge Univerity Press.

[3] Catania, A. C., & Harnad, S. (Eds.). (1988). *The selection of behavior. The operant behaviorism of B. F. Skinner: Comments and consequences.* New York: Cambridge University Press.

[4] Chamberlain, S. C., & Barlow, R. B. (1982). Retinotopic organization of lateral eye input to Limulus brain. *Journal of Neurophysiology, 48*, 505-520.

[5] Dietrich, E. (1990). Computationalism. *Social Epistemology ,4,* 135–154.

[6] Dietrich, E. (1993). The ubiquity of computation. *Think* [Special Issue on Machine Learning] Vol 15, pp. 86–99.

[7] Brooks, R. A. (1993) The engineering of physical grounding. *Proceedings of the Fifteenth Annual Meeting of the Cognitive Science Society.* Hillsdale, NJ: Lawrence Erlbaum Associates.

[8] Christiansen, M., & Chater, N. (1992). Connectionism, learning and meaning. *Connectionism,4,* 227–252.

[9] Christiansen, M. H., & Chater, N. (1993). Symbol grounding—The emperor's new theory of meaning? *Proceedings of the Fifteenth Annual Meeting of the Cognitive Science Society.* Hillsdale, NJ: Lawrence Erlbaum Associates.

[10] Fodor, J. A. (1975). *The language of thought.* New York: Crowell.

[11] Fodor, J. A., & Pylyshyn, Z. W. (1988). Connectionism and cognitive architecture: A critical appraisal. *Cognition,28,* 3–71.

[12] Hanson, & Burr, (1990). What connectionist models learn: Learning and Representation in connectionist networks. *Behavioral and Brain Sciences, 13,* 471–518.

[13] Harnad, S. (1982b) Neoconstructivism: A unifying theme for the cognitive sciences. In T. Simon & R. Scholes (Eds.), *Language, mind and brain* (pp. 1–11). Hillsdale, NJ: Lawrence Erlbaum Associates.

[14] Harnad, S. (1982a). Consciousness: An afterthought. *Cognition and Brain Theory, 5,* 29–47.

[15] Harnad, S. (1984b). What are the scope and limits of radical behaviorist theory? *Behavioral and Brain Sciences,7,* 720–721.

[16] Harnad, S. (1984a) Verifying machines' minds. (Review of "Consciousness: Natural and artificial". *Contemporary Psychology,29,* 389–391.

[17] Harnad, S. (1987). The induction and representation of categories. In S. Harnad (Ed.), *Categorical perception: The groundwork of cognition.* New York: Cambridge University Press.

[18] Harnad, S. (1989). Minds, machines and Searle. *Journal of theoretical and experimental artificial intelligence,1,* 5–25.

[19] Harnad, S. (1990a). The Symbol grounding problem. *Physica D 42,* 335–346.

[20] Harnad, S. (1990b). Symbols and nets: Cooperation vs. competition (Review of: *Connections and symbols connection*). *Science,2,* 257–260.

[21] Harnad, S. (1991). Other bodies, Other minds: A machine incarnation of an old philosophical problem. *Minds and Machines,1,* 43–54.

[22] Harnad, S. (1992a). Connecting object to symbol in modeling cognition. In A. Clarke & R. Lutz (Eds.), *Connectionism in context.* New York: Springer Verlag.

[23] Harnad, S. (1992b). The Turing test is not a trick: Turing indistinguishability is a scientific criterion. *SIGART Bulletin, 3*(4), 9–10.

[24] Harnad, S. (1993a). Grounding symbols in the analog world with neural nets. *Think* [Special Issue on Machine Learning]. Vol 15, pp. 155-175.

[25] Harnad, S. (1993b). Artificial life: Synthetic versus virtual. *Artificial Life III, Proceedings, Santa Fe Institute Studies in the Sciences of Complexity. Volume XVI.* Redwood City, Ca: Addison-Wesley. pp. 510–530.

[26] Harnad, S. (1993c). The origin of words: A psychophysical hypothesis. In W. Durham & B. Velichkovsky (Eds.), Explorations in psychophysics. Muenster: Nodus. pp. 230–240.

[27] Harnad, S. (1993d). Problems, problems: The frame problem as a symptom of the symbol grounding problem. *PSYCOLOQUY,4*(34), 11.

[28] Harnad, S. (1993e). Symbol grounding is an empirical problem: Neural nets are just a candidate component. In *Proceedings of the Fifteenth Annual Meeting of the Cognitive Science Society.* Hillsdale, NJ: Lawrence Erlbaum Associates. pp. 120–128.

[29] Harnad, S. (1993f). Exorcizing the ghost of mental imagery. Commentary on: J.I. Glasgow: "The imagery debate revisited." *Computational Intelligence.*

[30] Harnad, S. (in press). Computation is just interpretable symbol manipulation: Cognition isn't. *Minds and machines* [Special Issue on "What Is Computation"].

[31] Harnad, S., Hanson, S. J., & Lubin, J. (1991). Categorical perception and the evolution of supervised learning in neural nets. In D. W. Powers & L. Reeker (Eds.), Working papers of the AAAI spring symposium on machine learning of natural language and ontology. (pp. 65-74)

[32] Harnad, S., Hanson, S. J., & Lubin, J. (in press). Learned categorical perception in neural nets: Implications for symbol grounding. In V. Honavar & L. Uhr (Eds.), *Symbol processing and connectionist network models in artificial intelligence and cognitive modeling: Steps toward principled integration.*

[33] Jeannerod, M. (in press). The representing brain: neural correlates of motor intention and imagery. *Behavioral and Brain Sciences ,17*(2).

[34] Kentridge, R. W., (1993). Cognition, chaos, and nondeterministic symbolic computation: The chinese room problem solved? *Think* [Special Issue on Machine Learning]. Vol 15, pp. 230–245.

[35] Newell, A. (1980). Physical symbol systems. *Cognitive Science, 4,* 135–83.

[36] Pylyshyn, Z. W. (1984). *Computation and cognition.* Cambridge, MA: MIT Press, Bradford Books.

[37] Pylyshyn, Z. W. (Ed.). (1987). *The robot's dilemma: The frame problem in artificial intelligence.* Norwood NJ: Ablex

[38] Searle, J. R. (1980). Minds, brains and programs. *Behavioral and Brain Sciences,3,* 417–424.

[39] Searle, J. R. (1993). The failures of computationalism. *Think* [Special Issue on Machine Learning]. Vol 15, pp. 20–45.

[40] Steels, L. (1991). Towards a theory of emergent functionality. In J. A. Meyer & S. W. Wilson (Eds.), *From animals to animates.* (pp. 451–461). Cambridge, MA: MIT Press.

Index